WILD
AUSTRALIA

A GUIDE TO THE PLACES, PLANTS AND ANIMALS

GRAHAM EDGAR   **ROBERT EDGAR**   **ALLAN EDGAR**

Picture Credits

t = top, b = bottom, c= centre, l = left, r = right

All photographs are by the authors, except the following:

First published in Australia in 2006 by
Reed New Holland
an imprint of New Holland Publishers (Australia) Pty Ltd
Sydney · Auckland · London · Cape Town

14 Aquatic Drive Frenchs Forest NSW 2086 Australia
218 Lake Road Northcote Auckland New Zealand
86 Edgware Road London W2 2EA United Kingdom
80 McKenzie Street Cape Town 8001 South Africa

National Library of Australia Cataloguing-in-Publication Data:
Edgar, Graham.

Wild Australia : A guide to the places, plants and animals

Includes index.
ISBN 1 877069 33 7.

1. Animals - Australia. 2. Plants - Australia. I. Edgar, Robert. II. Title.

578.0994

Publisher: Martin Ford
Project Editor: Yani Silvana
Designers: Norman Baptista, Greg Lamont, Kerry Klinner
Cover Design: Kerry Klinner
Production: Monique Layt
Printer: SNP/Leefung Printing Co. Ltd. (China)

Title page: Wilpena Pound, Flinders Ranges, SA
Opposite: top Lord Howe Island; bottom Short-eared Rock Wallaby

Contents

Acknowledgements

We greatly appreciate help from many people in locating species, providing images, or offering advice on the habits of various species and on the manuscript. Particular thanks to: Kyra Ensbey and the staff at Coffs Harbour Zoo, Steve McEwan from Reptile World (Coffs Harbour), Ian Shaw, Neil Vaughan, Lindy Powells, Geoff McBride, Jodie Masters, Ron Mawbey, Sue Baker, John Chambers, Rudie Kuiter, Kelvin Aitken, Christine Crawford, Nev Barrett, James Brook, Lisa Gershwin, Bill Millington, Sophie and Michael Semmler, Ray Nichols, Jenny Maclean, Susan O'Sullivan, Adrian Meehan, Diana Fisher, Derek Shields, Reg Morrison, Nick Mooney, John Lawson and Arthur White. Louise Egerton's (formerly of New Holland Publishers) commitment to the project is also highly appreciated.

Many thanks to all those family members who provided support and encouragement during the compilation of this book. They include Joyce, Wendy, Jessie, Aroon, Kelvin, Robyn, Margaret, Sophie, Anna and Chris. Without their generosity of spirit the task would have been much more onerous.

This book is built upon the work of numerous researchers dedicated to the conservation of Australian biota. Without their labours this book would not be available to anyone with an interest in the natural world.

Tasmanian Waratah

How To Use this Book

Wild Australia will help travellers and others interested in natural history to identify common and iconic species of plants and animals throughout Australia. Although not comprehensive, it provides many examples of species within well-known animal and plant groups. You may encounter these species in our national parks and conservation areas, at picnic tables, or while snorkelling reefs or strolling along a beach.

The book is divided into four sections: Habitats, National Parks, Plants and Animals. Species are listed in order of increasing structural complexity, from seaweeds through ferns to pines, palms and flowering plants, and from corals and anemones to fishes, frogs, reptiles, birds and mammals. Closely related flowering plants are grouped and ordered approximately by size, from tall trees through shrubs and bushes to flowers and grasses. Within some larger groups, such as the eucalypts, species are arranged by geographic region so that it's easy to compare species present in a particular area. At the end of each species description, the flowering months (for plants), maximum size, and distribution are provided. Species distribution is described in an anticlockwise direction, hence 'sw WA to s NSW' means from south-western WA across the south of Australia to southern NSW, whereas NSW to WA implies a northern Australian distribution.

Because no single publication, whatever its size, can hope to cover the breadth of common plant and animal species found across Australia, a list of useful references and websites is provided at the end of the book. Use these reference sources to find out more about the species described, and to track down those not included. The use of internet cafés and libraries across Australia will enhance the book's usefulness. Take *Wild Australia* with you in the car, in your backpack or caravan—hopefully the dust from myriad locations will lodge between its covers.

Abbreviations

c	central	Fl	flowering	NSW	New South Wales
e	east/ern	Aus	Australia (excluding	Qld	Queensland
n	north/ern		Tasmania)	NT	Northern Territory
s	south/ern	WA	Western Australia	NZ	New Zealand
w	west/ern	SA	South Australia	GDR	Great Dividing Range
		Tas	Tasmania	GBR	Great Barrier Reef
		Vic	Victoria		

Scale Conversions

1 kilometre = 0.62 miles
1 metre = 3.28 feet
1 centimetre = 0.39 inches
1 square kilometre = 0.38 square miles
1 kilogram = 2.20 pounds

Introduction

Australia is the oldest continent on the planet. Very little volcanic activity or mountain building has occurred during the past 100 million years, and ancient rocks, some dating over 600 million years to the Precambrian geological period, are widely exposed. The consequences of great age include: flat eroded landforms; dry conditions—because rainfall is most reliably generated by air rising and condensing as it passes mountains; and poor soil—because most nutrients have leached from rocks and drained down rivers long ago. Australian plants and animals have adapted to this environment by tightly cycling water and nutrients within local foodwebs. These foodwebs can break down when new species, including humans, are introduced.

Australia is also the most isolated inhabited continent, lacking direct connections with other continents since separation from Antarctica 40 million years ago. With the exception of Antarctica, which broke from South America 25 million years ago, other continents are all connected to each other, or were joined during the last ice age.

After breaking from Antarctica, the distinctive Australian flora, including acacias, banksias, casuarinas, eucalypts, spinifex and grasstrees, adapted to changing local conditions and diversified. Monotreme, marsupial and placental mammals inhabited the continent at that time but placentals other than bats subsequently died out. The marsupials diversified, adapting to the increasing aridity caused by the northward movement of the Australian continental plate into hotter latitudes. This movement ultimately brought Australia into contact with Asia, resulting in a series of invasions of plants and animals, including many tropical rainforest plants, mangroves, corals, terrestrial and marine invertebrates, lizards, snakes, birds and placental mammals.

Hogan Island, Tas

Red Gorge, Karijini National Park, WA

Because of long isolation, evolution has taken a different course here. Time and again during the eighteenth and early nineteenth centuries, European naturalists in Australia discovered animals, such as the Australian Lungfish and the Tasmanian Mountain Shrimp, belonging to groups known only as long-extinct fossils. This process of unearthing 'living fossils' continues, with the discovery of a small population of archaic Wollemi Pines in a single New South Wales valley in 1994. European naturalists also encountered unimaginable animals in Australia, including an egg-laying duck-billed mammal—the platypus.

Australia's lengthy isolation from other landmasses also resulted in a very rich biota, with the majority of species not found elsewhere (endemic). Of the more than one million species of plants and animals native to Australia, about 85% of flowering plants, 90% of frogs, 90% of reptiles, 85% of mammals, 50% of birds, and 90% of freshwater and southern fishes are endemic.

Due to a paucity of plant nutrients, Australia's seas are less productive than seas surrounding other continents. However, the number of species is exceptionally high. The northern tropical zone has very high fish, mollusc and coral diversity, with the majority of species also spread widely throughout the western Pacific and Indian oceans. A number of the wide-ranging marine species, for example dugongs and marine turtles, find haven in Australia's coastal waters and have their highest population densities here. The eastern, western and southern temperate zones of Australia have fewer large species but the majority of species are endemic.

One additional striking feature of the Australian fauna is the number of examples of convergent evolution, where species with completely different ancestry have evolved a similar outward appearance—the features best adapted to fill a particular role in an ecosystem. The marsupial thylacine and its European parallel, the wolf, are examples of convergent evolution.

Yet this island continent, with its remarkable natural contrasts, is fragile, and most ecosystems have changed dramatically during the last 200 years. A variety of threatening processes have begun undermining Australia's biological richness, potentially leading to environmental

Christmas Bells

catastrophe. Global climate change is the greatest overriding threat. Rising temperatures are likely to cause mass extinctions of plant and animal communities adapted to cold climates, such as those in alpine areas and southern Tasmanian seas.

Land clearing is another major threat. Since European settlement more than 700 000 square kilometres of woodland and forest have been cleared or modified, and broad-scale clearing of our remaining native vegetation continues. Land clearing destroys the habitats and regional ecosystems on which native animals depend for food and shelter, ultimately leading to local extinctions. Clearing also has many indirect effects: it facilitates the spread of weeds and feral animals; it causes soil degradation through increased salinity and erosion; it increases greenhouse gas emissions; and it reduces water quality.

Other threatening processes include the incidental bycatch of seabirds, turtles, dugongs and dolphins through commercial fishing operations; increased coastal development; the spread of *Phytophthora* root-rot fungus; and pollution of our waterways with chemicals and runoff from urban and industrial areas and farmlands.

Human activity is responsible for all these threats, and their cumulative impact is now obvious for all to see. We are being forced to think about how we can interact with the landscape in an ecologically sustainable way and preserve Australia's natural wonders for future generations. With improved environmental management, rich rewards and breathtaking experiences will continue to await those who make the effort to explore this ancient continent, whether it be a weekend away or a year's journey visiting its wild places.

Australia is not a land where large herds of grazing mammals migrate across the

Euro

plains. Rather, it is a place where sightings of plants and animals often require patience and persistence. You may see more birds during a 20-minute rest while on a bushwalk than during four hours on the track, particularly if you're in a sunlit location in the forest. Most of our colourful flowers are patchily distributed across the landscape, in large part because vegetation is so diverse that individual species are scattered rather than massed together. Most mammals and frogs and many reptiles are nocturnal, so an hour walking with a spotlight in the evening reveals animals you won't otherwise see.

Patience in searching for Australian plants and animals is generally well rewarded. For example, although you won't see possums on every spotlighting trip into north Queensland rainforests, you're very likely to see them after two or three nightly visits. On another night you might see an unusual frog or lizard. The majority of photos used in this book were taken in the wild during a single year prior to book production. We found that the best locations to photograph wildlife were often national park camping grounds, where animals had adapted to the presence of people.

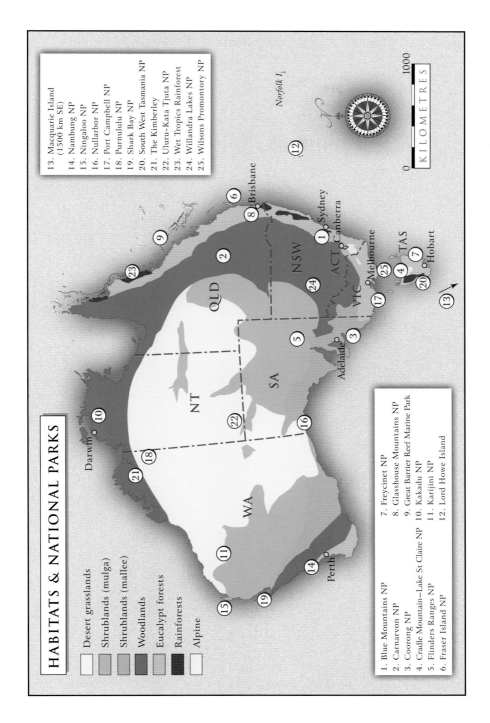

HABITATS & NATIONAL PARKS

- Desert grasslands
- Shrublands (mulga)
- Shrublands (mallee)
- Woodlands
- Eucalypt forests
- Rainforests
- Alpine

1. Blue Mountains NP
2. Carnarvon NP
3. Coorong NP
4. Cradle Mountain–Lake St Claire NP
5. Flinders Ranges NP
6. Fraser Island NP
7. Freycinet NP
8. Glasshouse Mountains NP
9. Great Barrier Reef Marine Park
10. Kakadu NP
11. Karijini NP
12. Lord Howe Island

13. Macquarie Island (1500 km SE)
14. Nambung NP
15. Ningaloo NP
16. Nullarbor NP
17. Port Campbell NP
18. Purnululu NP
19. Shark Bay NP
20. South West Tasmania NP
21. The Kimberley
22. Uluru–Kata Tjuta NP
23. Wet Tropics Rainforest
24. Willandra Lakes NP
25. Wilsons Promontory NP

Norfolk I.

KILOMETRES
0   1000

Darwin

WA   NT
          QLD
              SA
                   NSW
Perth   ACT
          Canberra
Adelaide VIC
          Melbourne
          Sydney
          Brisbane
          TAS
          Hobart

Habitats

Pieman River estuary, Tas

Australia is a country of climatic contrasts, from the tropical north, with its monsoonal summer rains and cyclones; to the eastern seaboard, with its hot, dry summers; to the dry interior west of the GDR, where rainfall averages less than 25cm per year. This climatic range, together with variability in geology and landforms and long isolation from other continents, has generated diverse habitat types.

DESERT GRASSLANDS ▼

Desert grasslands and stony (gibber) plains occupy much of central and western Australia, extending for 2000km north–south and 2500km east–west. Within this semi-arid region are six major deserts, each with a distinctive character—the Simpson, Great Sandy, Gibson, Great Victoria, Tanami and Sturt's Stony deserts. All have low and unpredictable rainfall (under 20cm) and a predominance of tussock grass, with pockets of stunted acacia and other shrubs.

Each desert has its own character. For example, the Simpson Desert includes about 1100 parallel sand-dune ridges, averaging 5–30m in height and 400m separation, whereas the Sturt Stony Desert in eastern WA comprises a vast 'gibber' plain covered by quartz pebbles, with little permanent vegetation.

Following heavy rain, desert grasslands burst into colour as the seeds of wildflowers that have lain dormant for years germinate. Parrots, finches, pigeons, honeyeaters and other birds follow the rain across the landscape, feasting on the sudden upsurge of pollen and nectar and the insects attracted to the flowers. Unlike grasslands elsewhere in the world, the major predators of Australian grasslands are lizards and snakes rather than

Mallee, Pooncarie, NSW

large mammals. Lizards are particularly diverse in our deserts, a major reason for Australia possessing more reptile species than any other country.

SHRUBLANDS ▲

Semi-arid regions of Australia with rainfall higher than that in the c deserts but still less than 30cm are typically dominated by a groundcover of saltbush, bluebush, small multi-stemmed acacias (known as 'mulga') and eucalypt shrubs (known as 'mallee'). These shrubs usually have bulbous root systems that are very hard, and sprout new stems after fire or attack by grazing animals. Mulga is more widespread than mallee, tolerating slightly drier conditions.

'Kwongan' heaths and woodlands of south-western WA are an unusual habitat type. Kwongan extends from Kalbarri to Albany, an area with winter rainfall, summer drought and nutrient-deficient soil. Over 5000 plant species live in this area, with most found nowhere else; they include many colourful species used in the cut-flower trade. The region is also home to many local animal species such as the Numbat and the Western Honey Possum. The kwongan ecosystem is recognised as one of 15 global hotspots with exceptional biodiversity coupled with major habitat loss. Over 80% of kwongan habitat has been destroyed for wheat production and grazing during the past century.

Gibber desert, Meekatharra, WA

WOODLANDS ▼

Woodlands possess scattered trees, with total canopy cover of less than 30%. Woodland understorey can include wiry bushes but grasses more often predominate, largely because of high grazing intensity due to farm stocking of cattle and sheep. Watercourses in eastern Australian woodlands are typically lined by River Red Gum or Coolabah.

Rhythms of life in the savannah woodlands of the tropical north are strongly influenced by monsoonal summer rains and bushfire. Most wildfires occur towards the end of the year immediately prior to the wet season, when the vegetation is tinder dry and frequent lightning strikes occur. Aboriginal groups traditionally managed hunting and gathering grounds by burning a patchwork mosaic of savannah woodland. In recent times, farmers have enthusiastically adopted the practice of burning to improve stock feed, albeit in a less controlled manner.

Blue Gum Forest, Blue Mountains, NSW

Savannah fire, Timber Creek, NT

EUCALYPT FORESTS ▲

The word 'sclerophyll' means 'thickened leaves', which in the Australian context generally means eucalypt; hence sclerophyll forests are eucalypt forests.

Sclerophyllous plants are adapted for dry conditions, with hard wax-coated leaves, woody fruits that lose little moisture, and deep roots. Eucalypts actively affect their environment by drawing water from deep underground, thereby lowering the water table, and by facilitating bushfires. Some plants are so dependent on fire that they need smoke or heat for successful seed germination.

Wet sclerophyll forests merge into rainforests, with both forest types occurring in areas with annual rainfall over 100cm. Wet sclerophyll forests are generally dominated by one or two giant tree species taller than 30m, but they lack a continuous canopy. Between 30% and 50% of sunlight typically reaches the ground, allowing grasses, flowers and small shrubs to develop on the forest floor. Much of Australia's unique flora, including eucalypts, banksias, hakeas and grevilleas, is thought to have evolved in wet sclerophyll forests as the continent dried out and rainforests contracted.

Dry sclerophyll forest is more open than wet forest (50–70% of sunlight reaches the ground), and generally includes smaller trees (less than 30m tall). It possesses an understorey of hard spiny shrubs such as wattles, hakeas and grevilleas. These forests are highly fire-adapted: they burn readily because they have an abundance of stringy flammable bark and leaves with a high oil, resin and wax content. Many eucalypts have buds buried deep under the bark that sprout after fire.

RAINFORESTS ➤

Rainforests occur patchily along the eastern mainland and western Tas coasts in areas of high rainfall. They lack eucalypts and have an almost unbroken canopy. Little sunlight reaches the damp ground, which is covered with deep leaf litter and has few flowers or grasses. Mosses and fungi grow abundantly on rocks and tree trunks, while in tropical and subtropical regions, epiphytes, vines and other climbing plants are common.

Australian rainforests differ between locations. The northernmost rainforests, most notably those at Iron Range National Park on Cape York, are relatively dry despite being strongly influenced by monsoonal summer rains, and have biological affinities with New Guinea.

Wet tropical rainforests further south possess the richest flora and fauna. They include many buttressed trees, strangler figs, palms, ferns, orchids and a floor blanketed with mosses.

Subtropical rainforests such as those near Dorrigo and Mt Warning in NSW generally occur on rich basaltic or alluvial soil on the eastern flanks of the GDR. They merge into eucalypt forests with more open canopy and occasional larger emergent trees.

Dorrigo, NSW

Temperate rainforests distributed southward from central NSW are less complex in both structure and composition, occupying less fertile soil and possessing lower canopies. They typically exist above 800m altitude and have few tree species: these include Sassafras and Antarctic Beech, with Huon, Celery Top and King Billy Pines present in Tas.

ALPINE ➤

Alpine ecosystems are characterised by meadows of grasses, herbs and ground-hugging shrubs living above the treeline on mountainsides and plateaus. The treeline is located at an elevation of 1800m in the Australian Alps (Vic, NSW) and about 1400m in the Tas highlands. Alpine herbfields are buried under snow for much of winter. Following spring thaws, plants emerge and flowers quickly bud and develop. Spectacular alpine wildflower displays peak in early summer.

Ben Lomond, Tas

Mystery Creek Cave, Tas

UNDERGROUND CAVES ◄

Underground habitats are widely but patchily distributed across Australia. The largest such habitat is the Great Artesian Basin, a sedimentary layer of rock permeated by water to 700m depth that underlies Qld, north-eastern SA, and northern NSW west of the GDR. This basin leaks naturally to the surface as desert mound springs, oases of life inhabited by unique aquatic faunas. The Great Artesian Basin is presently tapped by over 5000 wells to provide water for stock.

The most spectacular underground systems are formed by water dissolving limestone over tens of thousands of years, creating networks of caves and passages with fragile formations such as stalag-mites and stalactites. Such 'karst' systems occur in all States and Territories. They can be highly localised, such as near Jenolan Caves (NSW), or can extend for several hundred kilometres, such as the Nullarbor Plain (WA, SA). Each karst system contains a unique biological community, which can include such animals as bats, spiders, glow-worms, cockroaches, crayfishes, mountain shrimp and fishes, many of them blind.

LAKES AND RIVERS ➤

Because of dry conditions and a long erosional history, Australia has relatively few lakes and a poor aquatic fauna compared to other continents. The largest Australian lake—Lake Eyre— is usually dry, having filled across its 9300km^2 area only three times in the past century. Lake Eyre lies below sea level, acting as the final sink for rivers extending across 1.4 million km^2 of land. After rain-bearing cyclones flood ne Australia, the lake gradually fills and becomes a haven for waterbirds. Most large central Australian lakes are highly saline and ephemeral.

Red Rock Beach, NSW

Australia also has numerous freshwater lakes; however, virtually all large freshwater lakes are impounded for irrigation or hydro-electric production, and many are entirely human constructions. Australia's deepest lake, Lake St Clair in Tas, is unusual in that it remains unmodified, lying within a national park. The presence of downstream dams nevertheless blocks connections to the sea, eliminating migratory species such as eels from its waters.

Permanently flowing rivers are largely confined to regions with moderate or heavy rainfall—the tropics, eastern Qld, NSW and Vic, south-western WA, and Tas. The largest river system is the Murray–Darling, a network of creeks, rivers and swamps that drains most of inland NSW and northern Vic. Unfortunately, our longest river—the Darling—sometimes stops flowing for up to 18 months because of excessive irrigation demands, contracting to a series of slimy ponds. In former times, heavy rains on the east coast filled headwater creeks, generating floodwaters that could take weeks to pass along the whole system. The life cycles and productivity of plants and animals living in floodplain ecosystems depend on irregular flooding.

SANDY BEACHES ▲

Australia is justifiably famous for its white and golden sand beaches, including Bondi and Manly in Sydney and Wineglass Bay in Tas. They provide homes for beach worms, sand crabs, pipis and numerous other forms of marine life.

Franklin River, Tas

Conical Rocks, Tas

ROCKY SHORES ▲

The spectacular rocky shorelines of Australia are partly accessible by car or foot, although some can only be viewed from the sea. These shores host a diverse array of animal life, including cunjevoi, barnacles, limpets, sponges, sea worms, crabs, oysters and seaweed.

ESTUARIES ▼

Estuaries comprise the interface between rivers, sea, land and sky, with a mixture of mangroves, mudflats, seagrasses, sandy islands and rocky shores. They provide important feeding grounds for fish and birds, including seasonally migrating species from the northern hemisphere. Mangroves also provide important nursery sites for many fish species. However, be wary in tropical mangroves: they are home to dangerous estuarine crocodiles.

SEAGRASS BEDS ➤

Seagrass beds consist of meadows of flowering grass species. They occur widely in estuaries and sheltered coastal waters around the continent, providing nurseries for fish and prawn species, and feeding grounds for dugongs, turtles, sea snakes and cormorants. Seagrasses play an important role in enriching sediments, slowing down nutrient-laden water and allowing particles to drop out of currents onto the seabed.

Deal Island, Tas

CORAL REEFS ➤

Coral reefs develop slowly over thousands of years as coral polyps and encrusting calcareous seaweeds bind into the limestone reef base. In some reefs, most notably atolls, the limestone coral base is hundreds of metres thick. However, reefs can decline rapidly when coral dies because of physical erosion by waves and biological erosion from grazing fishes and boring animals.

Corindi, NSW

Many reefs are now declining in area. They are adversely affected by a combination of factors: rising water temperature and carbon dioxide levels causing 'bleaching'—the loss of symbiotic algae; the influx of nutrient-laden waters from mainland agricultural runoff resulting in excessive seaweed growth and the smothering of corals; and overfishing, which causes loss of the predators that control the numbers of animal grazers.

Erith Island, Tas

Coral reefs are largely confined to the tropics. They extend northward from Houtman Abrolhos (500km north of Perth) to Lord Howe Island and the Solitary Islands (500km north of Sydney). Individual corals attached to rock occur around the south coast. Much of the beauty of coral reefs results from the myriad fishes, molluscs, crustaceans and other living creatures that inhabit their nooks and crannies.

ROCKY REEFS ▲

Less well known than coral reefs are the hidden jewels of the Australian environment—underwater rocky reefs. Shallow rocky reefs are typically clothed in kelps and other seaweeds, whereas attached animals dominate areas with less light, such as under overhangs or in deeper water. Shaded rock habitats, particularly in areas with good current flow, are brilliantly coloured mosaics of sponges, sea squirts, sea whips, gorgonians, bryozoans and other animals.

In contrast to species associated with coral reefs, which typically have wide distributions extending from Africa to the Pacific islands, plants and animals associated with Australian rocky reefs are rarely found elsewhere. Approximately 80% of the flora and fauna on southern Australian rocky reefs is restricted to the region. Rocky reef communities below 60m depth remain virtually unknown—one of the great remaining unexplored habitats on Earth.

Beaver Cay, Great Barrier Reef, Qld

National Parks

Karijini National Park, WA

In recent decades, increasing understanding that Australia's wealth is ultimately underpinned by its rich natural heritage has led to a major increase in the amount of land managed as national parks and conservation reserves. The resulting mosaic of parks provides ready access to the myriad landforms and plant and animal communities that typify the nature of Australia.

KAKADU (NT) ➤

Kakadu National Park occupies 17 550km². It includes rivers, extensive floodplains, tropical woodlands and sandstone cliffs. A 200m high sandstone escarpment intersected by deep gorges delineates the eastern edge of this World Heritage Area. The Alligator River seasonally floods lowlands for two to six months in the wet season. These floodplains are extremely productive, hosting an amazing diversity of flora and fauna. In the dry season, from May to Sept, the drying pools and low-lying areas come alive with water birds.

Kakadu is home to over 280 bird species, 100 frogs and reptiles and 58 mammals, and includes some of the finest Aboriginal rock art in Australia.

ULURU–KATA TJUTA (NT) ▼

Uluru (Ayers Rock)—Australia's most famous geological landmark—is located 440km south-west of Alice Springs. This massive sandstone rock is over 8km in circumference and rises 350m above the red sandy plain. Uluru changes colour during the day as the sun passes overhead, turning from purple to a dull ochre red.

Kata Tjuta (the Olgas—pictured), a group of massive conglomerate domes located 27km west of Uluru, is considered by many to be more spectacular than Uluru. These domes rise 460m above the surrounding plain and include sheltered valleys accessible by foot, including the impressive Valley of the Winds. The Aboriginal name Kata Tjuta means 'many heads'.

Uluru and Kata Tjuta are of great cultural significance to Aboriginal people. Shortly after land title was restored to local indigenous people in 1985, the area was declared a World Heritage Area.

SHARK BAY (WA) ▼

The Shark Bay World Heritage Area includes two large bays with a total area of 4000km² that are separated by a long peninsula. A combination of restricted water movement, low rainfall and high rates of evaporation generates highly saline conditions in the south-eastern corner at Hamelin Pool. Stromatolites formed in this area are recognised as the simplest form of life on Earth and the world's oldest living fossils. Virtually identical fossils occur in rocks over 3500 million years old. Shark Bay also has the world's most extensive seagrass meadows—home to more than 10 000 dugongs, humpback whales (Aug–Sept), manta rays and green and loggerhead turtles. The most famous inhabitants are wild bottlenose dolphins that are hand-fed each morning on Monkey Mia beach under the supervision of rangers.

NAMBUNG (WA) ▲

This park, located 250km north of Perth, is famous for 'The Pinnacles'—thousands of columns of limestone that rise up to 5m high from the coloured sands. The columns were formed by the calcification of plant root systems that became exposed when erosion removed surrounding soils. Nambung National Park is also renowned for springtime wildflower displays, when multi-coloured blooms of a huge diversity of plant species carpet the landscape. Stromatolites occur nearby at Lake Thetis.

NINGALOO–CAPE RANGE (WA) ➤

Located 1200km north of Perth, Ningaloo Marine Park includes Australia's largest fringing reef, stretching 260km along the coastline. It approaches within 100m of land at its closest point and occurs 7km offshore at its furthest. Ningaloo Reef is home to over 500 species of fish and 240 species of coral, plus sea turtles, dolphins, sharks and other marine life. Its most charismatic animal is the whale shark, the world's largest fish. These giants appear off the reef Apr–June, their arrival coinciding with coral spawning.

Immediately landward of Ningaloo is Cape Range National Park, a semi-arid plateau dissected by gorges up to 300m deep. Extraordinary animals exist in subterranean pools and passages in the limestone rock, including primitive crustaceans and blind fish.

KARIJINI (WA) ▲

Karijini National Park (formerly known as Hamersley Ranges) lies 285km s of Port Hedland and covers 100 000km². It encompasses ancient mountain ranges containing the world's oldest fossils, and red earth plains dotted with spinifex, mulga scrub, white snappy gums and termite mounds. Several massive iron ore mines are located nearby. The undulating grassy plains of Karijini are intersected by spectacular deep red gorges with permanent pools and running streams fringed with ferns, palms and River Red Gums. The most visited location within Karijini is Oxer Lookout, a point of convergence of four different gorge systems.

THE KIMBERLEY/ PURNULULU (WA) ➤

The Kimberley comprises a huge region of northern WA with ancient ranges, gorges, plateaus, plains and coastal swamps. It includes six isolated national parks. Fifty kilometres south of Lake Argyle, in Purnululu National Park in the East Kimberley, lies the World Heritage-listed Bungle Bungle massif. Hundreds of black- and orange-banded beehive formations, some rising 300m above the sandstone plain, have been formed from sandstone originally laid down 360 million years ago.

saltbush and bluebush with occasional mallee scrub near the coast. More than 100 caves have been found in the area, many with spectacular rock art, fossil sites and underground lakes and rivers. The head of the Great Australian Bight, on Yalata Aboriginal ground, adjoins the

NULLARBOR PLAIN (WA, SA) ▲

The Nullarbor Plain is the world's largest area of karst limestone, occupying 250 000km² of south-eastern WA and south-western SA. The plain has few obvious features, its vegetation consisting of low-growing

e boundary of the park. For 200km to the west, the southern edge of the Nullarbor ends in high cliffs dropping vertically into the Great Australian Bight. Southern Right Whales can be seen calving from vantage points on the cliffs between May and October.

FLINDERS RANGES (SA) ▲

The 784km² Flinders Ranges National Park lies 150km north of Port Augusta. During the last 500 million years, softer rocks have been worn away, leaving a number of crater-like formations called pounds. Wilpena Pound, the largest and most spectacular of these, is surrounded by cliffs and saw-toothed rocks. The vegetation adapted to this arid region is noticeably different from that further south and hosts over 100 bird and 356 reptile species. A walk through Brachina Gorge will reveal some of the oldest multicellular fossils on Earth.

COORONG (SA) ▼

The 500km² Coorong National Park includes a variety of coastal landscape features such as estuarine

lagoons, wetlands and sandy peninsulas that have been generated over thousands of years by interactions between the Murray River and the sea. This region is a particularly important refuge for birds, including numerous migratory species and those forced to the coast during times of inland drought. The Coorong also provides a haven for mammals, fish and other animals, and has a long history of Aboriginal occupation, with many middens and burial sites.

PORT CAMPBELL (VIC) ▲

The Twelve Apostles lie 250km south-west of Melbourne along the Great Ocean Road near Port Campbell. Wave action has eroded the soft sedimentary cliffs, forming magnificent natural sculptures of islands, arches, blowholes, bridges and gorges. Cliffs and islands within this park provide nesting sites for shearwaters and penguins.

WILSON'S PROMONTORY (VIC) ▲

The oldest national park in Vic lies 230km south-east of Melbourne. Covering 490km², the park has more than 80km of walking tracks through rugged hills and sandy beaches. It contains eucalypt forests, patches of rainforest and coastal heathlands, with occasional stands of Southern Beech, a remnant of former connections to Tas that were submerged 12 000 years ago. A series of spectacular granite islands, many with seal haul-out sites, extend south-east from Wilsons Promontory to the Kent Group National Park in Tas (pictured top).

A 25km circular track winds through coastal heaths, secluded beaches, rocky cliff tops and eucalypt forests.

CRADLE MOUNTAIN-LAKE ST CLAIR (TAS) ▲

This 1400km^2 park is most famous for its scenery and the 80km Overland Track bushwalk. In the north, near Cradle Mountain, towering dolerite ridges rise from a plateau of heathlands, tussocky grasslands, low shrubs and clear shallow pools. In the south, the Overland Track skirts Lake St Clair through eucalypt and Southern Beech forests.

SOUTHWEST (TAS) ▲

The World Heritage-listed Southwest National Park covers 4420km^2. It is one of Australia's great wilderness areas and a mecca for bushwalkers. Almost completely uninhabited, with an annual rainfall of 2500mm, it combines rugged mountains, gorges, virgin temperate rainforests, trees more than 1000 years old, plains, rivers and some of the world's oldest and best preserved ancient rock-art galleries and middens.

FREYCINET (TAS) ▼

Freycinet National Park lies 200km north-east of Hobart. This 1000km^2 park includes Schouten Island, which may be visited by boat. The pink granite mountains of 614m-high Mt Freycinet in the south and Mt Dove in the north dominate the park.

MACQUARIE ISLAND (TAS) ▲

Macquarie Island, 34km long, 5km wide and with an area of 128km^2, is 1500km south-east of Tas. It is the only place on Earth where rocks from the Earth's mantle are actively being exposed above sea level. Fur and Elephant seals breed on the island, as do four albatross and four penguin species. During the breeding season, more than a million King Penguins (pictured) inhabit the island's southern rookery.

WILLANDRA LAKES/MUNGO (NSW) ▼

Willandra Lakes/Mungo National Park, 110km north of Mildura, is a World Heritage Area that includes 17 dry lakes over 2 million years old, and fossils of megafaunal animals including Tasmanian Tigers, Echidnas, Hairy-nosed Wombats and 3m-high kangaroos. At the edge of Lake Mungo is a 3km formation known as the 'Walls of China'. Exposed in the Walls through erosion are ancient Aboriginal artefacts and stone tools. Human remains from people who lived in the area when the lakes were full have been dated between 24 000 and 30 000 years old. These burial sites provide some of the earliest evidence of funeral rites and cremation.

BLUE MOUNTAINS (NSW) ▲

The World Heritage-listed Greater Blue Mountains Area includes Blue Mountains National Park 122 km west of Sydney; and Wollemi National Park to the north, a wilderness area comprising 5000km^2. Both parks offer magnificent views from high ridges and sandstone escarpments into valleys that remain much as they were when first encountered by European colonists 200 years ago.

At Katoomba, three weathered sandstone pinnacles called 'The Three Sisters' (pictured) perch on the edge of the sandstone escarpment. According to Aboriginal legend, the pinnacles represent three sisters turned into stone.

WARRUMBUNGLES (NSW) ▼

The Warrumbungles lie 490km north-west of Sydney and were formed during volcanic upheavals 13 to 5 million years ago. Subsequent weathering has created a series of spectacular eroded peaks and valleys, making it a favourite for hikers and rock climbers. The park is home to a mix of species from the arid and east zones. A third of Australia's parrot species are found here.

LORD HOWE ISLAND (NSW) ▲

Lord Howe Island, which lies 770km north-east of Sydney and occupies an area of 1463km², is one of the smallest areas with World Heritage listing. This volcanic island is bounded by a number of smaller uninhabited islands, including Balls Pyramid, which rises almost vertically 551m from the deep ocean floor.

The coral reef on the western side of the island is the southernmost coral reef in the world. Kentia Palms occupy a large part of the island, particularly on the slopes of the island's two mountains. Much of the island's flora and fauna is not found elsewhere. The island supports a population of approximately 250 permanent residents, with only 400 visitors allowed at any one time.

GLASSHOUSE MOUNTAINS (QLD) ➤

The 13 Glasshouse Mountains lie about 70km north of Brisbane. Four of these eroded volcanic plugs, some with narrow spires and others more rounded, are protected within the Glasshouse National Park. The area is favoured by bushwalkers, and climbs to the top of the plugs are difficult enough to test the most experienced rock climbers.

WET TROPICS RAINFOREST (QLD) ➤

The World Heritage Wet Tropics Rainforest covers 8940km² of the GDR and adjacent coastal plains between Townsville and Cooktown in north-eastern Qld. It contains the greatest concentration of primitive flowering plants in the world.

Of the 19 known families of primitive flowering plants, 12 are found here.

The Wet Tropics Rainforest is one of the oldest continuously existing rainforests on Earth, contracting with ice ages and expanding during warmer periods within the same area for over 100 million years. Although this rainforest occupies only 0.1% of the continent, it contains 30% of Australia's marsupial species, 60% of bat species, 30% of frog species, 23% of reptile species, 62% of butterfly species and 92% of fern species.

CARNARVON (QLD) ▼

Carnarvon National Park is located 750km north-west of Brisbane on the western slopes of the GDR. The most accessible part of the park is at Carnarvon Gorge where Carnarvon Creek has carved a 180m-high passage through the sandstone. This gorge, which extends for 21km, has many smaller side gorges with Aboriginal rock art, subtropical palm forests, rare ferns, ancient cycads and eucalypt forests. Good walking tracks pass through the gorge onto the higher plateau, providing splendid views and sightings of birds and mammals.

GREAT BARRIER REEF (QLD) ➤

The GBR is the largest and best known coral reef in the world—the only living structure that can be seen from the moon. It comprises a network of over 2000 separate coral reefs and 500 islands and cays that stretch 2300km along the Qld coast from the Gulf of Papua to Lady Elliot Island near Gladstone. The GBR Marine Park also includes continental islands, mangrove forests, seagrass beds and deeper inter-reef areas.

Over 1500 fish, 400 coral and 4000 mollusc species inhabit the reef, with crustaceans, anemones, marine worms, sponges, sea snakes and turtles also conspicuous. One of the great natural phenomena of the world is the synchronised spawning of coral species following the first full moon in November. While snorkelling is safe on the outer reef, the presence of deadly box

jellyfish makes swimming in the coastal waters during the wet season dangerous .

FRASER ISLAND (QLD) ▲

World Heritage-listed Fraser Island, the world's largest sand island, lies 190km north of Brisbane. This huge sand mass holds up to 30% of its volume as water, and also possesses numerous fresh-water creeks lined with palms and giant ferns. More than 40 perched freshwater lakes, some up to 200m above sea level, exist on the island, their bases cemented by chemical bonding between mineral sands and organic material. Lake Mackenzie, with its shallow aquamarine waters, is a favourite for swimming.

The dunes, which are among the highest in the world, support tall rainforest trees. Local Dingos, with a distinctive reddish colour, white socks and white-tipped tail, are recognised as the purest strain of this wild dog remaining in Australia.

Plants

Australian landscapes are immediately recognisable in photos and film because of their distinctive plant species. Rather than the soft leafy foliage evident across much of the globe, most Australian habitats are adapted to fire, drought and nutrient-deficient soil. Consequently, leaves are often narrow, sharp and waxy, and much light penetrates through the canopy to the ground because competition for light is not as important as competition for water and nutrients. About 18 000 plant species are officially recorded from Australia, but over 30 000 species are thought to exist here. Over 6000 known species are present in south-western WA alone.

Seaweeds and Seagrasses

Australia is the most diverse country worldwide for seaweeds, with over 500 species in the tropical north and about 1250 species on s coasts. Most southern species are unique to this country, including an unusually high proportion of the lacey red seaweeds. Seagrasses are unrelated to seaweeds; they are a group of terrestrial grasses adapted to live submerged in coastal environments. Over half of the about 70 seagrass species worldwide live in Australia, with many found nowhere else.

GIANT STRING KELP ▼
(Macrocystis pyrifera)
This giant rope-like kelp possesses a holdfast on the seabed connected by numerous stalks to a leafy surface canopy, which is buoyed by gas bladders. The dense surface canopy dampens wave action and blocks light, creating a unique marine environment. Divers relate swimming through the shafts of light in an underwater kelp forest to floating through a rainforest. This kelp is the fastest growing plant on Earth, with fronds growing up to 50cm per day. Australian kelp beds have declined in recent years, probably because of rising sea temperatures. 35m. s Vic, Tas.

BULLKELP ▲
(Durvillaea potatorum)
Bullkelp possesses a massive stalk and frond, and tends to dominate the low tidal zone on exposed southern shores. Huge quantities are deposited onto beaches by storms. The plant is harvested on King Island (Bass Strait) for a chemical used to solidify ice cream and toothpaste. Drift plants washed onto the shore also provide a food source for grazing cattle. Tas Aborigines used dried fronds as containers for transporting food and water. 8m. s Vic, Tas.

COMMON KELP *(Ecklonia radiata)* ➤
This palm-like kelp has a single branched frond, often with small surface spines, and a stalk 0.2–1m long. It tolerates low light conditions and grows abundantly on reefs to greater depths than other large seaweeds. Detached fronds drift onto Sydney surf beaches in large masses after storms, prickling the legs of surfers. 2m. sw WA to se Qld, Tas.

CRAYWEED ▲
(Phyllospora comosa)
This common large brown seaweed can be recognised by its flat branches with spines along the edges and spindle-shaped floats. Fishermen regard its presence as an indication that rock lobsters are living nearby. 3m. se SA to ce NSW, Tas.

SPIRAL SARGASSUM ➤
(Sargassum verruculosum)
The sargassums are a large group of seaweeds, with over 200 species worldwide. They are well represented in Australia, with one major subgroup restricted to southern Australia and NZ. Spiral Saragassum is the most abundant and widely distributed species of this subgroup, dominating sheltered habitats. 1m. sw WA to ce NSW, Tas.

NEPTUNE'S NECKLACE ▼
(Hormosira banksii)
This is the most distinctive of Australian seaweeds—a living string of beads. It is also the most abundant intertidal species on sheltered shores along the southern coast. 30cm. sw WA to ne NSW, Tas.

LABILLARDIERE'S STRINGWEED ▼
(Cystophora retroflexa)
Closely related to the sargassums, stringweeds (*Cystophora* species) comprise a second group of brown seaweeds that have evolved into numerous species in southern Australia. Each of the 23 species has distinctive characteristics to survive particular environmental conditions.

Labillardiere's is the most abundant species, found in sheltered bays and estuaries. 2m. cs SA to ce NSW, Tas.

STRAPWEED ▼
(Posidonia australis)

This common seagrass thrives in sheltered bays and estuaries, where it tolerates wide extremes of salinity and temperature. It forms large meadows composed of millions of tough, flat, strap-like leaves. These leaves grow very quickly and differ from other local seagrasses in having rounded rather than broken ends. 1.5m. Coastal sw WA to ce NSW, Tas.

CAULERPAS ▲

Interspersed among the brown and red seaweeds on rocky reefs are the green caulerpas. Caulerpa fronds grow seasonally from runners and often have a cactus- or fern-like form. Three different species on a SA reef are shown in the image— elongate bluish green Beaded Caulerpa (*Caulerpa vesiculifera*), grass-green Fern Caulerpa (*Caulerpa flexilis*), and dark green Bushy Caulerpa (*Caulerpa obscura*). 40cm. Aus, Tas.

RED SEALACE ➤
(Claudea elegans)

Described by the greatest nineteenth-century British seaweed expert as 'the most beautiful of all algae', this distinctive species has curved delicate lace-like fronds. It is most often seen by divers near sand in areas with good water flow, but is just one of over 800 red seaweed species present along the southern Australian coast. 45cm. s WA to cs Vic, n Tas.

Ferns

Ferns first appeared on Earth some 400 million years ago. They reproduce using fine brown spores released from under leaves, and have a well-developed internal transport system with roots and stems. Well over 300 species occur in Australia.

GIANT TREE FERN ▼
(Cyathea australis)
About 15 giant tree fern species are present in Australia, and another 800 are known worldwide. They are distinguished by their tall slender trunks and rough bark.

This species has fronds up to 4.5m long radiating from a central stem. The frond stems have rough lumps on the surface. Like most ferns they prefer cool, wet rainforest gullies. 10m. Coast and GDR s Vic to ce Qld, Tas.

SOUTHERN TREE FERN ▲
(Dicksonia antarctica)
This plant carpets alpine gullies of southern Australia. Its trunk is normally hidden by fronds, which tend to remain on the trunk rather than falling after they die. This is the only fern that can be moved by cutting the trunk and relocating. It is widely used by landscape gardeners. 15m. Coast and GDR Vic, NSW, Tas.

ELKHORN ▼
(Platycerium birfurcatum)
The Elkhorn generally grows as an epiphyte on the trunks of rainforest trees but can also be found on rocks in well-sheltered rainforests. It produces numerous brown spores on the tips of fronds. This fern is widely cultivated in domestic gardens. Fronds to 2m. Rainforests of NSW and Qld.

BIRD'S NEST FERN ◄
(Asplenium australasicum)
This rainforest species grows high up as an epiphyte on the trunks of trees, or lower down, sometimes even on the forest floor. The bright green fronds make it an attractive plant when cultivated in shaded gardens. Fronds to 3m. se NSW to ne Qld.

Most pines, also known as conifers, are evergreen trees that produce cones and lack flowers. The leaves are usually narrow, often resembling needles, or are reduced to small scales along the branchlets. A few species have broader leaves, such as the Kauri Pine, while the Celery Top Pine has flattened leaf-like branchlets. Australia is home to 43 known species.

HUON PINE ➤
(Lagarostrobos franklinii)

This slow-growing pine can reach 2300 years old. It generally has a straight trunk, weeping cypress-like leaves and reddish pollen cones. it usually grows along the banks of rivers in cool temperate rainforest. Its close-grained honey-coloured rot-resistant timber is famous for boat building and furniture. Over the past two centuries, the tree has been heavily exploited throughout its restricted range, to the extent that populations have contracted to remote wilderness refuges. 38m. sw Tas.

CELERY TOP PINE ▼
(Phyllocladus aspleniifolius)

This species has celery-like dark green foliage clustered at the ends of branches. It grows in cool temperate rainforest and wet eucalypt forest. A slow-growing, long-lived species, its timber has been used for railway sleepers, flooring, boat building and joinery. 30m. Tas.

PLUM PINE, ILLAWARRA PINE ▼
(Podocarpus elatus)

A subtropical rainforest tree, this species typically grows on sandy or deep alluvial soil near waterways. It has narrow oblong leaves, a dark green crown and fibrous dark brown bark. The fruit is plum-like, bluish black and edible, ripening Mar–July. 40m. ce NSW to ne Qld.

WOLLEMI PINE ➤
(Wollemia nobilis)

This attractive pine with dark green foliage was discovered in 1994 in a rainforest gorge in Wollemi National Park. It belongs to the araucaria pines, which dominated landscapes from 90 to 200 million years ago. Cultivated specimens have been requested by national parks and botanic gardens worldwide. 40m. Blue Mountains, NSW.

BUNYA PINE ➤
(Araucaria bidwilli)

Bunya pines are generally similar to their close local relative, the cultivated Hoop Pine (*Araucaria cunninghamii*), but have a distinctive domed rather than straight-edged appearance and almost black bark. They emerge above other canopy trees in tropical rainforests. The leaves are glossy green with sharp points. The

PENCIL PINE ▲
(Athrotaxis cupressoides)

Rough-barked pencil pines often grow in a group, forming high-altitude forests in Tas. The tree bears spherical cones 1.5cm in diameter and has reduced scale-like leaves on narrow branched stems. 15m. c, w and s Tas.

KING BILLY PINE ➤
(Athrotaxis selaginoides)

A close relative of the Pencil Pine, this wet-forest species grows taller and has spiny leaves, but otherwise is very similar. These two Tasmanian pines are related to the Giant Redwoods of California and have no other close relatives in the southern hemisphere. 40m. c and w Tas.

football-sized (20–30cm diameter) cones contain 50–100 large nuts, and are dangerous projectiles when they fall. Aborigines congregated in large numbers to feast upon the protein- and oil-rich seeds. 45m. se Qld near Nambour and ne Qld near Mt Lewis.

NORFOLK ISLAND PINE ▼

(Araucaria heterophylla)

This highly salt-tolerant species has distinctive incurved leaves. Its timber was used for spars in the rigging of sailing vessels during the nineteenth century. 60m. Norfolk Island, but now widely cultivated.

KAURI PINE ▲

(Agathis microstachya)

This pine extends above the canopy in tropical rainforest. It is characterised by flaky coarse bark and a straight trunk that only begins to taper at the start of the crown. The leaves have numerous longitudinal veins. Kauri timber is used for flooring, framing and joinery. 50m. Atherton, n Qld.

WHITE CYPRESS PINE ➤

(Callitris columellaris)

An arid-zone tree, this pine has tiny green leaves with triangular tips in whorls of three or four. Both male and female cones are present, the 2cm-diameter female cones occurring on separate branchlets. Seeds are 4mm wide with two wings. 15m. Inland Aus.

PORT JACKSON PINE, OYSTER BAY PINE ▲

(Callitris rhomboidea)

This small, widely distributed tree grows on sandy soil, particularly near the coast. The rounded cones are composed of large scales that taper to a blunt point. Leaves are ridged and 4–5mm long. 10m. se Aus, Tas.

Cycads

The 69 species of cycad known from Australia can be recognised by a crown of large compound leaves and a short, stout trunk. Today they are found as a minor floral component in tropical and subtropical regions, but 200 million years ago they were common worldwide. Because of their large attractive leaves and striking growth habit, many species are now cultivated in gardens.

GIANT ZAMIA ▼
(Macrozamia reidlei)
This species grows in relatively infertile sandy soil. It has a palm-like form with tough leathery fronds arising from a short trunk. Reddish seeds are contained within spiny, stalked, cone-like structures. Aborigines developed methods for leaching the toxins from the seeds, including soaking and ageing, to provide a starchy food. 5m. sw WA.

BURRAWANG ▲
(Macrozamia communis)
The male and female cones of the Burrawang look like pineapples and occur on separate plants. Aborigines ate the large seeds after washing them to remove toxins. 2m. ce NSW.

LITCHFIELD CYCAD ◄
(Cycas calcicola)
This plant has flat, stiff fronds with numerous long leaflets. New growth is sometimes coated by a fine white substance after fire, making this cycad stand out against its rocky sandstone habitat. The species burns easily but recovers by quickly producing new leaves. The two sexes can be distinguished by the different fruiting bodies: the male produces a large spike and the female numerous drumstick-like nuts. 5m. cn NT.

Palms comprise another early group of flowering plants. They are thought to have originated in India and spread across the ancient n and s supercontinents. Palms have been present in Australia for at least 55 million years; however, many Australian species are recent migrants from South-East Asia. Over 50 Australian palm species are known, with most found in the tropics or along the east coast to Vic. Many are cultivated as ornamental plants.

BANGALOW PALM ▼
(Archontophoenix cunninghamiana)

This species is naturally found in gullies and along creek banks, sometimes in pure stands. It has also been widely planted in urban areas. The dark green leaves grow to 2m long, forming a distinctive umbrella-shaped crown. Lilac flowers transform into globular red 1cm-diameter fruits. Fl Feb–June. 20m. se NSW to ce Qld.

WALKING STICK PALM ▲
(Linospadix monostachya)

This small single-stemmed rainforest palm has a slender trunk and leaves about 1m long. The flower spikes grow to 50cm long, eventually producing numerous small red berries. 5m. ce NSW to e Qld.

CABBAGE TREE PALM ▼

(Livistona australis)

This species has a slender stem topped with a crown of dark green leaves. The large fan-shaped leaves grow on stems up to 2m, with short curved spines projecting from the lower stem. The lower crown includes dead leaves that hang for some time before dropping. Fl Dec–Feb. 25m. Coast se Vic to ce Qld.

SAND PALM ➤

(Livistona humilis)

This stunted species occurs most commonly in savannah shrubland south of Darwin. Like most other plants in that region, it is adapted to fire. Although the leaves burn quickly, the vulnerable core of the plant is protected by tough bark and new shoots appear rapidly. 5m. n NT.

LICUALA PALM ▲

(Licuala ramsayi)

This species typically grows in shaded areas adjacent to stream banks or poorly drained areas. Its most striking feature is a crown of fan-like leaves up to 2m in diameter. Adult trees sometimes emerge above the canopy in rainforest. 15m. ne Qld.

LAWYER VINE, WAIT-A-WHILE ➤

(Calamus species)

These climbers have numerous stems growing in a tangled mass. The stems are

cloaked in spines, which dig into the flesh and clothes of anyone pushing past, hence the common names. The spines are an adaptation for climbing up larger trees towards light. Aborigines used lawyer vines in several ways: the cut stems as a source of water, the leaves to build shelters, and the stems to weave into baskets and to use as aids when climbing trees. Stem length 100m. ne NSW to ne Qld.

Trees, Shrubs and Flowers

Trees, shrubs and flowers are grouped with palms as flowering plants, the most conspicuous and diverse of all plant groups. Their flowers carry reproductive organs and can contain either male or female structures, or both. Many species produce a nectar or pollen reward for pollinators (insects, birds, small mammals and other organisms) to attract them to the flowers and induce them to assist in pollination. The colours and scents of flowers help pollinators to find fertile plants. Australia has over 14 000 species of flowering plants.

SPIRAL SCREW PALM, SPIRAL PANDANUS ▼
(Pandanus spiralis)
These small, spreading palm-like plants have branches almost the same diameter as the trunk. Their fibrous, spirally arranged leaves taper to a point and are edged with sharp teeth. Inconspicuous flowers develop into a fruiting body up to 40cm in diameter.

Most other screw pine species live next to river banks or the seashore, but this one extends inland a considerable distance in the northern savannah. 4m. n NT.

gourd-like fruits maturing after leaves drop. The foliage provides fodder for cattle during droughts. Aborigines used water trapped in deep hollows and the white powder in seed pods to produce 'bread'. 12m. ne WA, nw NT.

BOAB ➤
(Adansonia gregori)
This tree has a distinctive bottle-shaped trunk up to 16m in circumference. It is deciduous, producing new leaves Oct–Dec. Large white flowers appear when the tree is in leaf, the

MORETON BAY FIG ▼
(Ficus macrophylla)
Australia has 42 fig species, all producing edible fruits with numerous small seeds. A milky-coloured sap exudes from broken stems. Some species bear fruits directly from the trunk or branches. Many are large rainforest trees, including this giant tree with its characteristic buttressed trunk.

the year. Aborigines used the bark to make string. 50m. ce NSW to ne Qld.

RED CEDAR ▲
(Toona ciliata)
European timber getters explored the east coast largely in search of this tree. Its timber is light, soft, durable and highly valued for furniture and ornamental woodwork. With a buttressed trunk up to 3m in diameter, this deciduous rainforest species is now comparatively rare. 70m. ce NSW to ne Qld.

MACADAMIA ➤
(Macadamia integrifolia)
This small rainforest tree is an economically important plant both in Australia and overseas. Large-scale macadamia plantations in NSW and Qld produce the oil-rich 'macadamia nut', which can be eaten raw or lightly roasted. Under natural conditions, the tree bears fruit only after six to seven years. 20m. ne NSW to se Qld.

This fig is commonly seen beside major road systems and is often the only remaining tree in paddocks. The edible fruits ripen throughout

STRANGLER FIG ▲
(Ficus watkinsiana)
This species begins life when seeds lodge in the branch of a host tree. The seeds then germinate, sending down aerial roots that grow in size, ultimately killing the host tree. The succulent dark purplish fruits, 3–6cm long, are covered in small spots. 50m. ce NSW to ne Qld.

SOUTHERN BEECH, ANTARCTIC BEECH, MYRTLE ▼
(Nothofagus cunninghamii)
This rainforest tree has an ancient Gondwanan lineage, with close relatives in South America and NZ. New spring foliage is a rich bronze colour before turning a deep green. The soft reddish timber is used in cabinet making. 33m. s Vic, Tas.

YELLOW CARABEAN
(Sloanea woollsii) ➤
This NSW rainforest tree has buttresses that can extend 2–5m up the base of the trunk. The dark grey bark is furrowed and the toothed yellow–green leaves grow to 19cm long. It produces star-shaped flowers in spring, followed by small spiky seed capsules enclosing the fruit. 40m. ce NSW to se Qld.

ROSEWOOD ▲
(Dysoxylum fraserianum)
This large tree has yellow–grey scaly bark, a thick trunk to 1.5m diameter and a dense shiny green crown. It grows in subtropical rainforest, often on moderate slopes of coastal ranges. The underbark and sap have a rose-like fragrance. The timber is used for furniture, woodturning and joinery. 40m. ce NSW to se Qld.

SASSAFRAS ▼
(Doryphora sassafras)
This tree typically has a compact, small crown with branches positioned almost at right angles to the trunk. It lives in a variety of coastal rainforest sites from sea level to 1000m, including gullies and plateau areas. The sapwood, bark and leaves have an aromatic odour. Another tree also locally known as the Sassafras (*Atherosperma moschatum*) grows in wet forest situations from Tas to south-eastern Qld. That species can be recognised by its pale, mottled trunk and distinctive serrated-edged leaves. 42m. se NSW to se Qld.

Wild Australia

BUMPY SATINASH ▼
(Syzygium cormiflorum)

This rainforest tree has an erect growth habit, with buttressed trunks in mature individuals. New leaves are purple to pink; adult leaves are large and glossy green. The large white flowers are borne on the trunk and main branches. It has edible pink to white fruits to 6cm diameter. Fl Sept–Nov. 35m. ne Qld.

ROSE BUTTERNUT ▲
(Blepharocarya involucrigera)

This tall rainforest tree has a buttressed trunk topped with a crown of fern-like leaves. New leaf growth is red. The timber is commonly used for joinery, interior panelling and furniture. 35m. ne Qld.

LILLY PILLY ➤
(Acmena smithii)

This plant varies from a tall tree in wet forests to a shrub in exposed coastal conditions. It grows on a wide variety of soil types, but prefers sites along the banks of waterways. The white to pink or purplish fruits have a slightly acidic, aromatic flavour and can be made into jam. Aborigines relish them as a bushfood. Fl Oct–Feb. 20m. se Vic to ne Qld.

SWEET PITTOSPORUM ▲
(Pittosporum undulatum)

This dense bushy tree has dark glossy green leaves in whorls at the ends of branches. It produces clusters of white to cream flowers and distinctive orange fruits. Pittosporum has been widely planted in urban areas for shade. Fl July–Oct. 14m. ne Vic to se Qld.

RIVER SHEOAK ▼
(Casuarina cunninghamiana)

The sheoaks or casuarinas superficially resemble pines but use green branchlets for trapping light, the true leaves being reduced to a whorl of small triangular teeth at joints along the branchlets. A close association with nitrogen-fixing bacteria allows them to grow in poor soil.

This is the largest Australian sheoak and typically grows along the margins of waterways. It has been used for ornamental plantings as well as for providing shade and stabilising eroded river banks. The woody head of each flower forms a 'cone'. 35m. se NSW to ne Qld, n NT.

and open forests, although in drier areas plants are usually stunted. The hard wood makes good fuel and is used for building and by woodturners. 20m. se WA, n SA, nw Vic, w NSW.

DWARF SHEOAK ▲
(Casuarina monilifera)

This small sheoak commonly occurs in coastal heaths, where it rarely exceeds 1m in height. The largest plants (to 4m) are found on the central plateau in Tas. Coastal Vic, Tas.

GREY MANGROVE ▲
(Avicennia marina)

Mangroves are trees adapted to survive tidal inundation by seawater. About 60 mangrove species are known in Australia. They belong to a range of different plant families, with most confined to the tropics.

The Grey Mangrove extends much further south than other species. It has spreading glossy green foliage and an aerial root system of pencil-like pneumatophores (breathing structures) that poke up from the mudflat. The fruit was cooked and eaten by Aborigines. 8m. Coastal se, e and n Aus.

BELAH ➤
(Casuarina cristata)

This sheoak forms dense stands of medium-sized trees in river flats and depressions. It also occurs in woodlands

BLACK KURRAJONG ▼
(Brachychiton populneus)

About 30 compact, densely foliaged kurrajong species occur in Australia. Many are widely cultivated as shade trees and for livestock fodder during drought periods. Kurrajongs grow on a variety of soils, often preferring those derived from limestone.

The Black Kurrajong has a stout trunk, spreading crown, and distinctive leaves and seeds. This plant provides good fodder in drought conditions for cattle. Aborigines used its fibrous bark to construct nets. 20m. w GDR from c Vic to c Qld.

ILLAWARRA FLAME TREE ➤
(Brachychiton acerifolius)

This kurrajong is one of the most colourful Australian trees. Scarlet bell-shaped flowers cover the tree after the leaves have been shed. The edible seeds have a nutty taste. Fl Nov–Dec. 40m. ce NSW to ne Qld.

ALPINE ASH, STRINGYBARK ➤

(Eucalyptus delegatensis)

About 600 species of eucalypt or gum tree are known. Most possess a tree-like form, while others, known as 'mallees' in semi-arid regions, have thickened rootstock (a 'lignotuber') from which several stems arise.

The Alpine Ash dominates mountain forests of se Australia and Tas, particularly between 1000 and 1300m altitude, and is the second tallest eucalypt. It has dark, stringy, fibrous bark towards

the base of the trunk, while upper branches have smooth white–yellow bark. It is harvested for building framing, plywood, veneers, flooring and paper pulp, and produces gums and honey. 85m. se Vic, se NSW, Tas.

BLACK PEPPERMINT ▲

(Eucalyptus amygdalina)

This eucalypt has rough grey–brown bark to the bases of the larger branches, which are smooth barked, sometimes with ribbons of hanging bark. Long, narrow, aromatic leaves are characteristic of this and other peppermints. The timber is used for fuel, joinery and fencing. 30m. e and ne Tas.

CIDER GUM ➤

(Eucalyptus gunnii)

The mottled bark of this eucalypt occurs in various colours and flakes into small pieces. This gum usually grows on poorly drained sites in cold highland areas. Its sap flows feely, tastes like maple syrup, and is a favourite of animals such as sugar gliders. Early settlers used the sap to brew cider-like drinks, and Aborigines used it as a medicine. 25m. Tas.

MOUNTAIN ASH, SWAMP GUM ➤

(Eucalyptus regnans)

This is the tallest hardwood tree in the world, only exceeded in size by the softwood Californian Redwoods. Heights over 100m are attributed to this species, although the tallest accurately measured trees just reach 90m. It has rough, fibrous bark at the trunk base, and smooth bark above. Ribbons of hanging bark decorate the upper

branches. This species has been heavily exploited for its fine hardwood timber. 90m. s Vic, Tas.

ROUND-LEAFED GUM, MOUNTAIN BLUE GUM ◄

(Eucalyptus deanei)

This eucalypt has a smooth, mottled cream bark apart from some scaly grey bark at the base of the trunk. It usually grows in well-watered valleys, where it can occur in large stands, most notably in the Blue Mountains. The wood is used for construction, flooring and panelling. 65m. ce NSW to se Qld.

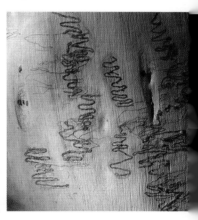

SOUTHERN BLUE GUM, TASMANIAN BLUE GUM ▲

(Eucalyptus globulus)

This eucalpyt is the floral emblem of Tas. Its trunk is mostly smooth and the leaves on mature plants are large and glossy green. It is widely exploited in native forests for pulp and timber production, as well as being grown in large plantations in Australia and overseas. 45m. s Vic to ce NSW, Tas.

TASMANIAN SNOW GUM ➤

(Eucalyptus coccifera)

Depending upon the environment, this eucalypt can grow as a tree or a mallee-like shrub. Its thickened rootstock helps it regenerate quickly after fire. The light grey to pink bark is smooth, with the occasional loose grey piece at the base. The Snow Gum (*Eucalyptus pauciflora*) of alpine areas of Vic and NSW is similar. Both eucalypt species typically grow at cold mountainous sites just below the tree line. 15m. c, w and s Tas.

SCRIBBLY GUM ▲

(Eucalyptus haemostoma)

This species has smooth mottled grey, cream or pale orange bark. The prominent scribbles are the empty tunnels of moth grubs that burrow along the boundary between old- and new-season bark. The Scribbly Gum is used for timber, fuel, honey production and medicine. Fl Sept–Dec. 15m. e NSW.

RIVER RED GUM ▲
(Eucalyptus camaldulensis)
This is one of our best known trees and the most widespread eucalypt. It provided the fuel that powered steamboats plying the Murray River in the nineteenth and early twentieth centuries. The River Red Gum generally grows beside permanent or seasonal water bodies. It has smooth, pale-coloured mottled bark. Its wood has a variety of uses, including flooring, railway sleepers, fencing, gums, oils and medicines. 45m. Aus.

WHITE MALLEE ▼
(Eucalyptus dumosa)
The lower stems of the White Mallee have rough grey–brown bark. Ribbons of bark are shed from the upper stems and branches. Leaves on mature plants are a dull grey–green and flowers are white. 10m. e SA, nw Vic, sw NSW.

SNAPPY GUM ▼
(Eucalyptus leucophloia)
With its white twisted form and dull green leaves, this species is conspicuous across the WA Pilbara region. It grows on grassy hillsides and in stony gullies. 12m. cn WA.

COOLABAH ▲
(Eucalyptus microtheca)
This eucalypt occurs on seasonally flooded heavy-soiled plains and river banks. Mature trees have a straggly appearance, always with some rough basal bark. The upper trunk and branches are smooth and pale, and the adult leaves are a dull greyish green. The timber is used for firewood and fencing. 10m. Inland Aus.

WANDOO ▼
(Eucalyptus wandoo)
This small tree has spotty bark and dull blue– to grey–green leaves. It is the dominant plant in open woodlands. Wandoo timber is very dense, strong and durable. 18m. sw WA.

RED TINGLE ▼
(Eucalyptus jacksonii)
This huge eucalypt has a moderately buttressed base and rough bark up to the smaller branches. The deep pink to reddish brown wood is used for heavy construction and railway sleepers. This

species has a highly restricted distribution on well-drained soil of coastal river valleys. 65m. sw WA.

BUSHY YATE ▲
(Eucalyptus lehmannii)
A mallee-like tree with thickened rootstock, this eucalypt has smooth stems with whitish grey to orange–brown bark that is shed in strips. The bud and fruit clusters are large and distinctive. The plant is widely used in urban plantings. 3m. Coastal sw and c WA.

SALMON GUM ▲
(Eucalyptus salmonophloia)
This tree grows surprisingly tall in semi-arid habitats. Its smooth bark is a pale cream to grey in winter and spring, turning a striking salmon colour in summer and autumn. The wood is strong and durable, and was once used extensively for mining supports, railway sleepers and firewood. 25m. cs WA.

JARRAH ▲
(Eucalyptus marginata)
This eucalypt can occur as a tall forest tree or as a mallee, depending on soil and climate. The dark red to reddish brown timber is well known for its hardness and durability. Among other functions, Jarrah is used in flooring and the manufacture of high-quality furniture. The flowers also help generate large quantities of nutty-flavoured honey. 35m. sw WA.

KARRI ▲
(Eucalyptus diversicolor)
This is the largest of the south-western eucalypts and one of the largest trees in the world. Mature Karri have smooth, mottled cream–grey

bark with a seasonal orange tinge. The striking red timber is moderately durable and was widely used in the past for flooring and building construction. 80m. sw WA.

MOTTLECAH ▲
(Eucalyptus macrocarpa)
Its massive red flowers and compact appearance make this eucalypt a favourite ornamental. It has a mallee-like growth form and smooth yellow– to grey–brown bark,

which is shed in short ribbons. 3m. sw WA.

GUNGURRU ▼
(Eucalyptus caesia)
This eucalypt has a mallee-like growth form. Its large flowers of pink filaments topped with yellow anthers complement the dull green leaves and fruits. It naturally grows adjacent to granite outcrops but has been planted widely, including in the eastern States. Fl June–Sept. 15m. sw WA.

PILBARA DESERT BLOODWOOD ▲
(Corymbia deserticola)

Recent studies indicate that the bloodwoods and Ghost Gums are more closely related to the smooth-barked apples than to other eucalypts, hence they are now grouped in a different genus, *Corymbia*. They share a number of features not seen in *Eucalyptus* species, including shape of gumnuts.

Like the other 100 plus bloodwood species, the Pilbara Desert Bloodwood has rough, ridged bark over most of the trunk, and flowers on branchlets. It grows on stony plains and rocky hills. 8m. c and nw WA.

GHOST GUM ➤
(Corymbia aparrerinja)

This gum has become the iconic species of central Australian deserts, receiving widespread national recognition as the focal point in landscape paintings by the Aboriginal artist Albert Namatjira. Smooth, powdery white to light grey bark covers the entire trunk. Ghost Gums generally grow on stony hillsides. 15m. NT, w Qld.

SMOOTH-BARKED APPLE ➤
(Angophora costata)

This smooth-barked tree is a close relative of the eucalypts, but with ridged gumnuts and leaf stems arising opposite each other on branchlets. The trunks are twisted and branches are often dead and liable to fall, creating cavities for nesting birds, gliders and possums. It has cream flowers and is a popular ornamental tree. 30m. Coastal ce to ne NSW.

TURPENTINE ▼
(Syncarpia glomulifera)

This close relative of the eucalypts prefers deep, fertile soil in forested valley bottoms. Its thick brown bark peels in strings, and gumnuts are fused together into a ball. The common name is derived from its red resinous sap, which protects the tree from termites and borers. Its highly durable timber is used in marine construction. 70m. Coastal ce NSW to se Qld.

WESTERN AUSTRALIAN CHRISTMAS BUSH ◄
(Nuytsia floribunda)

This odd species is a giant parasitic mistletoe, gaining nutrients by tapping into the roots of host trees, some of which may be up to 100m distant. Around Christmas the plant puts on a brilliant display of golden flowers. The species commonly grows on sandplains, slopes and at the bases of rocky outcrops. Fl Oct–Jan. 10m. sw WA.

CHRISTMAS BUSH ▲
(Ceratopetalum gummiferum)

This shub grows adjacent to sandstone outcrops. It typically has a shrubby form but can reach tree proportions. Possessing three-lobed leaves, it is commonly cultivated for its profuse summer display of bright red flowers. Fl Nov–Feb. 10m. ce to ne NSW.

GIANT STINGING TREE ▼
(Dendrocnide excelsa)

This species commonly grows as a small tree in rainforest clearings. It has very large heart-shaped and serrated-edged leaves that grow to 20cm long and are densely covered by stinging hairs. A sting from this plant, or worse still its larger relative in north Qld rainforests, causes excruciating pain. Giant Stinging Trees produce white fruits that resemble raspberries, also covered in stinging hairs. Although edible once the hairs are removed, these fruits are best left alone. 40m. Coastal ce NSW to se Qld.

LEATHERWOOD ▼
(Eucryphia lucida)

This tree and the smaller Dwarf Leatherwood (*Eucryphia milliganii*) are confined to temperate Tas rainforests. The five Australian leatherwoods have changed little over the past 100 million years; their nearest relatives are in South America. All Australian species produce numerous delicate white flowers with four rounded petals that carpet the forest floor after windfall. Apiarists set beehives near Leatherwood stands to exploit the copious nectar produced by flowers. Leatherwood honey has a distinctive flavour. Fl Dec–Feb. 30m. sw Tas.

WOODY PEAR ➤
(Xylomelum angustifolium)

This large shrub has white to cream flowers and pear-shaped woody fruits that take several years to mature. Winged seeds are released from the fruit, aiding dispersal from the parent plant. Fl Sept–Feb. 10m. cw WA.

MOUNTAIN PEPPER, SUGAR BUSH ▲
(Tasmannia lanceolata)

This species can grow as a small tree but is more commonly found as a shrub. The stems are red and the leaves are dark green to reddish with smooth margins. The leaves and reddish black fruit are edible and are increasingly used in cooking to provide a peppery taste. The ironic name 'sugar bush' is most often used when an unsuspecting victim is offered the leaves to taste. Fl Dec–Feb. 4m. Alpine se Aus, Tas.

DESERT QUANDONG ▲
(Santalum acuminatum)

This shrub grows in woodlands on sandy and stony soil. It has paired olive green leaves on drooping stems. The fruits are shiny bright red, ripening in spring. They are a well-known 'bushtucker', with high Vitamin C content and a pleasant, slightly acidic taste valued by Aborigines. The quandong is a root parasite, gaining many of its nutrients from a host tree. Fl year-round. 7m. Inland Aus.

KAPOK BUSH ▼
(Cochlospermum fraseri)

This deciduous shrub of the savannah woodlands produces large yellow flowers that are highly visible during the northern dry season. Large green globular fruits develop and eventually open to release seed. The small black seeds are embedded within a dense mat of fine silky hairs. Fl Mar–Sept. 6m. ne NT to n WA.

NATIVE CHERRY ➤
(Exocarpos cupressiformis)

This species resembles a conifer but is actually a semi-parasitic shrub associated with the root system of host trees such as eucalypts. The dense foliage is yellowish green to dark green. Cream-coloured inconspicuous flowers develop into an edible bright red fruit with a small nut attached to the end. Fl Oct–Apr. 8m. Coast and GDR se SA to ce Qld, e Tas.

SILVER WATTLE ➤
(Acacia dealbata)

The acacias or wattles comprise a large group of about 660 described species, with many more undescribed. They are the dominant vegetation in many semi-arid regions, with fewer species in the tropics. Acacias have a symbiotic relationship with nitrogen-fixing bacteria, and consequently play a key role in soil enrichment in forest environments. They are easily recognised by their bean-like pods and fluffy golden flowers that are either globular or clustered in cylindrical spikes. Leaves, when present, are flattened and fern-like.

The Silver Wattle has dark green leaves with 10–20 paired leaflets. The golden ball-shaped flowers are clustered in groups of 25–30. Often planted in urban areas, this tree is frequently attacked by boring insects. Fl July–Aug. 30m. se Vic to e NSW, Tas.

BLACKWOOD ▲
(Acacia melanoxylon)

This highly variable acacia can grow as a tree to 30m, or as a small shrub to 3m. It grows in diverse habitats but prefers flat areas at the bottom of valleys and sites with good rainfall. What look like lance-shaped leaves with long veins on this and most other acacia species are actually extensions of the bark known as phyllodes. Blackwood timber is prized for panelling, cabinet work and stringed instruments. Fl July–Sept. 30m. Coast and GDR se SA to ne Qld, Tas.

GOLDEN WATTLE ➤
(Acacia pycnantha)

This shrub is Australia's national floral emblem. It typically grows on sandy shallow soil in drier areas as a tall shrub or tree; small, spindly forms can also occur. The bark is a rich source of tannin, while the gum was eaten by Aborigines. Fl July–Nov. 8m. sc SA, Vic, s and cw NSW.

COOTAMUNDRA WATTLE ▲
(Acacia baileyana)

Although short-lived, this shrub is fast-growing, frost-resistant and hardy, with a spectacular floral display. It is widely cultivated in parks and gardens and is now established in all States. The light green leaves are finely branched in a fishbone arrangement. Fl June–Sep. 9m. sc NSW.

MULGA ➤
(Acacia aneura)

This highly variable shrub can be difficult to identify, but usually has greyish foliage and branches that bend upwards. It generally grows on sandy soil or on rocky soil on hills. Domestic stock and native mammals both use this plant as fodder during drought. Fl Mar–May. 7m. Inland Aus.

Trees, Shrubs and Flowers

COASTAL WATTLE, BOOBYALLA ▲

(Acacia sophorae)

This acacia commonly grows on coastal dunes and in forests. It has a sprawling growth habit, with stems usually turned upwards. The yellow flowers are grouped in elongated flower spikes. Cylindrical green pods develop during early summer. It has been used extensively to stabilise sand dunes.

Fl June–Oct. 5m. Coastal se SA to ne NSW, Tas.

PRICKLY MIMOSA ▼

(Acacia verticillata)

In place of leaves, this species has spine-like phyllodes up to 2cm long. The pale yellow flowers are clustered in short spikes. This acacia commonly occurs in saline areas and lower mountain slopes, and varies in size from a compact bush to a small tree. Fl July–Dec. 10m. se SA to se NSW, Tas.

KARIJINI WATTLE ▼

(Acacia marramamba)

The round flowers of this species have a distinctive reddish tinge and the leaf-like pyllodes are broad with a pointed end. This smooth-barked shrub grows on thin sandy soil among rocky hills and spinifex grasslands and woodlands. Fl May–July. 5m. nw WA.

related to paperbarks and have open white five-petalled flowers and a distinctive woody seed capsule.

This one is an erect or spreading shrub, with white or occasionally pinkish flowers massed along the stems. It generally grows as an under-storey plant in moist habitats in forests or heathlands. Many garden varieties have been derived from this species. Fl Oct–Feb. 3m. Coastal s Vic to ce NSW, Tas.

SILVER-LEAFED PAPERBARK ▲

(Melaleuca argentea)

Around 150 species of melaleucas are known. The large melaleucas, commonly called paperbarks, are conspicuous in swampy areas along rivers and floodplains, and can dominate the vegetation. The name 'paperbark' derives from the flaky nature of the bark, which peels off in large sheets. Many species contain oils that are used in medicinal treatments.

The Silver-leafed Paperbark can be recognised by the colour of its leaf tips. The flowers are yellow, cream or white. It grows on sand or clay along watercourses,

swamps and coastal lagoons. Fl July–Nov. 18m. Coastal ne Qld to nw WA.

BROAD-LEAFED PAPERBARK ➤

(Melaleuca quinquenervia)

This tree commonly occurs in pure stands on land adjoining mangrove swamps, or in low-lying swampy areas next to estuaries. The bark is thick, papery and greyish white, and is capable of protecting the living tissues beneath from the effects of moderate fires. Fl Feb–July. 20m. Coastal ce NSW to ne Qld.

MANUKA ➤

(Leptospermum scoparium)

This is one of many species of 'tea tree'. They are closely

watercourses. The flower spikes are a brilliant red tipped with yellow and are up to 10cm long. Fl Sept–Jan. 6m. ce WA to s WA.

SCARLET FEATHERFLOWER ▲
(Verticordia grandis)
This straggly shrub has numerous branches with bright red flowers partly hidden among the flattened leaves. Plants commonly grow among heaths on sand. They flower sporadically throughout the year, with a spring peak. 1.5m. sw WA.

SANDPLAIN BOTTLEBRUSH ▼
(Beaufortia squarrosa)
The compact leaves of this rounded shrub are arranged in two opposite rows. The scarlet flowers sit on the ends of the branches. Plants grow profusely in low-lying sandy areas, most commonly near limestone. Fl Aug–May. 4m. cw to s WA.

LESSER BOTTLEBRUSH ▲
(Callistemon phoeniceus)
A spectacular species when in flower, this widely cultivated shrub grows on sandy soil, often along

CRIMSON KUNZEA ▼
(Kunzea baxteri)
The dense branches of this rough-barked shrub grow close to the ground, giving it a rounded appearance. Bright scarlet flowers are borne on spikes. It grows in sandy soil among granitic hills. Fl July–Mar. 3m. Coastal s WA.

CRANBROOK BELL ▼
(Darwinia meeboldii)

This erect spindly shrub grows on peaty soil and adjacent hillsides. The flowers are produced from, and enclosed by, pale petal-like leaves with red tips. Numerous flowers are clustered together in a head. Fl Aug–Nov. 3m. Stirling Ranges, WA.

VIOLET EREMAEA ▲
(Eremaea violacea)

This low-lying shrub produces copious intense violet flowers with golden tips. Plants generally grow on coastal sandplains. Fl Sept–Dec. 1m. Geraldton, WA.

CLAWFLOWER ▼
(Calothamnus blepharospermus)

Over 40 different clawflower species are known, all restricted to s WA. This small shrub has pine-like foliage. The vivid red flowers tend to be clustered on one side of the branches. It grows on sandplains, dunes and clay. Fl Jan–July. 3m. Shark Bay to Geraldton, WA.

COPPERCUPS ▼
(Pileanthus peduncularis)

The profuse bright salmon flowers of this low-lying plant contrast with its thick stubby leaves. The species occurs on sandy soil, primarily near the coast. Fl Aug–Dec. 1.5m. cw WA.

COAST BANKSIA ▼
(Banksia integrifolia)

This large shrub is the most widespread of numerous banksias along the e coast. It produces a pale yellow flower spike about 12cm long, and has wide smooth-margined leaves with a dark green upper surface. The lower leaf surface is white and covered with fine hairs. Fl Dec–June. 25m. Coastal s Vic to se Qld.

SILVER BANKSIA, HONEYSUCKLE ▼
(Banksia marginata)

This abundant shrub has squat flower heads and narrow leaves with a white undersurface. It grows in a wide range of habitats, from coastal heaths to mountain scrub. Fl year-round. 12m. se SA to se NSW, Tas.

OLD MAN BANKSIA ▲
(Banksia serrata)

The 70 or so banksia species are restricted to Australia other than one that extends to New Guinea. Their discovery during the 1770 James Cook expedition by naturalist Joseph Banks created much excitement among European naturalists. Banksias are utilised widely in the cut-flower trade. They have large heads (technically known as spikes) made up of several hundred cream, red, yellow or orange flowers. Living flower spikes provide a critical food source for nectar-eating birds, mammals and insects, particularly during late autumn and early winter when few other native plants are flowering. The distinctive shaggy old flower heads with protruding woody fruits persist for many months.

Old Man Banksia is common in e Australia, particularly the Sydney region. It has long, serrated leaves, large flower heads and a corky furrowed trunk. The withered flower spikes of this shrub resemble the head of a dishevelled senior citizen. Because of this appearance, the bad 'banksia man' has entered children's folklore through cartoons and popular literature, most particularly May Gibbs' *Snugglepot and Cuddlepie* books. Fl Jan–June. 16m. se Vic to se Qld, n Tas.

HEATH BANKSIA ▼
(Banksia ericifolia)
This species is restricted to NSW coastal sandplains, extending inland as far as the Blue Mountains. It has elongated cylindrical orange–red flower spikes. Fl May–Sept. 6m. ce to ne NSW.

RED OR ALBANY BANKSIA ➤
(Banksia coccinea)
A small eye-catching shrub, this banksia has scarlet flower heads protruding vertically on branchlets. The species is widely used in the cut-flower trade. Fl July–Jan. 4m. Albany to Hopetoun, WA.

MENZIES' OR FIREWOOD BANKSIA ◄
(Banksia menziesii)
This distinctive straggling banksia has numerous furrowed acorn-shaped flower spikes. The species commonly adorns roadsides on coastal sandplains. Fl Feb–Aug. 15m. Kalbarri to Perth, WA.

ACORN OR ORANGE BANKSIA ➤
(Banksia prionotes)
The greatest diversity of banksias (about two-thirds of known species, including the most spectacular) grow in south-western WA. This flamboyant shrub has white acorn-shaped flower heads protruding from a woolly orange base. Fl Nov–Aug. 10m. sw WA.

ROUND-FRUITED BANKSIA ▼

(Banksia sphaerocarpa)

This shrub differs from other banksias in its relatively small, rounded flower spikes and narrow leaves. It lives among coastal heaths. Fl Jan–July. 3m. sw WA.

GOLDEN DRYANDRA

(Dryandra nobilis) ◀

Closely related to the banksias, the 100 or so dryandra species also have prominent flower spikes composed of numerous individual flowers. The flowers have a protea-like shape and are surrounded by leaf-like structures known as bracts. Given their similarity to banksias, it is appropriate that their name refers to a Swedish naturalist who catalogued plants for Joseph Banks— Jonas Dryander. All dryandras are restricted to south-western WA, where they grow on sandy soil.

A large shrub with serrated leaves and colourful flowers, the Golden Dryandra is one of the most wide-spread and spectacular species. It prefers woodland habitats and gravelly soil. Fl July–Jan. 5m. sw WA.

PARROT BUSH ▲

(Dryandra sessilis)

This dryandra has a variable growth habit, but most often grows as a shrub. It is relatively common on sand, limestone or granite-derived soil. The flowers are a cream to yellow and the leaves are wedge-shaped with prickly triangular lobes. Fl Aug–Nov. 5m. sw WA.

PINK DRYANDRA ▼

(Dryandra carlinioides)

This small dryandra grows as a compact, rounded bush on clay loam, sand or gravel. The flowers are white to pink. Fl Aug–Nov. 1.2m. Geraldton to Perth, WA.

NARROW-LEAFED GEEBUNG ▲

(Persoonia linearis)

Geebungs are a group of about 65 species restricted to Australia except for one NZ species. They have elongated yellow or white flowers with four petals and undivided leaves. The rounded green fruit occurs in clusters and is edible but bitter. Aborigines prized the fleshy fruit and their name for it, 'geebung', entered popular usage.

This one is an erect shrub or small tree with flaky bark, young branchlets with a hairy appearance, and yellow flowers. The fruits ripen when they fall to the ground. Commonly found in woodland or forest on coastal plains. Fl Dec–Feb. 5m. ne Vic to se Qld.

SYDNEY WARATAH ▼

(Telopea speciosissima)

All five waratah species are unmistakeable when flowering, brightening the landscape with intense scarlet flowers.

The Sydney Waratah is Australia's best known flower. It is restricted to NSW and is that State's floral emblem. The massive 15cm dome-shaped heads formed by up to 250 individual flowers contrast with the green serrated leaves. Sydney Waratah commonly occurs as a slender shrub in dry open forest on sandstone from Sydney to the Blue Mountains and down the south coast. Fl Sept–Nov. 3m. se NSW.

TASMANIAN WARATAH ▲

(Telopea truncata)

This waratah occurs as a spreading shrub or small tree with numerous spider-shaped flowers. The flowers produce copious amounts of sweet nectar, which drips from the plants as a lickable treat. It occurs widely on forested slopes of Tas mountains at 600–1200m altitude. Fl Nov–Dec. 8m. Tas.

MANY-FLOWERED HONEYSUCKLE ▲
(Lambertia multiflora)

The native honeysuckles are a small group of about 11 bushy shrubs with flower heads that contain five to seven colourful flowers. All except one occur in southern WA. This species grows as a multi-stemmed plant with yellow to red flowers, generally on sandy soil, particularly that derived from granite and limestone. Fl June–Dec. 2.5m. sw WA.

MOUNTAIN DEVIL ▲
(Lambertia formosa)

This prickly erect shrub has a terminal flower cluster that is similar but slightly more compacted than the Many-flowered Honeysuckle. Plants also have stiff, narrow leaves tipped with a sharp point, and a woody fruit with a wolf face and horns, hence the common name Mountain Devil. This species occurs widely in heath and dry eucalypt forest on coastal plains and ranges, particularly near Sydney. Fl year-round. 3m. ce to ne NSW.

CORKBUSH, ➤ WITINTI
(Hakea lorea)

Hakeas have dense flower spikes composed of many individual flowers. They look similar to grevilleas, but have a hard, woody nut-like fruit that can remain on the bush for several years. Fire is needed in some cases to split the fruit and release the seed. About 140 species are known, all restricted to Australia.

The Corkbush has an erect, sparsely branched appearance and distinctive corky bark. The pendulous leaves are circular in cross-section and up to 60cm long, while the creamy yellow flower spikes reach 15cm. 6m. Inland n Qld to n WA.

NEEDLEBUSH ▼
(Hakea lissosperma)

This common shrub has stiff needle-like leaves that reach 7cm, and small white flowers arranged in clusters at the base of leaves. The small tough, rounded, woody fruits have an upturned beak and open to release the winged seed. Fl Sept–Nov. 6m. s Vic to se NSW, Tas.

PINCUSHION HAKEA ▼

(Hakea laurina)

This hakea grows as a large shrub with an erect or spreading form. The narrow elliptical leaves are widely spaced, up to 15cm long, and have prominent veins. The cherry red pincushion-shaped flower heads are 5cm in diameter, with projecting pale pink to white spines. Fl Apr–Aug. 6m. Coastal cs WA.

SILKY OAK ➤

(Grevillea robusta)

Australia has about 360 grevillea species, each producing distinctive flower heads formed from up to 100 small individual flowers. Most species live in areas with relatively frequent bushfires. They are prolific bird attractors due their plentiful supply of nectar.

The Silky Oak is a semi-deciduous tree with distinctive fern-like foliage

and yellow–orange flowers. It usually grows near streams, but also occurs on exposed hillsides. The timber has a distinctive 'silky' lustre and is used for furniture and indoor feature walls. Fl Sept–Nov. 40m. Coastal ne NSW to se Qld.

OLD SOCKS, WHITE PLUME GREVILLEA ➤

(Grevillea leucopteris)

This shrub has a spreading growth form with divided leaves up to 30cm long. It produces masses of cream to yellow flowers on raised spikes. At night it generates an aroma described as 'smelly socks', which is used to attract pollinating beetles. Fl July–Dec. 3.5m. Geraldton, WA.

ROUGH LEAF GREVILLEA ➤

(Grevillea aspera)

This spreading shrub grows on open heathland and rocky

slopes. The oblong-shaped leaves can reach 8cm long. It bears cream to red flowers in tight drooping clusters. Fl May–Nov. 2.5m. cs SA.

PINK POKERS ▲
(Grevillea petrophilioides)
This grevillea grows as an erect shrub with pinkish red flowers and a rounded growth form. The needle-like leaves are divided into segments. It usually grows on sandy or rocky soil. Fl July–Oct. 3m. Inland sw WA.

SPREADING CONEBUSH ▼
(Isopogon divergens)
About 35 *Isopogon* species are known, all restricted to Australia. This species has divided twiggy leaves, pink flowers, and rounded 3cm-diameter fruit. Like many other conebushes, it grows in heaths. Fl June–Oct. 2m. sw WA.

PIXIE MOP ▲
(Petrophile linearis)
This low bush is one of about 40 'conestick' species, so named because the flowers fall away, leaving a large globular fruit at the end of the stem. It has pink mop-like flower heads covered in soft hairs. This species occurs in heaths and open woodlands, including remnant bushland near Perth. It is pollinated by native bees. Fl Sept–Nov. 1m. sw WA.

PRICKLY CONESTICK ▲
(Petrophile canescens)
This conestick has an open, erect growth form and divided leaves about 10cm long. It has creamy yellow flower heads and woody grey fruit. Fl Sept–Oct. 3m. c and e NSW, se Qld.

SPINY SYNAPHEA ▼
(Synaphea spinulosa)
About 50 synaphea species are known, all restricted to southern WA. They have yellow flower heads and often flattened leaves. This one grows as a dense bush in heaths from coastal areas to 100km inland. Fl June–Dec. 1.2m. sw WA.

MOUNTAIN ROCKET ▲
(Bellendena montana)
During summer and early autumn, this bush is the most conspicuous plant on most Tas mountain herbfields. White flowers are evident in Dec, but as the season progresses these give way to bright flame-coloured heads of flattened hanging seeds, the source of the name 'rocket'. Fl Dec–Jan. 60cm. Tas.

SCOPARIA ➤
(Richea scoparia)
This prickly bush belongs to a group of heaths that characterise alpine areas of Tas. Of the 10 known species, nine are restricted to Tas

while the other occurs in Vic and NSW highlands. Richeas are easily recognised by the sharp pointed leaves densely arranged up the stems, and colourful white, yellow, orange, pink or red flower spikes.

Scoparia is well known as an obstacle to bushwalkers because of its hard pointed leaves and densely compacted form. When flowering, they also provide one of the most beautiful sights in the highlands, each plant producing hundreds of colourful 10cm-long flower spikes with tubular caps of joined petals. The flowers release copious butterscotch-flavoured nectar, which can be sucked. Fl Jan. 3m. Tas.

SMOKEBUSHES ➤
(Conospermum species)
This group of shrubby plants is also centred in south-western WA, although several of the 50 or so species are found in e Australia. Their name derives from whitish grey flowers that look from a distance like a puff of smoke rising from the heath. They are characteristic plants of heaths. 2m. sw, s and e Aus.

PANDANI ▼
(Richea pandanifolia)
This is the world's tallest heath. The leaves, which are extremely long, tapered and serrated, initially project up from the crown but droop down the stem as they age and die. The red or pink flowers are large but partly hidden among leaves in the crown. This distinctive plant occurs commonly in rainforest, with stunted plants also present in highlands. Fl Nov–Jan. 12m. sw Tas.

CHEESEBERRY ➤
(Cyathodes straminea)
This spreading shrub with small, sharply pointed leaves is common in mountain areas. It produces masses of small white tubular flowers

that transform into flattened red berries after pollination. Fl Dec–Jan, fruit present most of the year. 1.5m. Tas.

COASTAL OR COMMON HEATH ▲
(Epacris impressa)
About 40 species of epacrid heaths are known. They mainly occur as small shrubs in habitats ranging from subalpine grassfields to coastal plains. A few species are present in NZ and New Caledonia, but most are restricted to Australia.

This heath, the floral emblem of Vic, is usually a small straggly shrub with pink tubular flowers strung in a row. The scientific name arises

from the small depressions at the base of each flower. It grows in sandy soil. Fl Mar–Oct. 3m. Coastal se SA to se NSW, Tas.

WINGED BORONIA ▲
(Boronia alata)
The boronias comprise about 100 species of mostly small shrubby plants with pink to mauve flowers. Some are cultivated commercially for their fragrant oil.

This species is an aromatic shrub with simple oblong leaves in pairs and star-like four-petalled pink flowers. Fl Oct–Jan. 3m. sw WA.

Australia, with most growing in semi-arid regions. The common name derives from a resemblance between their distinctive winged fruits and hops. This one has fern-shaped leaves and inconspicuous flowers offset by bright red winged fruiting capsules. 3m. c and nw NSW, sw Qld.

Some of the 80 or so Australian species can be eaten as bushtucker, while others have deadly poisons.

This large-leafed species of the semi-arid zone has purple flowers and non-edible fruit. It occurs most commonly in disturbed habitats. Fl July–Nov. 50cm. Inland SA, NT, WA.

GERALDTON WAX ▲
(Chamelaucium uncinatum)

This colourful shrub of the coastal sandplains is widely used in the cut-flower industry. Its long thin leaves are finely hooked at the end. The flowers maintain their pink–purple or occasionally white colouration and shape for over a week when picked. Fl Aug–Dec. 5m. Kalbarri to Perth, WA.

PINK HOPBUSH ▼
(Dodonaea sinuolata)

About 60 of the 70 hopbush species are restricted to

FLANNELBUSH ▲
(Solanum lasiophyllum)

This plant belongs to the very large *Solanum* group, which contains about 1700 species worldwide including such important crops as the potato, tomato and eggplant.

MORNING GLORY ▲
(Ipomoea brasiliensis)

A common plant of seashore dune areas, this species has a characteristic sprawling growth form. It is perfectly adapted to this environment and can survive being buried by windblown sand. The large flowers normally open for a day before the petals collapse. It flowers year-round. Other morning glory species occur Australia-wide, particularly in semi-arid regions. Coastal e and n Aus.

CLIMBING GUINEA FLOWER ▼
(Hibbertia scandens)
Guinea flowers are a group of about 150 species with large yellow buttercup-like flowers. This species can be recognised by its climbing habit and glossy, rounded leaves. It is common on coastal dunes. Fl year-round. 4m. e Aus.

NATIVE GINGER ▼
(Alpinia caerula)
This plant grows along rainforest margins, especially near tracks and roads. It has 2m-long fronds and produces obvious blue fruits approximately 1.5cm in diameter. The pulp of the fruits is edible, as are the

underground stems, which have a gingery taste. Fl Sept–Nov. 3m. ce NSW to ne Qld.

STURT'S DESERT ROSE ◄
(Gossypium sturtianum)
This small shrub with magnificent purple flowers up to 12cm in diameter is the floral emblem of the NT. It can flower year-round following rain in some of the most arid parts of Australia. 2m. Inland Aus.

DESERT HIBISCUS ▲
(Alyogyne huegellii)
This shrub of the semi-arid zone has bright green deeply lobed leaves. Each large mauve flower remains open for only one or two days but new flowers continue to open over several weeks. Fl Oct–May. 2.5m. sw WA to cs SA.

CRIMSON TURKEYBUSH ➤

(Eremophila latrobei)

This is one of a large group of about 220 species known as emubushes, all restricted to Australia. Most have sticky leaves, cream to purple flowers, and grow in semi-arid conditions. This one has tubular red to purple flowers 2–3cm long. Fl June–Oct. 3m. Inland Aus.

HILL RIVER LESCHENAULTIA ▲

(Leschenaultia hirsuta)

Most of the 30 or so species of leschenaultia are restricted to kwongan heaths of sw WA. This one differs from relatives in having hairy stems and bright red flowers. Native bees that pollinate other leschenaultia flowers cannot distinguish red, so this species relies on birds for pollination. Fl Aug–Oct. 50cm. cw WA.

EYEBRIGHT ➤

(Euphrasia gibbsiae)

This alpine herb has stems arising from the base and hairy fleshy leaves with three- to five-lobed margins. Flowers are arranged in terminal spikes. This species is semi-parasitic on the roots of other plants. It typically grows in wet habitats on mountains above 1100m. Fl Nov–Feb. 12cm. se Vic, Tas.

ORANGE EVERLASTING DAISY ▲

(Xerochrysum subundulatum)

This colourful long-lived daisy grows as an erect shrub in alpine areas, with plants spreading to 1m and forming extensive mats. The oval leaves reach 80mm long. Fl May–Sept. 30cm. ce Vic to s NSW, c Tas.

Trees, Shrubs and Flowers

FRAGRANT WAITZIA ➤

(Waitzia suaveolens)

This striking everlasting has a crisp white daisy flower head composed of numerous individual yellow florets clustered together and surrounded by white petal-shaped bracts. It is common in a wide range of grassland and woodland habitats. Fl July–Sept. 40cm. w and c WA.

STURT'S DESERT PEA ▼

(Swainsona formosa)

The pea family has more than 12 000 species worldwide and 1200 species in Australia. Pea species are used as food, animal fodder, medicines and dyes.

This species is one of Australia's emblematic wildflowers—the floral emblem of SA. It is ground dwelling, with light green feathery leaves and brilliant red flowers up to 10cm long.

The black-centred flowers are most often seen in semi-arid sandy soil, often at the side of roads. Fl June–Nov. 2m. Inland Aus.

COCKIE'S TONGUE ▼

(Templetonia retusa)

This spreading bush produces clusters of deep pink flowers to 6cm long, followed by rectangular pods. It grows on sandy coastal plains, prefer-ring areas near limestone habitats. Fl May–Dec. 4m. sw and s WA.

FLAME PEA ▲
(Chorizema species)

The flame peas include about 18 species, all except one restricted to south-western WA. They are characterised by bright red and orange pea-shaped flowers. Flame peas are indirectly responsible for the survival of such mammal species as the numbat in WA. They produce a toxin that enters the food web and kills introduced mammals such as foxes. Local native animals are naturally adapted to this toxin, which is the basis of the commercial poison 1080. Fl June–Feb. 1.5m. sw WA.

CUNJEVOI ▲
(Alocasia macrorrhiza)

An inhabitant of moist gullies and rainforest, this plant has large 1.5m heart-shaped leaves that arise from an underground rhizome. The leaves, yellow flowers and red fruits are poisonous, and have been responsible for the deaths of children. Aborigines detoxified the starchy rhizome by soaking, pounding and forming it into cakes for roasting. Fl Sept–May. 2m. Coastal se NSW to ce Qld.

CHRISTMAS BELL ▼
(Blandfordia grandiflora)

Christmas bells have large red funnel-shaped flowers with three sepals and three petals forming a bell. Up to 20 flowers may occur on a single stem. They primarily grow in sandy swamps. Fl Dec–Feb. 50cm. e NSW.

TWINING FRINGED LILY ▼
(Thysanotus patersonii)

An inhabitant of heaths, mallees and woodlands, this small, leafless, wiry creeper twines its way among grass and low branches of other species. Its tubers and stems were eaten by Aborigines. Each flower opens only once, in the morning. Fl July–Dec. 80cm. se WA to se NSW, Tas.

RED AND GREEN KANGAROO PAW ▼
(Anigozanthos manglesii)

The 12 kangaroo paw species have elongate leaves arising from underground runners and curved flowers clustered at the ends of long stalks. They are emblematic of WA, with this species the floral emblem of that State. Its curved, green, finger-like flowers project from a red central stem. Plants are pollinated by honeyeaters and other birds, which perch precariously on the stem.

This species thrives on sandy soil along the WA coast, including remnant bushland near Perth. Fl Aug–Nov. 1m. Shark Bay to Cape Leeuwin, sw WA.

GYMEA LILY ▲
(Doryanthes excelsa)

A spectacular plant when in flower, this lily has brilliant red tubular flowers clustered atop a single flowering stem to 5m high. The leaves are 1–2m in length, 15cm wide, with a pointed tip. The seeds are winged to aid dispersal from the host plant. Fl Sept–Feb. 5m. ce NSW to se Qld.

LONG-STALKED PURPLE IRIS ▼
(Patersonia longiscapa)

This is one of a number of native irises with purple flowers. As its name suggests, the flowering stem of this

species is longer than the elongate leaves. Each plant produces many flowering stems, with plants in the one area flowering together. Fl Nov–Jan. 40cm. Coastal se SA to ce NSW, Tas.

GOLDEN COTTONHEADS ▲
(Conostylus robusta)

The cottonheads are a group of over 50 species closely related to the kangaroo paws, and like them, plants have a number of strap-like leaves and flowers clustered towards the ends of stalks.

This one has bright yellow tubular flowers forming a head at the end of long stalks. It grows in heaths on coastal sandplains. Fl July–Oct. 40cm. cw WA.

CATSPAW ▲
(Anigozanthos humilis)

This relatively small kangaroo paw has hairy orange–yellow flowers on a single terminal spike. It grows widely in heath and woodland, most often in disturbed habitats such as roadside verges. Fl July–Oct. 30cm. sw WA.

BLACK KANGAROO PAW ▼
(Macropidia fuliginosa)

This kangaroo paw differs markedly from the others in seed structure and flower shape. It is also one of very few black flowers in the world; the colour results from a felt of black hairs. Each stem includes several large flowers that bend down after pollination and are replaced by new flowers. Individual plants can survive for over 30 years. Fl Aug–Nov. 1m. sw WA.

CANDLESTICKS ➤
(Stackhousia monogyna)

This long-lived plant grows in heaths and open forests. The erect stems support numerous crowded white flowers, giving the plant its common name. Fl July–Dec. 80cm. se WA, se SA to ne Qld, Tas.

SUMMER SPIDER ORCHID ➤

(Caladenia helvina)

The orchids form the largest family of plants with well over 30 000 species worldwide. About 80% of the 1400 or so Australian species are found nowhere else. Orchids live for many years and typically possess bulb-like creeping stems or tubers that persist throughout the year. Seasonal leaves and flowers may develop and disappear rapidly.

This and most other spider orchids produce flowers that mimic a wingless female wasp, enticing the male wasp to try to mate, thereby effecting pollination. To enhance attraction to male wasps, glandular areas on the flower produce sexual attractants. Like other southern Australian orchids it grows

on the ground. It flowers later in the year than most other spider orchids. Fl Dec-Jan. 50cm. e Tas.

WHITE SPIDER ORCHID ➤

(Caladenia longicauda)

The flowers of this highly variable species range from white to cream streaked with red. It grows on damp, sandy soil. Fl Sept–Nov. 30cm. sw WA.

SYDNEY ROCK ORCHID, NEW SOUTH WALES ROCK LILY ▼

(Thelychiton speciosus)

This plant usually grows on sunlit rocks in forests. The leaves are 12–24cm long, oval-shaped and tough. Stems are 2–5cm in diameter and 5–100cm long. Flowers range from yellow to white. Fl Aug–Oct. ne Vic to ne Qld.

PURPLE ENAMEL ORCHID ➤
(Elythranthera brunonis)

This common orchid produces glossy blue–purple flowers up to 3.5cm in diameter. It typically grows in groups in damp areas on sand and gravel, flowering most profusely after fire. Fl Aug–Nov. 40cm. sw WA.

COOKTOWN ORCHID ▾
(Dendrobium phalaenopsis)

Orchids are particularly diverse in the tropics, where most grow epiphytically on the trunks and branches of trees, receiving nutrients from leaf litter accumulating around the trees' roots.

This famous epiphytic orchid—the floral emblem of Qld—has dark green pointed leaves clustered towards the end of the stem, while the mauve to pink flowers occur in 40cm-long heads. Fl June–Aug. 1m. ne Qld.

HYACINTH ORCHID ▲
(Dipodium punctatum)

This species relies for nutrition on decaying organic matter in the soil. It is wholly dependent on an association with a fungus that resides in the fleshy root system of the plant and aids in absorbing nutrients. It has small, bright pink flowers but no leaves. Fl Nov–Feb. 90cm. Coast and GDR se SA to ne Qld, NT, Tas.

FLANNEL FLOWER ▾
(Actinotus helianthi)

This plant is widespread in sandy heaths, open forests and coastal dunes. The leaves are divided into lobes and are green–grey above and whitish below, both surfaces covered by hairs. The white flower heads are composed of a globular central cluster of flowers ringed by a star of petal-like bracts. Fl Aug–Feb. 1m. ce NSW to se Qld.

COASTAL PIGFACE ▲
(Carpobrotus rossii)
The leaves of this ground-dwelling species are succulent, triangular in cross section and reach 10cm in length. They store water, allowing the plant to survive dry summer conditions beside the sea. Historically, mariners used this plant to treat scurvy. The fleshy fruits taste like salty apples and were eaten by Aborigines. Fl Sept–Feb. Coastal sw WA to e Vic, Tas.

CUSHION PLANT ▼
These hard, compact domes grow among alpine grasslands. Close inspection shows that they are composed of thousands of individual shoots, often from several plant species, connected together into one mass. Different cushion plant species are not closely related although they have a similar form. Although most cushion plants can support a person's weight, they will eventually break down following trampling so avoid treading on them when bushwalking. Diameter 3m. Alpine Vic, NSW, Tas.

SOUTHERN TRIGGER PLANT ▼
(Stylidium graminifolium)
Many trigger plant species occur in Australia, with over

130 species recorded from south-western WA alone. They have a spring-loaded mechanism for actively transferring pollen to visiting insects. When the insect brushes against the trigger, a pollen-coated spring column snaps across the face of the flower. This one has stems up to 40cm long with numerous pink flowers. Fl Sept–Dec. 40cm. s Vic to se Qld, Tas.

BLADDERWORT, FAIRIES' APRON ▲
(Utricularia dichotoma)
This bog plant occurs in a range of peat habitats from the seaside to mountain peaks. It deploys trap-like bladders submerged in mud to catch small aquatic animals, which it then digests. Bladderworts have minute leaves and slender erect stems, each with one or more deep purple flowers at the end. Fl Dec–Jan. 15cm. se SA to se Qld, Tas.

QUEENSLAND PITCHER PLANT ▼

(Nepenthes mirabilis)

This plant has light green leaves with the tips modified into large pitchers up to 20cm long. It thrives in boggy nutrient-poor locations, obtaining much of its nutrition through the digestion of animals trapped in the pitcher. 40cm. ne Qld.

ALBANY PITCHER PLANT ◄

(Cephalotus follicularis)

This plant has uniquely designed pitchers to catch insects, which are attracted to secretions, fall into the pitcher, and are digested to provide nutrients lacking in local soil. The plant has green flowers on a long vertical spike. The 5cm-high pitchers occur at ground level and are difficult to find in thick vegetation, becoming most noticeable after bushfire. Fl Dec–Feb. 40cm. sw WA.

RED INK SUNDEW ►

(Drosera erythrorhiza)

Like other sundews, this green and red plant exudes sap to attract insects, which become trapped among sticky hairs on its leaves. The hairs bend inwards, further trapping the insect, which the plant digests. This sundew generally grows in boggy areas. It has white flowers on an erect spike. Fl Apr–June. 12 cm. sw WA.

BLUEBUSH ▼

(Maireana sedifolia)

These hardy bushes are capable of withstanding high temperatures and long periods of dry weather in salty environments. They have hairy, ovoid blue–grey leaves about 8mm long with a narrow constriction at the base. Sheep readily eat these plants during drought. Fl Jul–Oct. 1m. Inland Aus.

SALTBUSHES ▲

(Atriplex species)

Saltbushes are erect greyish green shrubs that often dominate landscapes in the hot, dry interior. About 45 Australian species are known, and about 200 worldwide. The flowers are usually insignificant and the salty-tasting leaves provide food for sheep in the inland. Fl Sept–Oct. 3m. Inland Aus.

DESERT SPINIFEX, PORCUPINE GRASS ▼

(Triodia irritans)

This grass of the semi-arid zone has a characteristic clumped growth form and needle-like leaves that jab unprotected legs. Fl Oct–Dec. 1m. Inland Aus.

SOUTHERN GRASS TREE ▼

(Xanthorrhoea australis)

The 28 species of grass tree form a distinctive component of the Australian landscape. They are easily recognised by the long stem blackened by fire, hanging skirt of old dead leaves, narrow spiky green leaves extending from the crown, and elongate flower spike.

This species has a thickened, fire-blackened trunk that may divide into two or three branches, but most often is undivided. The leaves can exceed 1m in length yet are only 1–4mm wide. A creamy white flower spike to 5m long is produced after fire. Plants generally live in heaths and open forests. 5m. se SA to ce NSW, Tas.

flowers are inconspicuous, while fruits are edible and bright red to attract seed-dispersing birds. Fl Oct–Feb. 0.5m. Alpine Vic, NSW, Tas.

BUTTONGRASS ▼
(Gymnoschoenus sphaerocephalus)

This grass with short underground rhizomes grows in poor acid soil and covers large expanses of southern and western Tas. The narrow leaves are up to 2m long. Rounded flower heads are produced at the ends of long stems. Fl Oct–Feb. Coastal se SA to ce NSW, Tas.

DWARF GRASS TREE ▼
(Xanthorrhoea nana)

This midget grass tree lacks an extended trunk and has a compact club-shaped flower spike. It occurs in heaths. Fl Aug–July. 2m. s Aus, Tas.

DRUMSTICKS ▲
(Kingia australis)

This strange plant has no close relatives. It looks like a grass tree but with drumstick-like flower heads projecting from the crown rather than a spike. Drumsticks respond to fire by flowering profusely, then producing nuts with a single seed. Large individuals can exceed 800 years of age. 8m. sw WA.

PINEAPPLE GRASS ➤
(Astelia alpina)

Large clumps of sword-shaped silvery leaves to 60cm in diameter characterise this grass. The

Animals

Other than placental mammals and newts, all major groups of animals are well represented in Australia, including many of the most primitive species known worldwide. They can be found in all habitat types, from the highest mountains to underground springs and the deep sea. Although mammals and birds attract most attention, the smaller, less obvious animals also show an amazing range of shapes, colours and behaviour patterns, and are equally worth spending time observing.

Sponges, Corals, Anemones, Jellyfish and Sea Squirts

These invertebrate animals dominate shallow coastal reefs in the tropics and shaded reefs in cooler seas. Sponges have a relatively simple body structure without complex organs. Most sponges are marine but a few occur in fresh water. Of the 6000 or so species known worldwide, over 20% are found off Australia.

Corals and anemones are closely related, both possessing tubular bodies ringed at the open end with a crown of tentacles. Some species reproduce by division into a large colony, while others are solitary. Unlike anemones, corals produce an outer protective wall of limestone, which forms the basic unit of coral reefs. Jellyfish are also related, but have escaped the seabed by using body contractions and their tentacles to propel themselves backwards through water.

Sea squirts (or ascidians) superficially look like encrusting sponges or fat anemones without tentacles, but are in fact more closely related to fishes. They comprise a diverse group with a tadpole-like larval stage that attaches to the seabed and develops into a filter-feeding adult. Larvae have a primitive backbone, an indication of their linkage with fishes.

ORGAN-PIPE SPONGE ▼
(Siphonochalina species)
This is one of the most distinctive sponges on southern reefs. Like other sponges, it has an important filtration function, extracting particles from passing water and reducing coastal turbidity. 60cm. SA, Vic.

BLUEBOTTLE, PORTUGUESE MAN-O-WAR (Physalia physalis) ➤
Most swimmers off eastern Australian surf beaches during summer will encounter this stinging jellyfish-like organism that floats on the sea surface. Although most stings are treated by removing tentacles and applying coldpacks, medical treatment is sometimes necessary. Each organism comprises a colony of many individual animals, some specialised for food capture or reproduction, and one to produce the gas-filled float. Float length to 30cm. Aus, Tas.

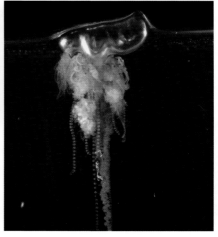

DEADLY BOX JELLY, SEA WASP ▲
(Chironex fleckeri)

Swimming off tropical beaches during summer and early autumn is restricted because of the presence of box jelly species that deliver an excruciatingly painful sting.

This box jelly can kill in minutes. It has 15–20 tentacles trailing from each corner of the body for up to 3m when extended. Each tentacle is covered with millions of stinging capsules. Apply copious amounts of vinegar immediately to any area of the body contacted by tentacles. Although they have a relatively simple body organisation, box jellies are active and proficient hunters with good vision. Bell width to 50cm. ce Qld to nw WA.

JIMBLE, JILGI ▼
(Charybdea rastoni)

The Jimble is the only box jelly that lives in cool Australian waters. A small species, it congregates in large numbers over sand patches during the day, dispersing over much wider areas to feed at night. The sting is relatively mild unless tentacles contact a sensitive area of the body such as the lips. Bell width to 4cm. s WA to se NSW, Tas.

WARATAH ANEMONE ▲
(Actinia tenebrosa)

This is the most commonly observed Australian anemone, appearing as a red blob under rocks and in intertidal rock pools when the tide is out. Most animals in close proximity are clones of each other. Juveniles usually develop in internal brood pouches of larger anemones and emerge from the mouth. 4cm. cw WA to ce Qld, Tas.

VARIABLE CORAL ➤
(Plesiastrea versipora)

Australia lies just south of the Indonesia–Philippines 'coral triangle' and consequently is home to numerous coral species. On both east and west coasts, reef coral species spawn synchronously on one or two nights of the year, generating a spectacular display for divers as packets of eggs drift to the sea surface. On the GBR (Qld) mass spawning occurs in the week following the full moon in Nov–Dec; at Ningaloo (WA) coral spawning follows a full moon in Mar–Apr.

Variable Coral comes in many different colours. It is unusual in that it can tolerate cool conditions, extending to the southern Australian coast. Colonies 30cm diameter. Aus, n Tas.

CUNJEVOI ▲
(Pyura stolonifera)

This sea squirt forms mats on rocky intertidal shores. Children deliberately tread on them to generate a long squirt of water. They are also used as bait by fishers, who knife open the tough outer body wall to gather the orange internal organs. 20cm. cw WA to se Qld, Tas.

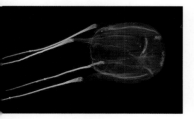

Insects

Insects are by far the most diverse of all animal groups, with over 10 million species thought to exist on the planet. More than 110 000 insect species have been scientifically described in Australia and there are many more undescribed species. Insects are arthropods characterised by a hard outer skeleton and a body divided into head, thorax and abdomen. Most species have two pairs of wings, enabling them to disperse widely. People tend to think of insects in terms of the harmful and annoying species such as flies and mosquitoes, but most species benefit the environment, including playing a key role in pollinating flowers.

GIANT STONEFLY ▼
(Eustenia spectabilis)

Stoneflies are a primitive group of insects with aquatic larvae. Adults are winged and characteristically have two long filaments projecting from the rear. As they are poor flyers, they rarely travel far from the creeks in which the larvae live.

This is the largest and most colourful Australian stonefly, with a lineage extending back to Gondwana and nearest relatives in Vic, NZ and South America. Both juveniles and adults have red, orange and black markings. Juveniles are ferocious predators of other insects in cool, fast-flowing streams. 6cm. s Tas.

GREENGROCER CICADA ▲▼
(Cyclochila australasiae)

Cicadas are central to the cacophony of sound heard throughout Australia during summer, when underground nymphs burrow to the surface, climb a nearby tree or shrub, break free of the nymphal shell (below) and emerge as adults (above). A pair of tympanic structures enable adults to produce large volumes of sound, which can be so loud as to be painful to listen to. The Greengrocer is primarily responsible for this noise in south-eastern Australia. 50mm. SA, Vic to s Qld.

GREEN TREE ANT ▼
(Oecophylla smaragdina)

This ant constructs complex nests in shrubs and trees. Some workers carry ant larvae to the building site, while others bind the leaves of plants together with larval silk, sometimes forming chains to span gaps by clinging to each other using jaws and legs. They vigorously defend their nests, often inflicting multiple stings on anyone incautiously brushing past. 8mm. e and n Qld, n NT, n WA.

BULLANT, BULLDOG ANT, INCHMAN ▲
(Myrmecia nigrocincta)

More ant species are thought to occur in Australia than on any other continent. Well over 5000 Australian species are known, but only about one-quarter of these have been scientifically named to date.

Bullants are one of 89 primitive ants in the *Myrmecia* genus. All are restricted to Australia or New Caledonia. Bullants are quick to defend both themselves and their nests, delivering a painful bite using slender, toothed jaws and a sting at the end of the body. Despite their fearsome appearance, adults feed primarily upon nectar and other plant material. 12mm. Vic to Qld, Tas.

JACK-JUMPER ANT ➤
(Myrmecia pilosula)

This ant is named for the short jerks and jumps with which it moves. Nests range from a single hole to large metre-wide mounds with multiple entrances that the

ants defend aggressively. A scattering of fine gravel typically surrounds nests. In Tas, deaths have resulted from allergic reactions to their stings. 6mm. Adelaide Hills SA, Vic, s NSW, Tas.

SUGAR ANT ▼

(Camponotus consobrinus)

This ant of suburban areas is especially common during warm weather as workers head out from their nest at dusk to forage for insects under lights. Although these ants are stingless they have strong biting jaws, and when threatened are able to spray acid from the abdomen.

Sugar Ants are closely related to Honeypot Ants *(Camponotus inflatus)* of the arid interior, which store regurgitated honeydew and nectar in the distended abdomen of a special class of 'workers' living in deep underground nest chambers. Aboriginal people use Honeypot Ants as a sweet food source.

Sugar Ant nests are located in holes among the roots of trees and shrubs or cracks between rocks or soil. 10mm. se SA to Qld; Tas.

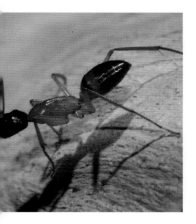

COMMON PYRGOMORPH ▲

(Monistria discrepens)

Over 3000 grasshopper and cricket species are known from Australia, including many brightly coloured animals and some of the most primitive species. They live in all terrestrial habitats, but occur in greatest numbers in semi-arid and coastal grasslands, and alpine areas.

This grasshopper has red to yellow spots and stripes across the body and startling scarlet hindwings that it exposes when threatened. It feeds during the day on green low-lying foliage. 30mm. SA to NSW.

CHRISTMAS BEETLE ▼

(Anoplognathus species)

Beetles dominate the Earth. About one in three known animal species is a beetle, including over 30 000 scientifically named in Australia. Adult beetles have two pairs of wings that meet in the centre of the body when folded—an outer pair that is hardened for protection and an inner membranous pair for flight.

Christmas beetle larvae feed underground on organic matter and the roots of plants, often causing serious damage to pasture crops. With others in the scarab family of beetles, the underground larvae are commonly called corby grubs or cockchafers. The adults also damage mature eucalypt trees, causing extensive defoliation and tree death when numbers are high. Adults typically emerge from underground around Christmas, hence the common name. 30mm. Aus, Tas.

PERPLEXED JEWEL BEETLE ▲
(Castiarina simulata)
This is one of the commonest WA jewel beetles, a group that includes some of the most brilliantly coloured of all Australian insects. In hot weather adults fly about actively in the sunlight and feed on flower nectar. The larvae feed on the woody tissues of plants. 12mm. sw WA.

SPOTTED LONGICORN BEETLE ▼
(Acalolepta species)
Species in the longicorn beetle family have elongate, slightly flattened bodies and long antennae that can be directed both forwards and backwards. Adults are active flyers, with species feeding on bark, foliage or flowers. The grub-like larvae feed on the

internal tissues of shrubs and trees. 35mm. Aus.

WEEVILS ➤
This family of beetles includes more species than any other on Earth. Adult weevils are characterised by the pointed head. Larvae of most species feed internally as grubs on various types of plants, while adults feed externally on plants, including pollen in some species and root tissues in others. 1–60mm. Aus, Tas.

FLIES ◄
Australia is justly famous for its number and variety of flies. The most annoying group are undoubtedly the biting midges or sandflies. In coastal areas, particularly near swamps, hundreds of these small and insignificant-looking flies can attack unnoticed at dusk, causing itching, swollen bites and sometimes allergic reactions. Sandfly larvae are aquatic, living in creeks and estuaries. The much larger marchflies or horseflies also use needle-like mouthparts to extract blood from mammals, and

give a painful, though harmless, sting in the process.

During the warmer months, numbers of the Australian Bushfly (Musca vetustissima) increase dramatically. Females feast on protein from the tears, saliva and nasal passages of

animals, then lay eggs in the nearest dung. A single pad of cow dung can produce 2000 flies. If temperatures drop below 12°C Bushflies become inactive. Most die off in the cooler southern areas of Australia during winter. Larger than the Bushfly, larvae of the (pictured) Australian Blowfly (Lucilia cuprina) feed on carrion. The blue–green metallic adults make an audible buzz when flying. Aus, Tas.

Wild Australia

SPITFIRE, LARGE GREEN SAWFLY ▼
(Perga affinis)

Spitfire grubs resemble caterpillars but are actually the larvae of a wasp-like animal rather than a butterfly or moth. Large numbers congregate during the day, dispersing to feed on eucalypt foliage at night. The name 'spitfire' comes from their habit of lifting the head and spitting out a green liquid of concentrated eucalypt oil when threatened. 60mm. se Aus, Tas.

CAIRNS BIRDWING ➤
(Ornithoptera priamus)

Adult butterflies and moths have two pairs of wings covered by minute scales. Their caterpillar larvae graze on plants and undergo complete metamorphosis to adult. Over 22 000 Australian butterfly and moth species have been scientifically named.

The Cairns Birdwing is Australia's largest butterfly. Males patrol areas near larval food plants such as the vine *Aristolochia tagala* in the hope of encountering newly emerged females. Mating can take place before the female's wings have dried. Animals are most active during early morning and late afternoon. 150mm. ne Qld.

ORCHARD SWALLOWTAIL ▲
(Papilio argeus)

This butterfly tends to hold its wings outspread when settled on vegetation. Its slow, erratic flight follows defined flight paths—but it moves rapidly when threatened. It lives in a variety of habitats, from drier inland woodlands to moist lowland rainforests. 108mm. Coast and GDR Vic to ne Qld.

ULYSSES SWALLOWTAIL BUTTERFLY ▼
(Papilio ulysses)

The metallic-blue upper-wing surfaces of this species catch the eye as brilliant flashes of reflected sunlight. In contrast, the underwings are drab, providing this large butterfly with camouflage when at rest. The species is commonly encountered adjacent to lookouts within rainforest areas. 108mm. ne Qld.

ORANGE LACEWING ▼
(Cethosia penthesilea)

A butterfly of tropical rainforests, this active flyer defends a fixed territory. It is common within its limited range. 50mm. n NT.

VARIED EGGFLY BUTTERFLY ▲
(Hypolimnas bolina)

Males establish territories from which they sally forth to challenge nearby males, or indeed any other butterflies. When at rest both sexes typically open their wings, thus displaying the colourful upper surfaces. During winter, females seek shelter in gullies, while vagrants disperse widely, including to semi-arid regions. 86mm. n Aus.

COMMON CROW, OLEANDER BUTTERFLY ▼
(Euploea core)

Often observed flying jerkily in sunlit glades within dry forests, mostly within 3m of the ground, this butterfly is also common in urban areas. Adults are most commonly observed Dec–May. Aggregations of Common Crow overwinter in sheltered tropical gullies, such as at Katherine Gorge. 80mm. e NSW, e and n Qld, n NT.

CRUISER BUTTERFLY ▲
(Vindula arsinoe)
This species is common within its range. It can often be seen feeding on flowers of introduced lantana plants or seeking moisture from wet sand fringing creeks. Flight has a strong, gliding motion. Females lay eggs in clusters on a variety of vines, particularly the Native Passion Vine (*Adenia heterophylla*). The pupal cocoon resembles an old, dead, twisted leaf. 82mm. Coastal ne and n Qld.

RINGED XENICA BUTTERFLY ▲
(Geitoneura acantha)
A woodland and dry eucalypt forest species, this butterfly lives in shaded gullies and along streams. It typically flies slowly and jerkily within 1m of the ground among sunlit patches. Larval food plants include grasses from the genus *Poa*. Females are generally inactive from Jan to early Feb, resting in shaded gullies and dense vegetation along creeks. 44mm. GDR from sw Vic to se Qld.

BOGONG MOTH ▼
(Agrostis infusa)
In general, moths differ from butterflies in possessing more feathery antennae without a terminal swelling.

Aborigines collected thousands of highly nutritious Bogong Moths, roasting them in hot ashes and mashing the bodies to make 'moth meat'.

During winter the larvae feed on leafy seedlings in the inland region from northern SA to southern Qld. They migrate in spring to caves in the Snowy Mountains, where they remain inactive throughout summer. In autumn, most fly north to mate and lay their eggs. 50mm. s Aus, Tas.

HERCULES MOTH ▲
(Coscinocera hercules)
This is the largest moth species in Australia. Females lack mouthparts and die soon after laying 80–100 rusty red eggs. These eggs superficially resemble leaf galls, providing an effective camouflage. 27cm. ne Qld.

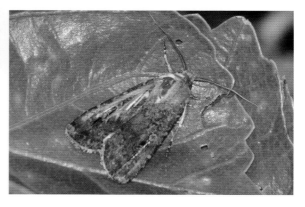

ORANGE-SPOTTED MOTH ▼
(Amata species)

Unlike most moths, this species is active during the day. It is partly protected from daytime predators by its distasteful flavour and body coloration, which mimics a wasp. At night and when in flight, adults emit regular ultrasonic clicks, thought to signal to bats that the moth is distasteful or poisonous to eat. 14mm. Aus, Tas.

GUM MOTH
(Opodipthera species) ▼

These large brown moths are often seen blundering around lights at night. The winged moth stage does not feed, spending its few days as an adult in search of mates. Gum moth caterpillars grow to a large size and feed on green foliage. 12cm. Aus, Tas.

WITCHETTY GRUB
(Xyleutes species) ▼

These large white grubs are larvae of the world's heaviest moth, a species with a wingspan up to 25cm. The grubs are prized as food by Aborigines, who usually eat them raw or lightly cooked in the ashes of a fire. Grubs can be detected by following the silk-lined tunnel they construct through soil to gain access to the roots of their food plant, the wattle *Acacia ligulata*. 12cm. n SA, s NT.

MAGNETIC TERMITE ▲
(Amitermes meridionalis)

Termites are commonly called 'white ants' but lack the large compound eyes, narrow waist and bent antennae of true ants, and are not closely related. They are best known for the enormous damage to houses and wooden structures caused by about 20 species. Less well known is the critically important role played by the other 400 plus species in enriching soil by breaking down plant material and moving nutrients underground.

The Magnetic Termite is the best known species because of its habit of constructing tall, thin parallel mounds. The mounds are designed to minimise exposure to sun and wind, so are locally aligned in the same direction but with different magnetic directions at different sites. 10mm. n Aus.

Spiders

Compared to insects, spiders are a relatively small group of arthropods, with only about 2000 species scientifically described from Australia. Regardless, they occur virtually everywhere across the continent and include some of the most dangerous and interesting animals found here.

SYDNEY FUNNEL-WEB SPIDER ▼ ➤
(Atrax robustus)

Bites of this species can cause death if not quickly treated. Attacks on humans increase during summer and autumn, when aggressive males leave their burrows in search of females. Wandering males (right) may be encountered in gardens, sheds and houses. Females (below) are often found under rocks and can live for 10 years. 45mm. ce NSW.

SAINT ANDREW'S CROSS SPIDER ➤
(Argiope keyserlingi)

This spider is named for its bright web decorations—zigzag ribbons of bluish white silk that form a cross through the centre of the orb web. This cross is assumed to help capture prey or avoid predators. The ribbon-like silk reflects ultraviolet light strongly, attracting flying insects that use ultraviolet light to locate food sources such as flowers. 16mm. e Aus.

REDBACK SPIDER ➤
(Latrodectus hasselti)

This spider prefers urban areas, sheds and junk piles on farms. They are particularly abundant in disturbed areas. Large females will 'steal' stored food from other spiders' webs. Females can store sperm for up to two years to lay several clutches of eggs. The bite of females can be deadly to humans. 10mm. Aus, Tas.

TASMANIAN GIANT CAVE SPIDER ▼
(Hickmania troglodytes)

This relict species is the last of an old Gondwanan lineage; its nearest relatives are in South America. It weaves a sheet web that may exceed 1m in diameter. Underground drainage and cave systems can support large numbers of spiders near cave entrances. The species lives in a variety of other dark, cool situations, ranging from hollow logs to the undersides of bridges. It is an icon species for faunal

conservation in Tas, especially in relation to cave management. 12cm. Tas.

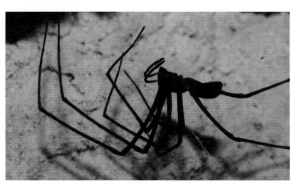

BANDED HUNTSMAN SPIDER ▲
(Isopeda insignis)

This large species shelters by day under the loose bark of eucalypts, venturing forth at night to forage. Females construct and guard a papery white egg sac until juveniles have hatched. The spiderlings remain near their mother until the first moult, after which they disperse. 40mm. Aus.

Crabs, Lobsters and Prawns

Crabs, lobsters and prawns are collectively called crustaceans—they have a hard, segmented external skeleton and the head is fused with the body. Most other crustaceans are microscopic in size. They comprise an important group of aquatic invertebrates, with over 5000 species inhabiting Australian freshwater and marine environments.

TASMANIAN MOUNTAIN SHRIMP ➤

(Anaspides tasmaniae)

While common as fossils, all members of this primitive group of crustaceans were considered long extinct until discovery of this species in Tas in the nineteenth century. This living fossil occurs commonly in freshwater streams, caves and lakes across much of Tas, particularly in water bodies at higher altitudes where predatory trout and native trout are absent. 5cm. Tas.

GIANT TASMANIAN CRAB ▼

(Pseudocarcinus gigas)

This deepwater crab is the largest true crab in the world, reaching over 12kg in weight. Because it rarely enters water less than 100m deep, the habits of this crab were largely unknown until large populations were discovered on the upper continental slope off Bass Strait, and a trap fishery developed there. Body width 60cm. s WA to se NSW, Tas.

ROCK CRAB, SWIFT-FOOTED CRAB ▲

(Leptograpsus variegatus)

This is an active predator and scavenger on intertidal rock platforms. Its purple body and relatively large claws are easily seen at a distance but the crab rapidly retreats under boulders or into crevices when approached. It is harvested in NSW for use as fish bait. Body width 8cm. cw WA to ce Qld, ne Tas.

MUD CRAB ▲
(Scylla serrata)
Several large crabs of similar appearance inhabit mangrove waterways and are targeted by fishermen. The Mud Crab is the largest and best known. It is an important commercial species in Qld and NT, and can be captured by setting baited traps or by searching holes in mudbanks at low tide. Body width 30cm. ce NSW to cw WA.

BLUE SWIMMER CRAB, BLUE MANNA CRAB, SAND CRAB ▼
(Portunus pelagicus)
This important commercial species can be recognised by the blue coloration, elongate claws and a long spine projecting from each side of the body. They are generally caught in baited traps, and can be seen while diving in sheltered bays, particularly at night. Body width 20cm. SA gulfs, se NSW to sw WA.

EASTERN KING PRAWN ▼
(Peneus plebejus)
Prawns (known as shrimps elsewhere in the world) can be distinguished from other shrimp-like animals by their relatively large size and the claws at the end of the first three pairs of walking limbs. They form the basis of major tropical fisheries and smaller fisheries in SA, NSW and WA.

The Eastern King is the largest prawn species commonly found on the east coast. Like many other prawn species, juveniles pass through several planktonic larval stages offshore and then migrate into estuaries and sheltered embayments, where they grow rapidly to maturity. Body width 30cm. cs Vic to ne Qld, ne Tas.

Gould's Giant Lobster (*Astacopsis gouldii*) in the north and Franklin's Giant Lobster (*Astacopsis franklinii*) in the south. Gould's is considered endangered because of its slow growth, exploitation by fishermen and ongoing destruction of the native forest streams in which it lives. It can grow to over 12kg in weight. Franklin's Lobster (below) is more widely distributed in lakes as well as rivers. Body width 50cm. Tas.

WESTERN ROCK LOBSTER ▲
(Panulirus cygnus)

This is Australia's most valuable fishery species, generating a catch worth over $200 million annually and supporting many WA coastal towns. This species shelters in caves for much of the day, venturing out at night across seagrass beds and reefs to feed. Following a larval stage of about a year in the open ocean, juveniles settle in large concentrations on coastal reefs at less than 10m depth. At about 20cm length, animals migrate to deep habitats offshore. Body width 50cm. cw and sw WA.

SOUTHERN ROCK LOBSTER, CRAYFISH, CRAY ➤
(Jasus edwardsii)

This rock lobster differs from tropical species in that it has relatively short central antennae that are unforked. It is captured in baited pots as part of a major fishery in Tas, Vic and SA. Body width 70cm. sw WA to ce NSW.

GIANT LOBSTER ➤
(Astacopsis species)

Tasmania has two species of giant lobster, the larger

MARRON ▼
(Cherax tenuimanus)

After the Tasmanian Giant Lobster, the Marron is one of the largest freshwater crayfish known. It can be recognised by its dark colouration and five ridges extending back along the top of the head. Recreational fishers capture Marron from permanently flowing streams and associated lakes, particularly during summer. The species is also commercially cultivated in aquaculture ponds, both within its native WA and also in the eastern States. 40cm. Perth to Albany, WA.

YABBY ▲
(Cherax destructor)

In contrast to most other species of freshwater crayfish, which prefer rivers and clear-water lakes, the Yabby inhabits muddy lakes and farm dams. It weakens dams and levee banks by creating extended

burrows, hence the scientific name *destructor*. Due to deliberate introductions, it is now very widespread. 10cm. Vic to s Qld; introduced to sw WA, SA, n Tas.

GHOST SHRIMP, NIPPER, YABBY ▼

Over 30 ghost shrimp species, including the Ceramic Nipper (*Biffarius ceramicus*) illustrated below, are known from Australian coastal waters. They primarily occur in estuaries, where they burrow in huge numbers in intertidal sandbanks, at some sites over 100

animals per square metre.

Ghost shrimps have a soft white body and large but weak claws. A great variety of fish eat them, including flathead, bream and whiting, and they are popularly used as bait. Fishers extract them from sediment using a piston pump that is repeatedly pushed into a sandflat. 80mm. Aus, Tas.

Shellfish, Squid and Octopus

These invertebrates are collectively known as molluscs, a group that includes bivalved oysters attached to the seabed, creeping snails, and fast-swimming squid. After the arthropods, the molluscs comprise the largest group of animals, with more than 100 000 species known worldwide, including more than 10 000 species in Australia. Octopus, cuttlefish and squid have independently evolved eyesight and intelligence to the level of some reptiles, birds and mammals.

GIANT CLAM ▼
(Tridacna gigas)

This is the largest of all molluscs. Although still common on the northern GBR, it has been overharvested by divers to extinction through much of the remainder of the Pacific. It obtains energy from microscopic plants embedded in its colourful fleshy mantle, hence survives only in shallow sunlit areas, most frequently in patches of sand between coral. 0.9m. ce to ne Qld.

SYDNEY ROCK OYSTER ◀
(Saccostrea glomeratus)

This oyster is regarded as a gastronomic delicacy; however, farmed populations are rapidly decreasing due to a combination of disease, pollution of estuarine waterways, and competition from the introduced Pacific Oyster. Although natural populations are also declining, dense populations remain attached to rock and mangrove roots in sheltered bays along the central NSW coast. 10cm. cs Vic to se Qld.

TASMANIAN SCALLOP, COMMERCIAL SCALLOP ▲
(Pecten fumatus)

This large, symmetrical scallop has a flat upper shell and cup-shaped lower shell. It forms the basis for a major commercial fishery that once occurred close to Melbourne, Adelaide and Hobart. Because of overfishing and disease, the fishery has progressively moved into deepwaters offshore, with most scallop dredging now undertaken as a 'boom and bust' operation in eastern Bass Strait. 15cm. cw WA to ce Qld, Tas.

PIPI, GOOLWA COCKLE ▲
(Donax deltoides)
Pipi shells are light pink on the outside, purple inside. Animals are sometimes cooked and eaten but the meat is tough and gritty, hence the species is more often used as bait. This clam lives buried in sand off surf beaches. It can be collected using your feet to feel for their hard shells in the shallows. 6cm. Aus.

BLACKLIP ABALONE ▲
(Haliotis rubra)
Blacklip Abalone shells can be recognised by their shape, large size and iridescent pink and green inner surface. This is the most valuable abalone worldwide, with most of the $100 million commercial catch taken in Tas. Animals still occur abundantly on shallow Tas, Vic and SA reefs; however, populations have greatly declined through overfishing in NSW and WA. 20cm. sw WA to ne NSW, Tas.

WONDER COWRY ➤
(Umbilia hesitata)
This is considered to be the most primitive cowry, and also one of the world's largest and most beautiful. It generally occurs in deepwater on soft sediment among sponges, but is also occasionally seen by divers in south-eastern Tas. 12cm. se Vic to ce Qld, Tas.

BLACK COWRY ▼
(Zoila friendii)
This is the most common of a group of large sponge-eating cowries that live off southern Australia and are prized by collectors. These cowries lack the planktonic larval stage of most other cowries; hence small regional populations have become isolated from each other and

evolved distinctive markings. Shells collected near Perth are much narrower and darker than those collected near Adelaide. 13cm. sw WA to sw Vic.

CAMPANILE ▲
(Campanile symbolicum)

Another 'living fossil', the Campanile is the only surviving species in a family that was dominant and widespread in shallow seas 60 million years ago. It has a pale chalky shell with a thin projecting outer lip. Large numbers of live and dead shells are present in mixed patches of sand, seagrass and reef near Perth. 20cm. sw WA.

LIGHTNING VOLUTE ➤
(Ericusa fulgetra)

Australia is the centre of diversity for volutes, a group of large, colourful shells prized by collectors. This one can be recognised by its size, rounded tip and dark brown wavy stripes. Like the Black Cowry, the pattern on the shell varies from site to site, with experts often able to specify the location and depth at which a shell was collected. 15cm. s WA to se SA.

PAPER NAUTILUS ➤
(Argonauta nodosa)

This octopus-like species produces a beautiful white egg case in which the female sits while swimming. The species generally inhabits the open ocean; however, each year large numbers of females enter eastern Bass Strait, where they release eggs and die. When this happens, shells wash ashore and are gathered on Vic and Flinders Island beaches. 35cm. Aus, Tas.

SOUTHERN CALAMARI ▾

(Sepioteuthis australis)

This species occurs abundantly off the southern Australian coast and is caught by both professional and recreational fishers using squid jigs (specialised lures with hooks). It is the only southern squid with sidefins extending the length of the body (in a similar way to cuttles). Like other squids and cuttles, it can change colour instantaneously. 38cm. cw WA to se Qld, Tas.

BLUE–RINGED OCTOPUS ▲

(Haplochlaena maculosa)

Treat this small octopus with extreme caution. Its bite delivers a powerful nerve toxin that has caused at least two human deaths. This species is often difficult to detect because of its brown–grey body camouflage in its preferred habitat under rocks at low tide and in shallows. However, when irritated, it displays characteristic neon blue rings on tentacles and body. 12cm. s WA to se Qld, n Tas.

GIANT CUTTLE ➤

(Sepia apama)

This is the largest and most abundant cuttle species of the southern Australian coast, recognisable by its large size and skin flaps behind its

eyes. Curious and aggressive, it often approaches and confronts divers. It has a rapid life cycle, dying shortly after reaching maturity at only one year of age. The 'cuttlebone' backbones of this and other cuttles are commonly seen washed onto surf beaches. 80cm. sw WA to ne NSW, n Tas.

Seastars (Starfish) and Sea Urchins

Seastars and sea urchins are both echinoderms, along with brittle stars, feather stars and sea cucumbers. They have the most unusual body plan of all invertebrates. They lack a head and brain, and the body is typically arranged in multiples of five rather than the equal-sided shape of most other animals.

CROWN-OF-THORNS SEASTAR ▼
(Acanthaster planci)

This large seastar has up to 23 arms, each covered with numerous long venomous spines that can inflict a painful wound. It feeds on reef corals and is considered partly responsible for the declining coral cover along much of the length of the GBR. Unless present in plague proportions, individuals generally hide in crevices during the day, moving out into the open to feed at night. 70cm. ne NSW to cw WA.

FIREBRICK SEASTAR ▲
(Asterodiscides truncatus)

This species is immediately recognisable due to the striking mauve, orange and red bumps projecting from its upper surface. Although most abundant in deep water, sufficient animals are present on shallow NSW reefs for the species to be well known and appreciated by divers. 17cm. s WA to ne NSW, ne Tas.

EIGHT-ARMED SEASTAR ➤
(Patiriella calcar)

While the shape of this seastar varies little, each animal has a unique combination of reds, browns, blues, greens and oranges on its upper surface. It occurs abundantly on intertidal shores around the south-east coast, with many individuals often present in a single rock pool. 5cm. s WA to se Qld, Tas.

along south-eastern Australian coasts. It occurs in such large aggregations that the combined grazing activity keeps rock surfaces bare of seaweed growth, creating the distinctive white rock or barren habitat type. It differs from the purple sea urchin in having longer, hollow iridescent spines. 10 cm. e Vic to n NSW, e Tas.

PINK BASKET STAR ▲
(Astroboa ernae)

This basket star is one of many spectacular invertebrates living on southern Australian reefs. During daylight and periods of low current flow, the animal generally contracts into a ball. At other times the long branched arms extend into the water to feed, often while the animal is perched on a sponge or gorgonian. 5cm. cw WA to cs SA.

PURPLE SEA URCHIN ➤
(Heliocidaris erythrogramma)

This common sea urchin supports a minor fishery in south-eastern Australia. Large aggregations can denude reefs of seaweeds. There are numerous colour forms based on three colours (purple, green, white) that can vary between spines and shell. Dead shells washed up on beaches without spines are commonly called 'sea eggs'. 9cm. cw WA to s Qld, Tas.

BLACK SEA URCHIN ➤
(Centrostephanus rodgersii)

Divers encounter this sea urchin more often than any other invertebrate species

Sharks and Rays

There are two major groups of fishes—those with a skeleton made from bone, and the sharks and rays, which have a skeleton of cartilage. Over 300 species of sharks and rays have been recorded from Australian waters, about one-third of the total worldwide.

PORT JACKSON SHARK ▼
(Heterodontus portusjacksoni)

This primitive shark has a blunt, rounded head, raised ridges above the eyes, dark stripes, and spines in front of each of the two upper (dorsal) fins. Females produce distinctive black-flanged spiral egg cases that are screwed by mouth into cracks in the reef. A juvenile emerges from each egg case after about five months. 1.7m. sw WA to ne NSW, Tas.

GREAT WHITE SHARK, WHITE POINTER ➤
(Carcharodon carcharias)

This huge shark has a grey upper and white lower body and single large dorsal fin. It is considered the most dangerous animal in the sea, a deserved reputation given its responsibility for about one Australian fatality per year. Nevertheless, to put this into context, this rate is similar to the number of deaths per year of people climbing Uluru. Most attacks are probably a result of black wet-suited swimmers being mistaken for seals by sharks. 6.4m. cw WA to se Qld, Tas.

ORNATE WOBBEGONG ▲
(Orectolobus ornatus)

Wobbegongs are flattened sharks with characteristic fleshy lobes projecting from the upper lip and two upper fins of similar size. This is one of about 12 species, most of which are confined to Australian waters. It has a camouflaged pattern of brown and grey blotches surrounded by black spots, and tends to remain immobile for long periods, ambushing passing fish, crabs and lobsters. 3m. Aus, ne Tas.

GREY NURSE SHARK ▲

(Carcharias taurus)

Once common along the NSW coast, populations of this shark have declined so much through fishing that it is now threatened, with valid fears for its long-term survival. Nevertheless, a few hotspots still exist where divers can reliably sight them, including Montague Island, Jervis Bay, Seal Rocks, South West Rocks, the Solitary Islands and Jurien Rocks. They typically occur in aggregations of several individuals, each remaining immobile or moving slowly about underwater gutters. Grey Nurses have two large dorsal fins, thin projecting teeth, and are grey, with white spots prominent in juveniles. 3.2m. Aus.

WHALE SHARK ➤

(Rhincodon typus)

With its spotted upper body, gaping mouth and oceanic habits, the world's largest fish is unmistakeable. For most of its life, the Whale Shark is solitary; however, Mar–May each year animals congregate off Ningaloo Reef, WA, probably in response to annual coral spawning and an associated explosion in planktonic food. 18m. se NSW to s WA.

ELEPHANT SHARK, ELEPHANTFISH ➤

(Callorhynchus millii)

This shark belongs to an archaic group of sharks known as the chimaeras or ghost sharks that first evolved around 400 million years ago. While almost all other members in the group live in deepwater, the Elephant Shark also moves into shallow bays and estuaries in late spring and early summer. This species cannot be confused with any other: it has a silvery scaleless body and protruding rubbery snout, which is a sensitive organ for detecting prey in sediment. 1.1m. s WA to ce NSW, Tas.

BANDED STINGAREE ➤

(Urolophus cruciatis)

Stingarees comprise a group of small stingrays with a short barbed tail and rounded

terminal fin. Over 12 species are known from southern Australia. This one has characteristic dark patches across the upper surface. It can occur in large numbers in sheltered bays; many are seen by divers. 50cm. se SA to se NSW, Tas.

Bony Fishes

About one-quarter of the world's 22 000 bony fish species have been identified in Australian seas, lakes and rivers. Most are marine. Considerably fewer freshwater species live here compared to other continents, probably because major river systems have dried out in the recent past, with extinction of many species.

AUSTRALIAN OR QUEENSLAND LUNGFISH ▼
(Neoceratodus forsteri)

This fish is appropriately regarded as a 'living fossil'—its closest known relatives inhabited Australia 100 million years ago. It is one of six living lungfish species, but is considered more primitive than the species in South America and Africa, which are eel-shaped and have thread-like fins and a double rather than single lung. Australian Lungfish generally breathe through gills but rely on the lung to survive during periods when water becomes stagnant. 2m. Mary and Burnett rivers, Qld; introduced elsewhere in se Qld.

GULF SARATOGA ➤
(Scleropages jardinii)

This primitive fish belongs to the bony-tongue family, a group with similar fossilised relatives dating back 40 million years. Six other living species are known, including the Saratoga (Scleropages leichhardtii) in central-eastern Qld. Both Australian species live in billabongs and still waters of coastal river systems, and are sometimes seen feeding near the water's edge. Females protect eggs by holding them in the mouth. 90cm. nw Qld to n NT.

SPOTTED GALAXIAS, SPOTTED NATIVE TROUT ▲
(Galaxius truttaceus)

This is one of about 20 Australian species of galaxiid, a southern hemisphere family of fishes mostly restricted to freshwater and related to northern hemisphere salmon. Spotted Galaxias spend the juvenile stage of their life cycle at sea, migrating when about 65mm long into rivers, where they grow to adulthood and spawn. Eggs drift back down rivers to the sea. 20cm. s WA to se Vic, Tas.

for a major decline in population numbers. The species mainly inhabits deep holes in slow-flowing rivers, preferring sites with submerged logs. 1.8m. se SA, n Vic, w and c NSW, s Qld.

AUSTRALIAN GRAYLING ⚊

(Prototroctes maraena)

This is the last remaining member of the southern grayling family. The only other species in the family, the New Zealand Grayling, suffered a catastrophic population crash in its native NZ and has been extinct for 80 years. Small adult populations of Australian Grayling persist in coastal rivers, spending their juvenile life at sea. 33cm. se SA to se NSW, Tas.

BLACKFISH, SLIPPERY ▼

(Gadopsis marmoratus)

Blackfish have a distinctive appearance and unclear relationships to other fish groups. They live in clear-flowing streams, lakes and dams, preferring sites with

vegetated banks. Females lay eggs under a log or rock, where one parent guards them for two weeks until they hatch. 60cm. se SA, Vic, c NSW, s Qld, n Tas.

MURRAY COD ▼

(Maccullochella peeli)

As Australia's largest freshwater fish, this species is much sought after by fishers. They can weigh up to 114kg and exceed 50 years of age. Overfishing and habitat destruction are responsible

GOLDEN PERCH, CALLOP, YELLOWBELLY ⚊

(Macquaria ambigua)

This species is related to the Murray Cod, with a slightly wider distribution, and similarly prefers turbid slow-flowing rivers and billabongs.

During periods of flood, adults move long distances upstream to spawn. Fishers heavily target this species. 75cm. e SA, n Vic, w and c NSW, sw Qld, se NT.

after reaching maturity to spawn. The largest individuals reach 50kg. 1.8m. Coastal se Qld to cw WA.

AUSTRALIAN BASS ▲
(Macquaria novemaculeata)
This fish is regarded as the best angling species in south-eastern rivers draining to the coast. Adults live mostly in the upper freshwater reaches of rivers, migrating into estuaries to spawn in winter. 55cm. cs Vic to se Qld.

BARRAMUNDI ▼
(Lates calcarifer)
The most famous angling species in our tropics, Barramundi also form the basis for a controversial commercial fishery involving gillnets. Juvenile Barramundi generally live upstream in rivers, migrating to estuaries

SEVEN-SPOT ARCHERFISH ▲
(Toxotes chatareus)
Like other archerfish, this species has a flat-topped head for surface feeding. It can squirt a jet of water from its mouth to knock insect prey from overhanging vegetation into pools. The species is commonly seen from the banks of estuaries and coastal river systems. 40cm. n Qld to n WA.

SOOTY GRUNTER ➤
(Hephaestus fuliginosus)
This is the largest of the approximately 20 grunter species inhabiting Australian rivers and lakes. It is common in streams draining towards the tropical n coast. Schools circle snorkellers in the clear pools of Litchfield and Kakadu national parks, NT. 45cm. n Qld to n NT.

Bony Fishes

MURRAY RIVER RAINBOWFISH ▼

(Melanotaenia fluviatilis)
The 50 or so rainbowfish species are all confined to Australia and New Guinea. Because of their bright colouration and hardy disposition, they are globally popular with aquarists. This species tolerates cooler conditions than its relatives, most of which are tropical. 12cm. ne SA, nw Vic, w NSW, sw Qld.

Australia's most threatened fish species, having almost disappeared in recent years due to habitat loss and competition from introduced pest species. 12cm. se Tas.

SHORT-HEADED SEAHORSE ➤

(Hippocampus abdominalis)
About half of the 250 species in the seahorse and pipefish family are found in Australia, many times more than other continents.

This is the largest and most frequently sighted Australian seahorse, easily recognised by its size, yellow colour and black spots. Like other seahorses, the male carries eggs and protects the young. It lives in a variety of habitats, including kelp forests, rocky reefs, seagrass beds and sandy rubble. 25cm. cs SA to ce NSW, Tas.

SPOTTED HANDFISH ➤

(Brachionichthys hirsutus)
Handfishes are a small family of about eight species confined to southern Australia and Tas. Like their relatives the anglerfishes, they dangle a modified fin as a lure in front of the body to attract prey, and walk about the seabed on leg-like fins. This species lives only near Hobart. It is regarded as

COMMON OR WEEDY SEADRAGON ▲

(Phyllopteryx taeniolatus)

This exotic-looking seadragon is regularly seen by divers on south-east Australian reefs. Rainbow-coloured adults typically live in coastal kelp forests; juveniles more often in sheltered bays. 46cm. sw WA to ce NSW, Tas.

spines, fleshy appendages, and bright and subtle colours merge and flow in all directions. This species occurs in relatively high numbers at localised sites, but its camouflage makes it difficult to find while diving among seaweeds and seagrass. 43cm. sw WA to cs Vic.

LEAFY SEADRAGON ▲

(Phycodurus eques)

This is perhaps the world's most astonishing-looking fish. Its living appearance cannot be captured by photo—

LATCHETFISH ➤

(Pterygotrigla polyommata)

This colourful and spiny fish is an important commercially trawled species. It generally lives in deepwater, but enters

diveable depths in some Tas estuaries. 62cm. sw WA to se NSW, Tas.

COMMON GURNARD PERCH ▲

(Neosebastes scorpaenoides)

This is the largest southern Australian scorpionfish, a family of fishes with venomous spines that can inflict excruciatingly painful wounds. Divers commonly encounter this species among broken rocks and sand near reef edges, where it sits inconspicuously on the bottom waiting to ambush shrimps and fishes. It is also caught with lines and gillnets. 40cm. cs SA to ce NSW, Tas.

REEF STONEFISH ▼
(Synanceia verrucosa)

This scorpionfish and its close relative, the Estuarine Stonefish (*Synanceia horrida*), are among the most feared fishes in the sea. They have extremely venomous spines that can cause death, and camouflage so good that they are almost impossible to see among rocks and coral. If stung, wounds should be immersed in water as hot as the victim can tolerate to break down the toxin proteins. 35cm. Tropics from se Qld to cw WA.

RED VELVETFISH ➤
(Gnathanacanthus goetzeei)

This flabby species has venomous spines and is related to the scorpionfishes, but sits alone in its own family. The orange–red colouration is strikingly bright when exposed to sunlight, but provides good camouflage underwater among kelp. 46cm. sw WA to cs Vic, Tas.

WARTY PROWFISH ➤
(Aetapcus maculatus)

This odd-looking fish is one of only three species in its family, all restricted to southern Australia. It lacks scales but has a soft outer skin that it periodically sheds like a snakeskin to remove fouling organisms accumulated on the body. 22cm. cw WA to cs Vic, n and e Tas.

SAND FLATHEAD ➤
(Platycephalus bassensis)

About 60 flathead species occur worldwide, with most present in Australia. Southern Australian anglers target these fishes from small boats and the shoreline because of their abundance and good eating qualities. Different species can be recognised by various combinations of stripes, blotches and colours on the tail, which is used as a flag for signalling potential mates and competitors.

The Sand Flathead has brown blotches on the upper half of the tail and a large black patch, sometimes broken by a white line, in the lower half. 46cm. s WA to se NSW, Tas.

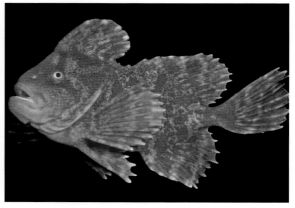

HARLEQUINFISH, CHINESE LANTERN ▲

(Othos dentex)

This brilliantly coloured species has blue spots on the upper body and yellow spots around the belly. It is among the most inquisitive fishes, watching and following divers for up to ten minutes. This curious behaviour has led to declining population numbers in areas accessible to spearfishers. 76cm. sw WA to cs SA.

species for human deaths, although none has been reliably documented. 2.7m. ce NSW to sw WA.

WESTERN BLUE DEVILFISH ▲

(Paraplesiops meleagris)

Divers often spot this colourful fish with iridescent blue spots at the mouth of caves. A shyer relative with stripes, the threatened

Eastern Blue Devilfish *(Paraplesiops bleekeri)*, frequents NSW reefs. 36cm. sw WA to cs Vic.

WESTRALIAN JEWFISH, DHUFISH ▼

(Glaucosoma hebraicum)

This is the most heavily targeted reef fish in Australia's south-west, being prized by both anglers and divers for its large size and excellent eating qualities. Individuals generally live on rugged offshore reefs near crevices and large holes. The horizontal body stripes tend to fade with age, although the line through the eye persists in the largest animals. 1.2m. sw to s WA.

QUEENSLAND GROPER, GIANT GROUPER ▲

(Epinephelus lanceolatus)

This fish grows to over 300kg in weight and is the largest coral reef fish worldwide. Popular stories blame this

indistinguishable species of Australian salmon occur in the south-east and south-west, with an area of overlap around Tas and central Vic. Juveniles of both species are

MULLOWAY, JEWFISH ▲

(Argyrosomus hololepidotus)

Although called a Jewfish in the eastern States, the Mulloway belongs to the croaker family and is not closely related to the Westralian Jewfish. Juvenile Mulloway, known as 'soapies', inhabit estuaries; adults generally live at sea, spawning off coastal beaches. The Mulloway's croaking sound travels long distances on still nights. 2m. cw WA to se Qld.

EASTERN SCHOOL WHITING ▼

(Sillago flindersi)

Australian whiting comprise about 20 elongate species with pointed snouts and small mouths that forage among sand. They are not closely related to European whiting. Most are popular

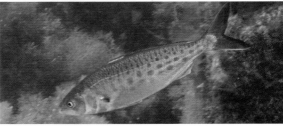

table fish. Adult Eastern School Whiting typically live in deepwater; juveniles forage over the sandy seabed of coastal bays and estuaries. 32cm. cs Vic to se Qld, e Tas.

EASTERN AUSTRALIAN OR BLACKBACK SALMON ▲

(Arripis trutta)

Australian salmon are not related to northern hemisphere salmon, although both groups are harvested in large quantities for canning. Different but virtually

commonly known as 'cocky salmon'. 90cm. cs Vic to se Qld, Tas.

YELLOWFIN BREAM ▼

(Acanthopagrus australis)

Common in estuaries and coastal bays, this fish has a silver body and yellow fins, and is one of the more popular angling species. Adults spawn at the mouths of estuaries, with small juveniles migrating into estuaries when about one month old. 66cm. se Vic to ce Qld.

hairstyle—short at top, long at back—also known as the 'mullet'. 80cm. Aus, Tas.

WESTERN TALMA, WESTERN CORALFISH ▼
(Chelmonops curiosus)
In contrast to most other

SNAPPER ▲
(Pagrus auratus)
A large relative of the Yellowfin Bream, the Snapper is a prized angling fish. Juveniles are abundant in estuaries and coastal bays, where the species is initially known as 'Squire' then later 'Cockney Bream'. Large adults typically occur on deep offshore reefs. Very large animals have a pronounced bump on the head. 1.3m. cw WA to ce Qld, ne Tas.

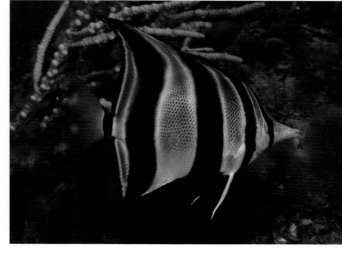

LUDERICK, BLACKFISH ▼
(Girella tricuspidata)
Luderick have about 10 thin vertical lines extending across the body. Juveniles primarily school in estuaries, while adults occur abundantly in

the surf zone off rocky shores, where they feed on plants. This is the only fish in the world that anglers capture with seaweed bait. 62cm. cs SA to se Qld, n Tas.

SEA MULLET ➤
(Mugil cephalus)
Several mullet species inhabit estuaries and sheltered bays around the continent. This is the largest, distinguishable by its rounded snout and large gelatinous eyelid. This fish inspired a distinctive

butterflyfishes, which are tropical, this species frequents cool-water reefs off the south coast. It generally moves about rocky reefs in pairs. 20cm. cw WA to se SA.

OLD WIFE ➤
(Enoplosus armatus)
A close relative of the tropical butterflyfishes, this species is placed in its own family because of distinctive characteristics such as two rather than one dorsal (upper) fin. Its name derives from the grating sound generated as it grinds its teeth together when stressed.

EASTERN BLUE GROPER ▼
(Achoerodus viridis)
These large wrasse follow divers like curious dogs, consequently population numbers have suffered greatly from spearfishing. They are now fully protected from spearfishers, although not from anglers. The species has been adopted as the fish emblem of NSW. A similar species, the Western Blue Groper (*Acheorodus goudii*), lives on southern Australian reefs. 1.6m. cs Vic to se Qld.

Pairs commonly occur on coastal reefs. Schools of mixed size also aggregate in sheltered bays and over seagrass beds. 31cm. sw WA to se Qld, n Tas.

a pink female, and finally transforming into the striped male (illustrated). 30cm. sw WA to n NSW, Tas.

SENATOR WRASSE ▲
(Pictilabrus laticlavius)
The wrasse family is one of the largest groups of fishes, with over 400 species in a huge range of sizes and shapes.

This is the most colourful wrasse of cooler Australian waters, and also the most widespread. It starts life as a mottled juvenile, changing to

LONG-SNOUTED BOARFISH ➤

(Pentaceropsis recurvirostris)

This striped species is a slow-moving inhabitant of cooler coastal reefs. Numbers appear to be slowly increasing in Tas following recent laws that protect it from spearfishing. The long spines are venomous. 60cm. sw WA to ce NSW, Tas.

MAGPIE PERCH ➤

(Cheilodactylus nigripes)

This fish belongs to the morwong family, a group of about 20 fish that primarily occur in southern Australia. They have rubbery lips and pectoral (side) fins with extended lower rays. The Magpie Perch feeds like a typical morwong, sucking in mouthfuls of food from the seabed. 40cm. s WA to se NSW, Tas.

HORSESHOE LEATHERJACKET ◄

(Meuschenia hippocrepis)

Over half of the world's total of about 100 leatherjacket species are found in Australia. They have a leathery skin with spiny embedded scales and a long first dorsal spine with associated locking spines. Numerous species are seen while diving southern Australian reefs, including this one, an inquisitive species with a distinctive horseshoe mark on the flanks. 50cm. sw WA to cs Vic, n Tas.

Because dry conditions prevail across much of Australia and frogs need water, we have relatively few frog species compared to other continents—about 200 in total. Nevertheless, many interesting species occur here, including the burrowing frogs of semi-arid country. These belong to our largest family, the Myobatrachidae.

The most remarkable Australian frogs are the two gastric-brooding frogs of eastern Qld. These unexceptional-looking species differ from all others worldwide in reproductive strategy. They lack a swimming tadpole stage; instead the female swallows the fertilised eggs, which develop into miniature adults in her stomach over a six-week period.

During the past two decades, frogs worldwide, including the two gastric-brooding species, have been catastrophically affected by a fatal epidemic involving a skin fungus. Gastric-brooding frogs were last seen in 1981 and are probably now extinct.

GREEN AND GOLDEN BELL FROG ▼
(Litoria aurea)

This frog belongs to the tree frog group of about 60 species, most of which inhabit the wetter regions of Australia. They all have horizontal eye pupils and suction pads on the tips of fingers and toes, an adaptation that allows them to cling to vertical surfaces, including glass windows. While many are tree dwellers, others rarely venture above the ground and have long limbs characteristic of terrestrial species.

Active by day and partly aquatic, the Green and Golden Bell Frog is cannibalistic and a voracious predator on freshwater invertebrates. Population numbers have declined dramatically in recent years. 85mm. ne Vic, e NSW.

GREEN TREE FROG ▼
(Litoria caerulea)

Perhaps the most commonly seen frog in Australia, this species likes urban areas, particularly where lights attract insects. It is also found in shaded gardens, outside toilets and shower blocks. Its presence is sometimes proclaimed by calls amplified by house drainpipes. 80mm. n Aus.

RED-EYED TREE FROG ▲
(Litoria chloris)
This species is similar to the Green Tree Frog, but has a red and golden eye. It is mostly confined to wet forests but can also be found in boggy grasslands after summer rains. 65mm. ce NSW to ce Qld.

GREEN-EYED TREE FROG ▲
(Litoria genimaculata)
This rainforest species is associated with rocky creeks. It usually perches on mossy seepages or among creekside vegetation. Females reproduce when they are two to three years old, producing from 200 to 1000 eggs annually. Their skin secretions have an antibiotic quality. 85mm. ne Qld.

BROWN TREE FROG ▼
(Litoria ewingii)
This abundant species frequents many habitats. Large aggregations occur during the breeding season at dams, ponds, waterholes and creeks. Males call throughout the year from low vegetation, on the ground, or when floating in water. 45mm. se Aus, Tas.

DAINTY TREE FROG ▼
(Litoria gracilenta)
The upper surface of this frog is a uniform pea-green, with a pale stripe extending from eardrum to nostril. The under-surface is bright yellow. It is commonly found in dense vegetation near water. This species can be attracted to house lights, where insects aggregate. Males call after rains during spring and summer. 45mm. ce NSW to ne Qld.

GREEN LEAF TREE FROG ▲
(Litoria phyllochroa)
....
Males can be heard calling Oct–Mar in low vegetation or on the ground near running water. Eggs are laid in clusters attached to leaves

temporary pools. Tadpoles are pale yellow with dark side stripes. This species is most commonly observed in trees near permanent water. Most individuals have a bright rusty red upper half of the iris. 55mm. Coastal ce Qld to n NT, ne WA.

GIANT ROCKETFROG ▼
(Litoria wotjulumensis)
....
This is a nocturnal terrestrial species of tree frog. It frequents shallow permanent swamps near rocky outcrops, but also forages widely through forest and grassland, sometimes at some distance

from water bodies. Breeding occurs Oct–Mar, during and after rainfall. 75mm. nw Qld, n NT, ne WA.

CORROBOREE FROG ▲
(Pseudophryne corroboree)
....
The most easily recognisable frog in Australia, this striking species is bright yellow and black. It is found in the Southern Alps above the treeline or in wet forests beside creeks, generally in its preferred breeding habitat of sphagnum bog. The population has declined dramatically recently, hence its threatened status. 30mm. Australian Alps, se NSW.

and sticks. The tadpoles are small and peppered with golden spots. 40mm. se SA, Vic, NSW, s Qld.

ROTH'S TREE FROG ▶
(Litoria rothii)
....
Males call throughout summer, with increased frequency after rainfall. Females lay eggs in any source of water, including

BANJO FROG, POBBLEBONK ▼

(Limnodynastes dumerilii)

The common name of this ground-dwelling species is derived from its call—a 'bonk' or 'plonk'. A call by one individual will often result in a series of calls from nearby frogs. Responses generally occur instantaneously, making it difficult to believe that more than one frog is calling. Commonly seen after rain in heaths and eucalypt forests, its genus name *Limnodynastes* means 'lord of the marshes'. 70mm. Coast and GDR se SA to se Qld, Tas.

as natural bushland. 65mm. Coast and GDR cs Vic to ne Qld, Tas.

RUSSELL'S TOADLET ▲

(Uperoleia russelli)

Prominent glands on its back, reddish orange spots on the back of the knee and groin, and a reddish patch on each shoulder characterise this species. It can be found well away from water after rain but is more commonly observed beside permanent river pools. 30mm. Coast and inland c WA.

STRIPED MARSH FROG ➤

(Limnodynastes peronii)

Males of this species call throughout the year while floating on water or sitting on vegetation at the water's edge. The call is a 'whuck' sound. This frog is highly adaptable, surviving in mildly polluted waters, urban areas and swimming pools, as well

MALLEE FROG, PAINTED BURROWING FROG ▲
(Neobatrachus sudelli)

This burrowing species can be observed in free-standing water after heavy summer rains. Only the males call. They issue a short trilling sound during a breeding season that is governed by rainfall. Females lay up to 1000 eggs among vegetation. Increasing soil salinity and habitat modification threaten the long-term survival of this species. 40mm. c and w Vic, interior of NSW, sw and s Qld.

COMMON FROGLET ▼
(Crinia signifera)

This is one of a group of similar small brown froglets that are best identified by genetic analysis or by their calls. The Common Froglet itself is highly variable in colour and pattern, and occurs in a wide variety of habitats from the coast to drier inland regions. It prefers slow-moving water bodies for breeding, and attaches egg masses to twigs or leaves. 30mm. se SA, Vic, NSW, se Qld, Tas.

GREAT BARRED FROG ▲
(Mixophyes iterates)

This large species and several close relatives have banded legs and a black stripe that extends from the eardrum through the eye to the snout. The eye itself has a vertical pupil; the upper half of the iris is a pale golden colour, whilst the lower half is darker. An inhabitant of rainforests and wet eucalypt forests, it can sometimes be observed close to running water. Breeding occurs Oct–Nov. 115mm. ce NSW to se Qld.

Crocodiles

Ancient relatives of the crocodiles were the first vertebrate animals to successfully colonise land. Like other reptiles, crocodiles are air-breathing and cold-blooded, with a scaly skin to reduce water loss from body surfaces. Two of the 21 species worldwide occur in Australia. They are superbly adapted to an amphibious life, with valves in their throat and nostrils, and a muscular tail for locomotion in water.

FRESHWATER CROCODILE, FRESHIE ➤

(Crocodylus johnstonii)

This crocodile lives in rivers, billabongs and lagoons in n Australia. Its slender, smooth snout allows it to sideswipe rapidly underwater when capturing prey such as fish, crustaceans, frogs, small reptiles, birds and mammals. Animals often sun themselves on river banks during daylight. Although sometimes considered harmless, these cocodiles can inflict nasty bites if annoyed. 3m. ne Qld to ne WA.

ESTUARINE CROCODILE, SALTIE ▼

(Crocodylus porosus)

This is the largest reptile in Australia and is responsible for human deaths. It has a muscular tail capable of propelling the animal in rapid bursts of speed, while its powerful jaws are capable of snapping the thigh bone of a large mammal. They swim stealthily, with only their nostrils and eyes breaking the water's surface. Estuarine crocodiles can remain submerged for up to an hour. 5m. Coastal swamps and rivers ce Qld to cn WA.

This successful group of reptiles has survived for the last 100 million years. Twenty freshwater species occur in Australia, all with clawed, webbed feet. The six marine species have limbs evolved into flippers without an ankle joint and with one or more claws on the front edge.

LONG-NECKED TURTLE, SLIDER ▼
(Chelodina longicollis)

The head and neck of this species are as long as the shell. It is carnivorous, catching molluscs, crustaceans and fish with a snake-like strike. When alarmed or handled it produces a foul-smelling fluid. During summer, individuals may migrate long distances overland between water bodies. Shell 25cm. se SA to ce Qld.

NORTHERN SNAPPING TURTLE ▲
(Elseya dentata)

This is the larger relative of the Saw-shelled Turtle, distinguishable by size and differences in the shape of shell plates. Individuals often exhibit macrocephaly, a condition in which the head becomes greatly enlarged. Shell 35cm. n Qld to ne WA.

VICTORIA RIVER TURTLE ➤
(Emydura victoriae)

This is one of six short-necked species in eastern and northern Australia. All have an extended head but the neck is shorter than the shell. They feed on plants and animals, preferring still rivers, lakes and billabongs. This turtle often basks on logs and rocks. Shell 30cm. n NT, ne WA.

marinus). Shell 28cm.
ne NSW to ne Qld.

GREEN TURTLE ▼
(Chelonia mydas)

During the first year of life, Green Turtles are carnivorous, later switching to a diet of seaweeds and seagrasses. Females return to the beach of their birth to lay up to 120 eggs in a nest dug in the sand, sometimes twice in a year. Some beaches will be visited by hundreds of females in a single night. Marine turtles are an important food for Aboriginal people of coastal northern Australia. Shell 1.5m. Aus.

SAW-SHELLED TURTLE ▲
(Elseya latisternum)

This turtle has a longish neck and a shell that is serrated along its rear edge, most noticeably in juveniles. The upper surface of the neck has numerous pointed tubercles. It feeds on a variety of aquatic plants, insects, crustaceans and fish. Importantly, it is a successful predator of the introduced Cane Toad (*Bufo*

Lizards

Because they can conserve body water and survive in arid lands, lizards are unusually diverse in Australia, particularly the semi-arid regions. Australia is home to about 120 geckos, 60 dragons, 300 skinks and 15 goannas.

NORTHERN LEAF–TAILED GECKO ▼
(Saltuarius cornutus)

Geckos are nocturnal soft-skinned lizards that occur throughout Australia other than alpine regions, south-eastern Vic and Tas. They generally shelter by day under bark or rocks, emerging at night to feed on insects, spiders and scorpions. Some species have padded toes with adhesive ridges, allowing them to climb vertical and overhanging surfaces. Others have simple clawed toes. Geckos are unable to blink, so use the tongue to clean their lidless eyes. If threatened they can voluntarily lose their tail, subsequently regenerating a new one.

The cryptic colouration of the Northern Leaf-tailed Gecko renders it almost invisible against rainforest trees and rocks. It can be recognised by its flattened heart-shaped tail and the long, hooked tubercules on its sides. 14cm. ne Qld.

TREE DTELLA ▼
(Gehyra variegata)

This gecko is one of the most abundant lizards in woodlands, shrublands and rocky ranges of drier areas. Generally a tree-climbing species, it shelters by day under loose bark or crevices in rocks. 54mm. Inland Aus.

THICK–TAILED GECKO ▼
(Underwoodisaurus milii)

An inhabitant of a variety of habitats from coastal heathlands to arid scrublands, this gecko emerges from shelter at night to forage in sandy or open grassed areas. If threatened it produces a loud barking sound, raises its body, and lunges at the aggressor. 96mm. s WA, SA, nw Vic, NSW, s Qld.

BYNOE'S GECKO ▲
(Heteronotia binoei)
This gecko is common in a diverse range of habitats from the semi-arid interior to wet coastal forests. It generally shelters among ground litter or in rock crevices, but forages in more open areas at night. Females in populations in central WA are capable of producing clones without the need for sexual reproduction. 50mm. Aus.

BURTON'S LEGLESS LIZARD ▼
(Lialis burtonis)
The most widespread Australian reptile, this snake-

like lizard lives in every habitat type other than cool alpine areas. It has small hindlimb flaps and a long, wedge-shaped snout. It feeds on small lizards and the occasional snake, constricting prey with a suffocating grip

around the chest area. Prey are swallowed head first. 29cm. Aus.

COMMON SCALY-FOOT ▲
(Pygopus lepidopodus)
A large legless lizard with conspicuous external ear openings, this species is highly variable in colour. It inhabits environments ranging from coastal heaths and sand dunes to inland mallee scrub and wet forests. Active during daylight, it forages through ground litter under low vegetation. 23cm. Coast and ranges from sw WA to se Qld.

FRILLED LIZARD ▼
(Chlamydosaurus kingii)

This is the best known of the dragon lizards, an egg-laying group that mainly forage on the ground by day. Many have large spines along the body.

The Frilled Lizard is active during the day, spending much of its time in trees but characteristically moving behind the trunk if approached. If confronted on the ground, it faces its attacker with open mouth and erected frill, which in large individuals may be up to 30cm wide. It can also run from danger on its hindlimbs to the nearest tree. Juveniles, such as the animal illustrated, are marked with streaks. 26cm. n Aus.

EASTERN WATER DRAGON ◄
(Physignathus lesueurii)

This dragon is most commonly seen on tree branches adjacent to rivers, including creeks in urban areas. If disturbed it will launch itself from the branch into the water and quickly swim by sinuous movements to a riverbank shelter, where it disappears from view. 25cm. Coastal se Vic to ne Qld.

BOYD'S FOREST DRAGON ▲
(Hypsilurus boydii)

This elusive day-foraging lizard is confined to tropical rainforest. It basks in sunlight after rainfall, often along roadsides, stream edges or walking tracks. This species moves slowly and attempts to hide from view by sliding around saplings or trunks. A large spined crest distinguishes it from other local dragons. 15cm. ne Qld.

COMMON BEARDED DRAGON ▲

(Pogona barbata)

One of the most commonly observed large lizards, this dragon often resides in urban areas. If approached it will initially remain still to avoid detection. However, it may then gape its mouth to show the yellowish pink interior, flatten its body, and extend its beard, while turning in confrontation. 25cm. Coast and ranges from s SA to ne Qld.

JACKY LIZARD ▼

(Amphibolurus muricatus)

This lizard commonly perches on shrubs, trees, fallen timber or fence posts. It is an opportunistic feeder on small insects and spiders in dry eucalypt forests, rocky ridges and coastal heathlands. When threatened it will run swiftly on its hindlimbs with an upright gait. 12cm. Coast and ranges from se SA to se Qld.

NORTHERN WATER DRAGON ▼

(Amphibolurus temporalis)

An inhabitant of woodlands and river margins, this species is most often seen perched on elevated objects amongst pandanus or melaleuca shrubs. It mainly feeds on ants and other lizards. Females lack the prominent broad whitish lateral stripe of the males. 12cm. n Aus.

CENTRAL-NETTED DRAGON ▲

(Ctenophorus nuchalis)

This is one of most abundant of the 22 species of fast-moving *Ctenophorus* dragons present in semi-arid areas. It shelters in burrows at the base of shrubs or stumps, plugging the entrances with soil during winter. 12cm. c and w Aus.

RED–BARRED DRAGON ▲

(Ctenophorus vadnappa)

This dragon perches on prominent, elevated sites on rocky outcrops. Males display with their tail coiled vertically, while engaging in a series of 'push-ups'. 85mm. n Flinders Ranges, SA.

MOUNTAIN DRAGON ▼

(Rankinia diemensis)

Most often encountered in low vegetation or among rocks or leaf litter, this is the world's most southerly dragon. Unlike other dragons, it tends to scuttle rather than run swiftly. Individuals reach largest size towards the south. 82mm. Coast and ranges from c Vic to cs NSW, n and e Tas.

THORNY DEVIL ▼

(Moloch horridus)

This unmistakeable lizard is a dietary specialist, feeding exclusively on ants, and ingesting up to 5000 per meal. It moves with a slow jerky motion, its tail held curved above the ground. When infrequent rain falls, raindrops striking the body are channelled to the lizard's mouth via a series of grooves on the body. 110mm. c and w WA.

commonly encountered in dry open habitats. It shelters in deep burrows. Large adults can stand erect on their hindlimbs, maintaining balance with their tail. 1.6m. Aus.

PERENTIE ▲
(Varanus giganteus)
This is the largest goanna in Australia. Like others it is carnivorous, foraging with a swaggering gait and constantly flicking its deeply forked tongue. An opportunistic feeder on carrion, this species also takes small animals, including some of our most venomous snakes. During the breeding season males engage in ritualised combat, lashing their long powerful tails aggressively back and forth like whips. It primarily lives on the ground near rocky outcrops and ranges, but also has sometimes been observed in sandy desert areas. 2.4m. w and c Aus.

SAND GOANNA ➤
(Varanus gouldii)
This widespread ground-dwelling lizard is most

LACE MONITOR ◄
(Varanus varius)
This tree-dwelling species feeds on nestling birds, mammals, reptiles and insects, although it is also often seen in picnic grounds and camping areas. It will quickly ascend a large tree if disturbed, spiralling upwards out of sight. 2.1m. e SA to ce Qld.

MERTEN'S WATER MONITOR ▲
(Varanus mertensi)

A semi-aquatic goanna with flattened tail and nostrils on the top of its snout, this species basks on the limbs of trees. When disturbed it will drop into water, where it swims to cover, or dives. It can remain submerged for many minutes. 1.1m. ne Qld to ne WA.

BLOTCHED BLUE-TONGUED LIZARD ▼
(Tiliqua nigrolutea)

This large short-limbed lizard belongs to the skink family, the largest and most widespread group of lizards in Australia. Although some skinks lay eggs, this species produces up to 25 live young. It forages across the ground in daylight, tending to slink away when approached. If threatened, it will flatten its body, gape its mouth, extend a flat blue tongue, and hiss loudly. Four similar species occur elsewhere across Australia, with at least one blue-tongue present at most locations. 30cm. se SA, s and e Vic, highlands s and c NSW, n and e Tas.

CUNNINGHAM'S SKINK ▲
(Egernia cunninghami)

This is one of about 30 moderate to large skinks in the *Egernia* group. Most are active during the day and produce up to six live young.

This one lives communally in rock crevices or under rock slabs and is often encountered on exposed rock surfaces near cover. It primarily eats seeds and fruit, but will also capture insects. 20cm. se SA, GDR from sw Vic to se Qld.

EASTERN WATER SKINK ▼
(Eulamprus quoyii)

This species lives in a variety of habitats, including rain-forests, eucalypt forests and heaths. It is most often seen beside creeks and among wetlands, where it frequently basks on logs or rocks. If disturbed it will promptly take to the water or disappear down crevices. It feeds on insects and smaller lizards. 12cm. se SA, c and e NSW, se and ce Qld.

WHITE'S SKINK ▲
(Egernia whitii)

Like Cunningham's Skink, White's will shelter within rock crevices; however, it will also excavate burrows or tunnels beneath rocks and logs. It can move quickly. 11cm. Coast and GDR s SA to se Qld, Tas.

SHINGLEBACK, BOBTAIL ◄
(Trachydosaurus rugosus)

This common skink is easily recognised by its short stumpy tail and large body scales. An omnivorous species, it mates for life and usually produces two young per litter. It is widely distributed in habitats ranging from dry forest and semi-arid shrublands to coastal heaths. 31cm. s WA, s SA, w Vic, w NSW, sw Qld.

Snakes

The Australian snake fauna is diverse and rich, comprising both terrestrial and aquatic species, with over 190 species described. The majority belong to the front-fanged snakes, of which 30 are dangerous to humans. Most feed on small vertebrates with lizards the primary prey, although frogs, birds and small mammals are also commonly preyed upon.

CARPET PYTHON ▼
(Morelia spilota)
Pythons are thick, slow-moving snakes that constrict their prey to kill them. All are non-venomous, but they may bite; most are nocturnal and lay eggs. The largest python in Australia—the Amethystine Python (*Morelia amethistina*)—can grow to 8m in length.

The colour of the Carpet Python varies greatly among habitats. It is one of the more commonly observed snakes in Australia, and can be found moving at night in urban areas, including ceilings of houses. Behaviour of individuals varies greatly—some will repeatedly strike if approached, while others will tolerate handling. 2.5m. ne and s WA, s SA, nw Vic, NSW, s, e and n Qld, n NT.

BLACK-HEADED PYTHON ➤
(Aspidites melanocephalus)
This inhabitant of woodlands, shrublands and rocky outcrops feeds mainly on reptiles, including venomous snakes. It lacks the heat sensory pits on the lips that are present on mammal- and bird-feeding pythons. It has

been suggested that the black head allows this species to absorb heat while exposing only a small part of its body from crevice shelters. 2.6m. n Aus.

SPOTTED PYTHON ▲
(Antaresia maculosa)
This inoffensive snake was once a popular pet. It inhabits rocky outcrops and woodlands, and will sometimes shelter in termite mounds. Spotted Pythons have been observed at cave entrances attempting to seize bats emerging at dusk. 1.0m. ne NSW to ne Qld.

GREEN TREE PYTHON ▲
(Chondropython viridis)
This rainforest species spends the day tightly coiled among tree hollows, branches and ferns, moving out to forage for birds and mammals at night. The green and yellow colours are characteristic. 1.2m. ne Qld.

BANDY-BANDY ▼
(Vermicelli annulata)
This burrowing venomous species is generally only encountered at night, and then after recent rain. When

threatened it thrashes about then twists its body into an upright loop. A specialist predator, it feeds exclusively on blind snakes. 76cm. se SA, nw and n Vic, NSW, Qld, ne NT.

TIGER SNAKE ▲
(Notechis scutatus)
This is one of our best known snakes, primarily because of its highly toxic venom and the number of fatalities caused by bites before an antivenom was developed. It is most active during daylight and at dusk, and is often seen searching for frogs near water. Populations on some Bass Strait islands feed exclusively on muttonbird chicks, fasting for much of the year. If provoked this species will raise its head, flatten its neck, and face the harasser. 2m. Coastal sw, se and e Aus, Tas.

COPPERHEAD ▲

(Austrelaps superbus)

This venomous snake is more tolerant of cool conditions than other Australian rear-fanged snakes. It has a strong preference for sites near water, particularly among tussock grasses, and feeds on frogs, tadpoles and lizards. 1.8m. s and c Vic, GDR NSW, Tas.

EASTERN BROWN SNAKE ▼

(Pseudonaja textilis)

This is the most venomous Australian snake, one of several brown snakes that have variable colour patterns and are difficult to distinguish. A similar fast-moving brown snake is the Dugite (*Pseudonaja affinis*), the most dangerous snake living near Perth, WA. Brown snakes typically defend themselves vigorously if threatened, with head and neck reared and mouth open, and striking repeatedly. The Eastern Brown is widely distributed over a range of habitats from forests to semi-arid regions. It feeds on frogs, lizards, birds and mammals. 2.5m. c and e Aus.

TAIPAN ▲

(Oxyuranus scutellatus)

An extremely dangerous snake if provoked, the taipan feeds predominantly on rats. It strikes with lightning speed, often more than once, injecting massive doses of highly toxic venom. Taipans then release the prey and wait until it succumbs before they start to feed. 2.8m. ne NSW to ne Qld, n NT, ne WA.

COMMON DEATH ADDER ➤

(Acanthophis antarcticus)

Death adders are a group of sluggish, viper-like snakes, with three Australian species. All have a broad triangular head, robust body and a narrow tail ending in a spine. They are among the most dangerous snakes in Australia, with relatively large fangs and highly toxic venom. This one is an ambush feeder, lying motionless beneath leaf litter or loose sand. It wriggles the tip of its grub-like tail to attract prey, including lizards, birds and small mammals. 80cm. s WA to s SA, NSW, Qld, ne NT.

MULGA SNAKE ▼

(Pseudechis australis)

Although also known as the King Brown Snake, this species is a member of the black snake rather than brown snake group. It primarily feeds at night or at dusk on frogs, lizards, other snakes, birds and mammals.

This highly venomous species lives in most habitats other than wet and alpine areas. 2.7m. n, w and c Aus.

RED–BELLIED BLACK SNAKE ▲

(Pseudechis porphyriacus)

This venomous species is common throughout its range, including the fringes of urban areas. It prefers damp areas, including swamps and the banks of rivers and lakes. An accomplished swimmer, it feeds mainly on frogs, although it has been observed attacking and killing other snakes. 2.0m. Coast and ranges se SA to se Qld.

COMMON TREE SNAKE ➤

(Dendrelaphis punctulata)
This snake moves swiftly and agilely through tree branches. Although non-venomous, it puts on an aggressive display if cornered, striking out at the harasser with flattened neck. It can release a pungent odour from anal glands when handled. 1.2m. Coast and ranges ce NSW to n WA.

BROWN TREE SNAKE ⋀

(Boiga irregularis)
This slender species has a well-defined head with prominent eyes and vertical pupils. It mainly feeds in trees at night on birds and small mammals, sheltering during the day in crevices, hollow logs and termite mounds. If threatened it will hiss loudly and lunge repeatedly with open mouth. It is a rear-fanged snake, producing a mild venom that is not considered dangerous to humans. 2m. Coast and ranges ce NSW to n WA.

STOKES' SEA SNAKE ▼

(Astrotia stokesii)
Sea snakes are allied to the terrestrial front-fanged snakes of Australia, and most of the world's species occur in this region. All are venomous and should be regarded as dangerous. They are adapted to an aquatic existence: they have valves in the nostrils, a paddle-shaped tail, and membranous tissues associated with the lungs to store air. This is one of the largest species, recognisable by a deep keel of scales and dark circular patches regularly distributed down the body. It inhabits both turbid inshore waters and habitats between reefs. 2m. Tropical waters se Qld to nw WA.

Wild Australia

Through flight and song, birds are the most conspicuous of all animals. In inhospitable areas, such as the open sea and the fringes of Antarctica, they are often the only animals to be seen. Seabird species include penguins, petrels, cormorants, pelicans and seagulls. Some seabirds, such as albatrosses, inhabit the open ocean. Others live along coastal shorelines and estuaries, including a few species that penetrate inland as far as the central Australian salt lakes.

LITTLE PENGUIN ▼
(Eudyptula minor)

Eleven species of penguins visit Australian shorelines. One breeds on the mainland and Tas, another four breed on Macquarie Island, and others are rare vagrants. All are flightless with a streamlined body shape and flattened feather shafts, giving the appearance from a distance that they are 'furred'. They have a tail gland that secretes oil to weatherproof feathers.

The Little Penguin is the smallest penguin worldwide. It is a star attraction on Phillip Island near Melbourne. It waddles up the beach at dusk after feeding on plankton and fish, emitting sharp barking sounds. Colonies are established around the s coastline in some unlikely places, including Sydney Harbour. 34cm. cw WA to ne NSW, Tas.

SHY ALBATROSS, MOLLYMAWK ▲
(Diomedia cauta)

Albatrosses have long narrow wings, short legs placed well back, large webbed feet without a hind toe, and a hooked bill with tube nostrils on either side. They can exist for weeks at sea without drinking fresh water, and secrete salt through a pore above the bill. The Shy Albatross is the most common local albatross, and the only one to breed off the Australian continent. It nests on Albatross Island in Bass Strait and two cliffy islands off southern Tas. It has a wingspan to 2.25m, and is frequently seen gliding at sea, where it often follows small fishing boats in search of fish, squid or crustaceans. 100cm. Offshore s Aus, Tas.

SHORT-TAILED SHEARWATER, MUTTONBIRD ▲
(Puffinus tenuirostris)

This seabird migrates during Sept from the far northern Pacific to breed on islands off south-eastern Australia and Tas, returning northward in autumn. Large flocks fly close to the water in summer, feeding on plankton. It is the only wild Australian bird that is commercially harvested for food, with thousands of fat chicks taken from nesting burrows each year in controlled harvesting operations. The name Muttonbird refers to the taste of the flesh. 45cm. Coastal s SA, Vic, NSW, se Qld, Tas.

PACIFIC GULL ▲
(Larus pacificus)

This is the only gull of the 42 species worldwide that is restricted to Australia. It is also the largest of the seven local species. The Pacific Gull eats the eggs and young of other birds, as well as fish, molluscs, crustaceans and snails, which it sometimes drops onto rocks to break open. It is generally seen singly or in pairs and breeds on islands. 60cm. s WA, s SA, s Vic, se NSW, Tas.

SILVER GULL ▼
(Larus novaehollandiae)

This noisy bird congregates in large flocks on the seashore, or moves inland in hundreds to scavenge refuse dumps. It forages on beaches for fish, plankton and carrion. This gull normally nests on offshore islands, but sometimes also on headlands. It is an unwelcome guest at coastal picnic areas. 40cm. Aus, Tas.

SOOTY OYSTERCATCHER ▲
(Haemanoptus fuliginosus)

This species specialises in prising molluscs from rocks or in picking bivalves and crustaceans out from under sand. Unlike the black and white Pied Oystercatcher (*Haematopus longirostis*), it occurs more often on rocky platforms than sandy beaches. It lays one to four eggs in a scrape between rocks. When disturbed it flies off with a loud complaining 'peep-peep-peep'. 50cm. Aus, Tas.

HOODED DOTTEREL ▼
(Charadrius rubricollis)
Like most dotterels, this small plover bobs its head continually when standing, and runs away when approached. It forages along the swash zone of beaches and saltlakes for insects, crustaceans and other small animals. Populations are declining and the species is considered threatened. 20cm. s Aus, Tas.

RED-CAPPED DOTTEREL ▼
(Charadrius ruficapillus)
This species runs across sandy foreshores foraging for insects, worms, molluscs and

the small seeds of aquatic plants. If an intruder approaches the nest, it pretends to have a broken wing to entice the intruder away. Juveniles play dead among dune plants, and can be closely approached. 15cm. Aus, Tas.

SPUR-WING LAPWING, MASKED LAPWING ➤
(Vanellus miles)
This and the other Australian lapwing, the Banded Plover (Vanellus tricolor), are named for their distinctive flight of hesitant beats. They are strongly territorial, attacking intruders who approach their nest too closely. Each wing has a spur. Its call is a loud, complaining 'keer-ki-ki-ki'. Food items include insects, worms and seeds. 35cm. Coastal Aus, Tas.

AUSTRALIAN PELICAN ▲
(Pelecanus conspicillatus)
In addition to coastal lagoons, this bird can be found almost anywhere in Australia where sufficient water exists to support fish and crustaceans. It is easily identifiable, whether soaring in the air or floating on water. Pelicans like a free feed and often wait for handouts near boat ramps. 170cm. Aus, Tas.

Ducks, geese and other waterfowl are adapted for swimming on water, and have webbed or partly webbed feet, waterproof plumage, and flattened bills. Herons, ibises and storks, on the other hand, have long unwebbed toes, and forage around the water's edge. Many waterbirds remain in the one area throughout their life, while others migrate long distances depending on the availability of food and water. Populations can grow rapidly when breeding in dry inland areas after heavy rain. Waterbirds do not tend to compete against each other for food as diets of different species at the same location generally vary.

LITTLE BLACK CORMORANT ▼
(Phalacrocorax sulcirostris)
Cormorants (or shags) are persecuted by some fishers due to their proficiency in catching fish. They can distort the lenses in their eyes and thus see well both above and below water. This one inhabits most coastal and inland waterways. The wings lack waterproofing, reducing buoyancy and helping the bird to reach the riverbed to feed. 65cm. Aus, Tas.

DARTER, SNAKEBIRD ▲
(Anhinga melanogaster)
This large brownish black bird has a brown bill and a thin white stripe below the eye. Its feathers do not repel water and quickly become waterlogged, hence the bird can often be seen drying its outstretched wings. Common in coastal and inland areas, it often swims with only its snake-like head above water. It spears fish with its sharp, pointed bill. 90cm. Aus.

BLACK SWAN ▼
(Cygnus atratus)
This large bird, the emblem of WA, has a long slender neck, a red bill, and black plumage, but with white wing tips that are noticeable during flight. After the breeding season, thousands of swans gather in wetlands, feeding on aquatic plants and marsh grasses. Their distinctive trumpeting call is sometimes heard when they are flying in a V formation at night. 130cm. Aus, Tas.

BLACK DUCK ▲
(Anas superciliosa)
Like other ducks and geese, this very common Australian duck is a strong swimmer. It is mostly found near water and normally feeds on aquatic plant seeds, insects and crustaceans, but is also accused by farmers of damaging crops. More brown than black, it has a dark line edged in white from the bill through to the eye. Females make a noisy 'quack'. 60cm. Aus, Tas.

WOOD OR BLACK-MANED DUCK ▼
(Chenonetta jubata)
This duck feeds almost exclusively on grasses adjacent to swamps, dams and rivers. It initially remains motionless when alarmed,

ready to fly laboriously away if approached too closely. Flocks of up to 2000 birds can sometimes be seen. It nests in tree hollows and its call is a drawn out 'quaark'. 50cm. Aus, Tas.

BURDEKIN DUCK ▲
(Tadorna radjah)
This duck prefers the brackish muddy reaches of tropical rivers and only visits freshwater streams and lagoons in the dry season. It feeds mostly on molluscs, worms and large insects, and occasionally on algae and sedges. It is noisy whether on the ground or in flight, the males making a hoarse whistle and the females a harsh rattling sound. 60cm. n Qld to n WA.

During the breeding season, it becomes aggressive towards any animal that threatens its eggs or chicks. Populations once declined due to hunting, but the species is now protected. 100cm. s WA, s SA, sw Vic, n Tas.

FRECKLED DUCK ▲
(Stictonetta naevosa)

This threatened species of freshwater swamps and creeks congregates in small numbers except during drought, when aggregations of up to 200 may be seen. It is a quiet feeder unless alarmed, when it utters a loud discordant 'quack' as it flies away. 60cm. sw WA, se SA, nw Vic, sw NSW.

MAGPIE GOOSE ▼
(Anseranas semipalmata)

This species has a knob on its head and a characteristic loud honking call. During the wet season, thousands flock together in the tropical freshwater floodplains to feed on aquatic plants. A heavy flier, it takes some time to become airborne. Birds roost at night in trees and shrubs. 95cm. se, e and n Aus.

CAPE BARREN GOOSE ➤
(Cereopsis novaehollandiae)

Small groups of this species are usually found on islands and open grassy coastal areas. It feeds almost exclusively on grasses.

BLACK-WINGED STILT ▼
(Himantopus himantopus)

This waterbird lives gregariously, even during the nesting season. Several nests can often be found together at sites adjacent to water. If disturbed it flies off with a complaining 'yap, yap, yap'. 38cm. Aus.

PIED HERON ▲

(Ardea picata)

This bird is smaller and less abundant than the White-faced Heron, but behaves similarly. In the breeding season, long dark plumes project from the back of the head and white plumes from the base of the neck. 50cm. n Aus.

WHITE-FACED HERON, BLUE CRANE ➤

(Ardea novaehollandiae)

This heron can be seen all over Australia wading in shallow water, foraging in fields, or perched in trees near water. It stalks its prey—birds, amphibians, snakes and grasshoppers—with its long G-shaped neck and head folded back close to the body, straightening its neck with a lightning-fast strike to impale its prey. 70cm. Aus, Tas.

NANKEEN NIGHT HERON ▲

(Nycticorax caledonicus)

This species is often seen in the late afternoon feeding in shallow water on yabbies, frogs, small fish and insects.

When disturbed it flies off with a loud complaining quack. It roosts and nests communally in high trees, often using the same roosting tree for many years. 60cm. Aus, Tas.

GREAT EGRET ▲
(Egretta alba)
Commonly seen standing in shallow water waiting quietly for fish, crustaceans, frogs or insects to approach, this bird nests in trees or bushes near water. Like other egrets and herons, hunters targeted this species for its plumes a century ago, when they were an important component of ladies' hats. 100cm. Aus, Tas.

fields for insects and grasshoppers. Ibises will travel up to 40km to feed, frequently using thermals to gain height before gliding down to new food sources. 70cm. Aus.

YELLOW–BILLED SPOONBILL ➤
(Platalea flavipes)
This bird wades slowly in shallow water, either singly or in large flocks. It waves its bill from side to side in the mud or water searching for insects, crustaceans, fish or molluscs. The tip of the bill is extremely sensitive, permitting it to quickly grasp prey. 90cm. Aus.

BLACK–NECKED STORK ▼
(Xenorhynchus asiaticus)
This is the only stork in Australia. Until recently it was known as the Jabiru; however, that name properly belongs

to a South American species. The Black-necked Stork frequents swamps, lakes and tidal flats, more frequently in pairs than in large numbers, standing quietly, waiting for prey to pass. It builds large stick nests in the tops of tall trees or on ground surrounded by water. 120cm. e and n Aus.

STRAW–NECKED IBIS ▲
(Threskiornis spinicollis)
Straw-like feathers cover the base of this bird's neck. It feeds in water, probing with its beak for insects and aquatic animals, and in open

Wild Australia

BROLGA ➤
(Grus rubicunda)

This is one of two species of crane in Australia. Both form long-term breeding pairs that utilise the same sites from year to year. Chicks can swim and run soon after hatching, but remain with their parents for up to ten months. The Brolga has exceptional dancing prowess, lining up, spreading wings, jumping and bowing, while emitting a deep trumpeting sound. It eats plant roots and insects, and nests in mounds of vegetation surrounded by shallow water. 130cm. se, e and n Aus.

TASMANIAN NATIVE HEN ▼
(Gallinula mortieri)

This flightless species, affectionately known as the 'turbo chook', is one of 16 rails in Australia. Some rails disperse great distances and can be found on oceanic islands. This one is commonly seen in pairs or small flocks on flats adjoining rivers, creeks and swamps. It runs quickly, flicking its short stubby tail when alarmed and complaining with a rasping call. 45cm. Tas.

DUSKY MOORHEN ➤
(Gallinula tenebrosa)

Shy in the wild but relatively tame in city parklands, this

rail can run rapidly but usually takes to water if threatened. Pairs or small flocks feed on seeds, insects and frogs on land adjoining water. It also feeds upended on underwater weeds. 35cm. sw WA, e SA, Vic, NSW, Qld.

Bush Birds

The large variation in habitats has greatly influenced the evolution of birds in Australia, with different species adapted to particular habitats. Around 800 of the 9000 bird species worldwide are recorded from Australia. Of these, about two-thirds live in grasslands or forests, and are collectively known as bush birds. They include the songbirds or perching birds, a very large group of birds with intricate voiceboxes that generate complex songs. Australian bush birds can be divided broadly into associations living in the tropical and subtropical region, the semi-arid interior, se Australia, and sw Australia.

EMU ➤
(Dromaius novaehollandiae)

This bird is grouped as a 'ratite' with other large flightless birds of the s continents, such as the cassowary, ostrich, kiwi and rhea. The emu is the second largest bird after the ostrich. It normally eats grasses, fruit and flowers but is not averse to insects. Emus are innately curious and can be attracted by lying on the ground and waving a piece of cloth. After the females have laid their eggs, they abandon them, leaving the males to incubate and raise the chicks. Some farmers regard the emu as a pest because it breaks fences. A stunted form of this species in Tas and a black species once present on King Island are both now extinct. 2m. Aus.

CASSOWARY ◄
(Casuarius casuarius)

This large flightless bird with a deep booming grunt is slightly smaller but heavier than the emu. Cassowaries eat fallen fruit from the rainforest as well as dead birds, rats and fish. Despite its size and bright neck colouration, this bird is difficult to see in the rainforest. The first indication of its presence may be a rustle of leaves or a loud hiss. It has been known to fatally wound humans with a slashing kick to the stomach. 2m. ne Qld.

AUSTRALIAN BRUSH TURKEY ▼
(Alectura lathami)
A common sight in rainforest camping grounds along the e coast, this bird forages on the ground for insects, seeds and fruits, but will fly to escape danger and to roost at night. It is one of three Australian mound-builders, a group of birds that incubate eggs in huge mounds of vegetation, sand or soil built by males. Heat generated by decaying leaves keeps the mound warm. Males tend the mound, maintaining the correct temperature and humidity

until the eggs hatch. The same nesting mounds are used year after year. After hatching, the chicks quickly disappear into the surrounding countryside, where they fend for themselves. 70cm. Coastal ce NSW to ne Qld.

MALLEE FOWL ▲
(Leipoa ocellata)
This quiet mound-builder has an occasional deep booming call and eats seeds and insects. Birds mate for life. During autumn they scoop out a small depression and build a mound to 1.5m high of sticks and dry leaves. Winter rains dampen the mound, beginning the internal heating process. Around 20 eggs are laid in spring. 60cm. sw WA, s SA, nw Vic, sw and cw NSW.

STUBBLE QUAIL ➤
(Coturnix pectoralis)
Although common, these small, plump, ground-hugging

birds are rarely seen. When flushed they rise with a rapid whirring of wings and then fly a short distance before diving into ground cover. They eat mainly seeds and small insects. 20cm. Aus.

BUSH STONE CURLEW ▲
(Esacus magnirostris)
This ground-loving species is mainly seen in pairs. When disturbed, it moves away in a crouched attitude with head bent, only flying as a last resort to escape. It eats mostly insects such as beetles and grasshoppers. Active at night, it emits an eerie long and melancholy 'wer-loo'. 55cm. Aus, Tas.

LAUGHING KOOKABURRA ▲
(Dacelo novaeguineae)

With a distinctive heavy bill and iridescent colours, kingfishers are among the most admired of birds. They often sit silently and conspicuously for long periods on sunlit perches before diving on unwary insects and other small animals.

This is the largest kingfisher worldwide. It is an important predator in open eucalypt forest of snakes, lizards, insects, frogs, birds, mice, and meat from barbecue plates. Unusually, it does not chase away its young when they are old enough to leave the nest. Family groups often start and finish their day with a loud laughing call (a rising 'kook-kook-kook', 'ha-ha-ha'). Its call has been plagiarised in numerous Hollywood jungle films but is the distinctive sound of Australian bushland. 45cm. se SA to e Qld; introduced sw WA, Tas.

BLUE-WINGED KOOKABURRA ➤
(Dacelo leachii)

This kingfisher surveys the ground for prey in open woodlands, forests and paperbark swamps. Its call is a harsh cackling. Nests are constructed in tree hollows and termite mounds. 45cm. n Aus.

FOREST KINGFISHER ▼
(Todiramphus macleayii)

Often seen sitting silently on power lines or on the branch of a tree looking for a meal, this bird feeds on frogs, spiders, caterpillars, insects and small reptiles. It nests in termite mounds, excavating the burrow with its sharp beak. 20cm. Coastal ne NSW to n WA.

OSPREY ▼
(Pandion haliaetus)

This bird of prey is commonly observed along the coast, on the margins of rivers and lakes, and on offshore islands. Despite a similar appearance, it is only distantly related to the eagles, hawks and kites. Its diet consists almost exclusively of fish, which it grasps with its talons from the water during flight. Ospreys possess a number of unique adaptations, including a closable nostril, a reversible outer toe, and spines under the foot. They build large stick nests high on rocky headlands, in trees, or on electricity transmission towers. 65cm. Coastal Aus, Tas.

WEDGE-TAILED EAGLE ➤
(Aquila audax)

Australia's largest bird of prey, this is one of the largest eagles worldwide. Like other raptors, the 'Wedgie' is feared by smaller birds, which warn others of its presence with alarm calls and harassment as it flies slowly near the ground. It can soar to great heights, fly swiftly at tree height, or perch on tall trees and telegraph poles. Both a predator and a scavenger, many are killed by cars while feeding on road-killed mammals. Although accused of attacking lambs, this rarely occurs, rabbits and carrion being its main food. 100cm, wingspan 250cm. Aus, Tas.

BLACK-SHOULDERED KITE ▲
(Elanus notatus)

This is one of the more common of the 17 raptor species (kites, hawks and eagles) in Australia. Lone

birds or pairs hover in open or lightly timbered country, or perch high above the ground, silently searching for small mammals, birds, reptiles and larger insects. When flying it appears white with dark wing tips and a black patch at the bend of the wing. 40cm. Aus, n Tas.

WHISTLING KITE ▲
(Haliastur sphenurus)

This scavenger preys on small birds, mammals, and insects, congregating wherever these are in plague proportions. Both the Whistling Kite and a similar relative, the Black Kite (Milvus migrans), often perch around country garbage tips, squabbling among them-selves. These two species are also generally the first to arrive at bushfires in search of fleeing prey or dead animals. 60cm. Aus.

BROWN GOSHAWK ▲
(Accipiter fasciatus)

Like all goshawks and sparrowhawks, the brown goshawk has short, rounded wings, a relatively long tail, and long legs, toes and claws. An ambush predator, it preys on rabbits, snakes, frogs, lizards and invertebrates. It builds a nest of twigs lined with leaves in the topmost branches of trees. 55cm. Aus, Tas.

PACIFIC BAZA ➤
(Aviceda subcristata)

This is the only Australian bird of prey with a crest. Pairs or small flocks move through rainforests and along well-timbered river courses, feeding on insects and small vertebrates. The flimsy nest of twigs lined with leaves is placed on a high horizontal tree limb. 45cm. Coastal ne NSW to ne Qld, n NT.

BROWN FALCON ➤
(Falco brerigora)

Falcons have long, pointed wings and relatively short tails. Six species are resident in Australia. Their bills have a special notch for severing the neck vertebrae of their prey. This is the most common species, particularly in open or lightly timbered country. It often uses the abandoned nest of another bird of prey or raven. 50cm. Aus, Tas.

RAINBOW BEE-EATER ➤
(Merops ornatus)

This beautiful bird migrates from northern to southern

Australia in summer. Normally seen in pairs, it nests in tunnels facing away from prevailing winds, in the banks of rivers or raised mounds. It has a characteristic high-pitched 'chitter-chitter' and often sits on power lines and low tree branches, darting out occasionally to catch flying insects such as grasshoppers. 25cm. Aus.

WELCOME SWALLOW ▲

(Hirundo neoxena)

All six Australian species of swallows and martins are sociable, have long wings and short broad bills for capturing flying insects, and are superb aerialists.

This swallow builds a mud and fibre nest on sheltered vertical faces beneath bridges, caves and buildings, including house eaves. It migrates s for the summer, when its presence is announced by a constant twittering. 15cm. Aus, Tas.

AUSTRALIAN BUSTARD ➤

(Ardeotis australis)

This large, heavy bird of open country has disappeared from the settled areas of Australia as a result of hunting and attacks by foxes and feral cats. The Bustard can survive long periods without drinking, being able to utilise water from the animals and plants it eats. 100cm. WA, SA, w NSW, w, s and n Qld, NT.

TORRES STRAIT PIGEON ▼

(Ducula spilorrhoa)

Australia is home to 25 pigeon and dove species, three of which are introduced. Most eat either fruit or grain, while several graze on plants. All pigeons take to the air with an audible whirr of the wings, and often fly only a short distance before landing. In the late afternoon, flocks are often seen heading for water.

Arriving from tropical islands further north in spring and summer, the white Torres Strait Pigeon rarely moves more than 80km inland. It feeds on fruit in tropical rainforests and mangroves. The call is a deep 'coo-ooh'. 38cm. Coastal ne Qld to nw NT.

PEACEFUL DOVE ▲

(Geopelia striata)

Pairs or small flocks frequent rivers in open forest country or on the sides of roads. It feeds on seeds of grasses and low shrubs. The call is a melodious, high-pitched 'doodle-doo'. 22cm. Coastal se SA to ne Qld, n NT, n WA.

WONGA PIGEON ▼
(Leucosarcia melanoleuca)
This bird lives in rainforest and heavily timbered regions, mostly alone or in pairs, feeding off the ground on fallen fruits and berries from low-lying bushes. The call is a monotonous 'coo-coo-coo' that can be heard at a distance. 40cm. Coastal se Vic, e NSW, se Qld.

CRESTED PIGEON ▼
(Ochyphaps lophotes)
Although normally seen in small flocks in lightly wooded areas, this bird sometimes congregates in large numbers near waterholes. It eats mainly seeds and plants. This species is timid, and flies off with a rapid beating tail when disturbed. The call is a single note 'hwoo', repeated endlessly. 35cm. Aus.

COMMON BRONZEWING ▲
(Phaps chalcoptera)
This bird is named for its beautiful iridescent bronze-coloured wing feathers. It warily approaches water at dusk to drink. Like some other pigeons, the Bronzewing is able to suck water, rather than sip, and hence does not toss its head back, reducing the risk of attack from predators. The call is a repetitious 'oom…oom…'. 34cm. Aus, Tas.

ROSE-CROWNED FRUIT-DOVE ▲
(Ptilinopus regina)
Despite its bright plumage, including pink crown, green wings, and yellow and pink belly, this dove can be difficult to see among the rainforest trees where it lives. It feeds on fruit and builds a small untidy nest of twigs for its one white egg. 24cm. Coastal se NSW to ne Qld, n NT, ne WA.

blossom, flocks descend en masse, individuals seemingly intent on feeding from as many flowers as possible. 22cm. Coast and ranges s SA to se Qld, Tas.

RAINBOW LORIKEET ▲

(Trichoglossus haematodus)

The 52 Australian parrot species all have two toes pointing forward and two back, a short strongly hooked bill, relatively short neck, short legs and a large head with prominent eyes.

This is one of Australia's most colourful parrots. It is noisy and gregarious, and can become tame enough to hand feed. Although usually moving about in small flocks, hundreds sometimes feed with their brush-like tongue on the blossom nectar of shrubs and trees. When disturbed they fly off with a complaining screech. 30cm. Coast and ranges se SA to ne Qld, ne Tas.

MUSK LORIKEET ▼

(Glossopsitta concinna)

This gregarious parrot is mostly seen in large flocks. When eucalypts are in

PURPLE-CROWNED LORIKEET ▲

(Glossopsitta porphyracephala)

More often seen in flocks than in pairs in dry mallee areas, this bird feeds on pollen, nectar, fruit and berries. Hundreds congregate on flowering eucalypts. Like the Musk Lorikeet, it has been accused of damaging fruit in orchards. 16cm. s WA, s SA, Vic.

SCALY-BREASTED LORIKEET ➤

(Trichoglossus chlorolepidotus)

This bird feeds on pollen, nectar, flowers and fruit. Although a noisy bird, when feeding it is often hard to see as its green colouring blends in with the tree foliage. 23cm. ce NSW to ne Qld.

EASTERN ROSELLA ▲

(Platycercus eximius)

Best known as the trademark for Arnott's biscuits, pairs are often seen feeding in parks on grass seeds. It also enjoys flower nectar and pollen. Unless alarmed, when it utters a loud and piercing screech, its call is a pleasant piping. 30cm. Vic, NSW, Tas.

CRIMSON ROSELLA ➤

(Platycercus elegans)

Pairs and small flocks of this colourful bird often frequent picnic and camping areas in rainforests, but are also found in open forests. It feeds on the seeds of acacias and eucalypts but is not averse to cultivated fruits, and can become quite tame. Its call is an ascending whistle-like note that changes to a screech when alarmed. 35cm. SA, Vic, NSW, s Qld.

PORT LINCOLN PARROT, TWENTY EIGHT PARROT, AUSTRALIAN RINGNECK ▼

(Barnardius zonarius)

Most frequently a ground feeder, this bird will also feed on flowers in trees. The usual call is a 'kwink-kwink'. It breeds year-round near the coast, and from spring to summer inland. It is commonly seen across s Australia in pairs or small flocks. 38cm. Inland Aus.

MULGA PARROT ▲
(Psephotus varius)
This parrot mostly feeds in pairs on the ground, quietly searching for grass seeds and herbs. When disturbed it flies to the nearest tree and waits for the danger to pass before returning to the ground. The call is a flute-like whistle repeated several times. 28cm. Mulga country WA, SA, Vic, NSW.

BUDGERIGAR ▼
(Melopsittacus undulatus)
Large flocks congregate in the semi-arid zone, the location depending on the availability of grass seeds and water. This extremely popular cage bird keeps up a constant chatter, both in the wild and in captivity. Wild specimens are green with the wings barred with yellow and black. 18cm. Inland Aus.

KING PARROT ▲
(Alisterus scapularis)
One of our most colourful and common parrots, this bird frequents coastal forests along rivers and streams, mostly in pairs, and is also occasionally seen in urban parks. It feeds mainly on seeds but favours bananas and other fruit. When disturbed, it flies off with a harsh screech. 45cm. c and e Vic, e NSW to ne Qld.

more a warble than a screech. Normally found in flocks, but occasionally in pairs, it feeds on a variety of seeds, herbs and grasses. 32cm. Inland Aus.

YELLOW–TAILED BLACK COCKATOO ▽
(Calyptorhynchus funereus)
This bird is sometimes seen in pairs but more often in large flocks, feeding on the seeds of casuarinas, banksias and hakeas. When flying it attracts attention with loud wailing cries, but it is a relatively silent feeder. The yellow cheek patch on the male is smaller and duller than on the female. 65cm. s SA, s Vic, e NSW, se Qld, Tas.

ECLECTUS PARROT ▲
(Eclectus roratus)
This bird is unusual in that the red and blue female is more colourful than the green male. It is a noisy rainforest bird, making its presence known with harsh screeches as it flies above the forest trees, or by melodious calls

as it feeds on fruit, nuts and nectar in the canopies of trees. 33cm. ne Qld.

COCKATIEL ▽
(Nymphicus hollandicus)
This popular aviary bird shows apparent affection and can learn a few words. Unlike other cockatoos, its call is

SULPHUR-CRESTED COCKATOO ▼

(Cacatua galerita)
Driving people to distraction with its loud raucous screeching, this bird is common and widespread. It damages crops by snipping the heads off plants when feeding. It is one of the few birds that can be taught to speak words, but its strong jaws can mean that it is a destructive pet. 50cm. n WA, se SA, Vic, e NSW, e Qld, n NT, Tas.

MAJOR MITCHELL'S COCKATOO ➤

(Cacatua leadbeateri)
This is an uncommon nomad of open woodlands. Its striking pink and yellow striped crest contrasts with its delicate pink and white body. It flies with hesitant wingbeats, each stroke revealing the deep salmon-coloured underwings. 40cm. Inland Aus.

GALAH ▲

(Cacatua roseicapilla)
This bird often behaves erratically, and so its name has become synonymous with idiotic human behaviour. The species is not popular with farmers because it assembles in large flocks that can damage crops. In cities and country towns it is more often seen in pairs or small groups. 36cm. Aus, Tas.

raucous, repetitive and penetrating call of 'krork-rork-rork' is not soon forgotten. It eats fruit, insects and sometimes nestling birds. 60cm. NSW, Qld, n NT, n WA.

LITTLE CORELLA ▲
(Cacatua sanguinea)

This species feeds on seeds and grasses during the day and roosts at night near water in flocks that may number thousands. When disturbed it takes to the air with an unforgettable screech. 38cm. Aus.

CHANNEL-BILLED CUCKOO ▼
(Scythrops novaehollandiae)

Most of the 13 resident Australian cuckoos are migratory, moving s in summer to lay eggs in the nests of other birds. The male distracts nesting host birds while the female deposits the egg. Juveniles eject the host nestlings. This species is the largest bird in the world with a parasitic juvenile. It migrates to Australia from New Guinea and Indonesia between Aug and Oct, laying its eggs in nests of crows, magpies and currawongs. Once heard, its

BOOBOOK OWL ▲
(Ninix novaeseelandiae)

Sometimes called the Mopoke because of its call, the Boobook is the smallest and most widespread of the 10 Australian owls. It roosts during daylight hours in tree hollows, caves or trees among thick vegetation. This owl often hunts in pairs, feeding on small rodents, small birds and insects. Like other owls, it has a large round head with forward projecting eyes, good binocular vision, and fully feathered legs. Adaptations to the flight feathers allow near silent flight. 30cm. Aus, Tas.

TAWNY FROGMOUTH ▼

(Podargus strigoides)

Unlike owls, which feed exclusively on mammals, frogmouths feed at night on insects, frogs, mice and small snakes. During the day indivduals or pairs sit motionless on a tree branch. If approached, it freezes with neck outstretched, imitating a dead branch. 50cm. Aus, Tas.

RAINBOW PITTA ▲

(Pitta iris)

The pittas are colourful ground-foraging birds that typically migrate seasonally and live in rainforests. This is the only one of four Australian pittas resident solely in Australia. It occurs commonly in monsoon rainforests but has secretive habits so is rarely seen. It preys on insects, frogs and snails, which it batters on rocks or timber to break the shell. 20cm. n NT, nw WA.

SUPERB BLUE WREN ▲

(Malurus cyaneus)

The fairy wrens comprise 16 species of social territorial birds that are restricted to Australia. They live in groups with a dominant brightly coloured male, a brown breeding female, and non-breeding birds.

This fairy wren is named for the colourful plumage of the males, and is relatively common around most urban areas. Females are brownish grey. Becoming quite tame in picnic areas, they search the ground for small insects, with their tails cocked. The call is a musical trill. 14cm. se SA, s Vic, e NSW, se Qld.

SPLENDID WREN ➤
(Malurus splendens)

Not as gregarious as the Superb Blue Wren, this fairy wren prefers to remain among cover, and also tends to forage higher in shrubs and trees. It builds a dome-shaped nest close to the ground in small bushes between Aug and Dec. 14cm. sw and c WA, c SA, cw Vic, w NSW, sc Qld, s NT.

SPOTTED PARDALOTE ⬠
(Pardalotus punctatus)

Pardalotes are all small and colourful with blunt short beaks, and are restricted to Australia. Several populations migrate seasonally, moving between wetter forests in southern areas to inland and northern coastal areas. This species lives mostly among the tree canopy, where it searches leaves for small insects. It builds its nest in earthen banks or tree hollows. 10cm. sw WA, se SA, Vic, NSW, e Qld, Tas.

WHITE-BROWED SCRUBWREN ▼
(Sericornis frontalis)

This inquisitive species is the most common of a number of small brown forest-dwelling birds. Its colour pattern varies considerably between regions; however, two small white stripes contrasted against black are always present at the base of the wing, and the head is streaked with white above and below the eye. 13cm. sw and s WA, s SA, Vic, c and e NSW, se and ce Qld.

NEW HOLLAND HONEYEATER ▲
(Phylidonyris novaehollandiae)

The honeyeaters comprise a diverse and emblematic Australian family of 67 birds, with at least one species inhabiting every terrestrial habitat. All have a brush-shaped tongue designed to collect nectar from flowers. Some species are sedentary, while others migrate seasonally in search of food. They are territorial, chasing away intruders of their own and other species. Breeding depends on the availability of food and generally occurs from July to Dec. Many plants rely on honeyeaters for pollination and seed dispersal.

The New Holland Honeyeater is the most widely distributed species, and the first honeyeater recorded here. Although seen on heaths, it is more likely to be found feeding on blossoms of eucalypts, banksias and other native trees. It can also swoop on insects in flight. Groups maintain a constant chatter when feeding. 18cm. Coastal se SA to se Qld; Tas.

WHITE-CHEEKED HONEYEATER ▼
(Phylidonyris nigra)

This looks similar to the New Holland Honeyeater, differing primarily in the size of the white patch on the cheek and in its more musical call. It lives in a wide range of forest and heath habitats. 19cm. sw WA, coast se NSW to ne Qld.

NOISY MINER ➤
(Manorina melanocephala)

This honeyeater is probably the best known in eastern Australia. A belligerent bird, it inhabits open woodlands, forests and urban areas. It frequently chases both larger and smaller birds from its territory. During the day it maintains a loud continuous chatter, but before dawn it emits a melodious whistle. The diet includes insects, nectar, native fruits and berries. 28cm. Vic to Qld; Tas.

EASTERN SPINEBILL ▼
(Acanthorhynchus tenuirostris)

This active honeyeater flies about erratically like a hummingbird, the wings making a whirring sound. Its long, down-curved beak allows it to feed on the nectar of tubular flowers, as well as on the smaller flowers of shrubs such as banksias. A relatively tame bird, pairs often flit around houses, piping shrilly. 14–16cm. Coast and ranges s SA to ne Qld, Tas.

It feeds on insects, fruit and nectar. 32cm. w Vic, e NSW, e Qld, n NT, ne WA.

NOISY FRIARBIRD ▲
(Philemon corniculatus)

This loud, raucous bird is easily recognised by the knob on its beak. It utters a noisy 'chok-chok-a chok' while feeding on fruit, nectar, berries, insects and grasshoppers. The featherless face is an adaptation for feeding on nectar-rich flowers, which otherwise would cause feathers to become matted with nectar. Friarbirds often chase each other and squabble among themselves. 35cm. e Aus.

BLUE–FACED HONEYEATER ➤
(Entomyzon cyanotis)

This large colourful bird moves in flocks in open forest near urban centres. Like other honeyeaters, it is territorial and chases other birds from its feeding areas.

LITTLE WATTLEBIRD ▲
(Anthochaera chrysoptera)
This is the smallest of the large honeyeaters known as wattlebirds, and the only one with no wattles at the side of the head. It follows banksia flowering from area to area, often across large distances. When feeding on insects and the nectar of banksias it will defend its territory vigorously, The call is a harsh 'quok-quok'. 31cm. sw WA, se SA; coastal Vic to s Qld.

LEWIN'S HONEYEATER ▼
(Meliphaga lewinii)
This friendly, sociable rainforest bird is bold and inquisitive. It feeds on fruit, insects and nectar. The call is a staccato chatter. It remains in the same area throughout the year. It has become quite tame in many camping grounds and will sometimes perch on a shoulder. 18cm. Coastal e Vic to ne Qld.

YELLOW–BELLIED SUNBIRD ▲
(Nectarinia jugularis)
Bright yellow plumage gives this bird its common name. This active species can live in urban areas, where it is seemingly unafraid of humans. The male has an iridescent blue breast. Nests hang suspended from branches, pieces of rope, or even clotheslines. Sunbirds dart rapidly from flower to flower, often hovering to sip nectar; they also pick spiders from their webs. 12cm. ce to n Qld.

SILVEREYE ▲
(Zosterops lateralis)
This species has been
intensively studied in
Australia because of its
variable behaviour. Some
populations are sedentary,
others are nomadic. Still
others embark on extensive
migrations. Silvereye numbers
have been severely reduced
by the removal of
undergrowth, which
protects the species from
predators. They feed on
nectar, fruit and insects, and
announce their presence with
a pleasant warbling. 12cm.
Coastal Aus.

SCARLET ROBIN ▼
(Petroica multicolor)
This small bird is sometimes
seen perched on branches or
sitting sideways on tree
trunks, scanning surroundings
for insects and other prey.
The species usually has a
pleasant warbling song, but
occasionally produces a more
abrasive sound. It frequents
highlands, woodland forests
and gardens, mostly in pairs.
The diet is mainly insects,
but unlike other robins,
Scarlet Robins rarely take
them in flight. 13cm. sw WA,
s SA, Vic, s and e NSW, se
Qld, Tas.

EASTERN YELLOW
ROBIN ◄
(Eopsaltria australis)
A flash of yellow among the
foliage of a wet forest or
rainforest heralds the arrival
of this small bird. Inquisitive
and tame, it sometimes lands
on picnic tables. Two to three
eggs are laid in a neat cup-
shaped bark nest. The call is
a repeated piping. 15cm.
Coast and ranges se SA to
ne Qld.

positioned downwards.

However, in contrast to the active movements of other fantails, this one often perches patiently, rarely fanning its tail. It prefers forest margins, where it watches for insects flying in the sunlight. 22cm. n Qld, n NT, ne WA.

GREY-CROWNED BABBLER ▲
(Pomatostomus temporalis)

This gregarious bird moves about energetically in small flocks. It generally forages across the ground and among tree limbs in grassy woodlands, searching for insects. 22cm. se SA, Vic, NSW, Qld, NT, nw, c and ce WA.

NORTHERN FANTAIL ▼
(Rhipidura rufiventris)

The four Australian fantails characteristically wave long fan-shaped tails sideways, while the wings are

WILLIE WAGTAIL ▲
(Rhipidura leucophrys)

One of the most common birds in urban areas across Australia, this black and white fantail is usually observed singly or in pairs. It moves constantly in search of insects, worms, spiders and flies, whilst wagging its tail and maintaining a constant repetitive chatter of 'sweet pretty creature'. It is one of the most easily approached Australian birds. 20cm. Aus.

DIAMOND FIRETAIL FINCH ➤

(Stagonopleura guttata)

Finches are small seed-eating birds that mostly inhabit open grasslands near water. They tend to move in large flocks but disperse in the breeding season. All species pair for breeding and perform elaborate courtship dances before mating. Many construct a colonial dome-shaped grass and twig nest with a side entrance.

This finch feeds in pairs or small groups in open grasslands, flying to nearby trees if disturbed. The call is a plaintive whistle that rises and falls. It drinks by suction rather than scooping with its beak, enabling it to drink quickly. 12cm. Coast and ranges s SA to se Qld.

GOULDIAN FINCH ▼

(Erythrura gouldiae)

One of Australia's most beautiful birds, this finch feeds in large flocks on grass seeds and insects in savannah. It is the only finch that nests in the hollow branches of trees or in termite mounds. The call is a soft 'sssitt'. Becoming increasingly rare in most areas, conservation efforts are now attempting to stabilise population numbers of this threatened species. 14cm. nw Qld to n WA.

CHESTNUT–BREASTED MANNIKIN ▲

(Lonchura castaneothora)

This is one of Australia's smallest birds. Flocks of several hundred sometimes gather in reed beds, canefields and grasslands. Farmers consider it a pest as it sometimes feeds on sorghum, barley and other cultivated crops. The call, often uttered in flight, is 'tarrt-tarrt'. 10cm. Coastal ne NSW, e and n Qld, n NT, n WA.

BLACK-FACED WOODSWALLOW ➤
(Artamus cinerus)

Woodswallows are a group of six highly gregarious species that rear their young communally. This one is a migratory species, ranging over most of Australia. It often sits huddled in rows along a branch or telegraph wire, darting out from time to time to feed on insects. It nests in low stumps or trees. 18cm. Aus.

MAGPIE-LARK, PEEWEE, PEEWIT ▼
(Grallina cyanoleuca)

This species has a distinctive 'pee-wee' call sung by pairs. It

spends most of its time foraging for insects on the ground. Its bowl-shaped mud nest is strengthened with grass and lined with grass or feathers. Three to five eggs are laid. 30cm. Aus.

EASTERN WHIPBIRD ▼
(Psophodes olivaceus)

Both whipbird species are excellent mimics. They inhabit thick vegetation, spending most of their time on the ground turning leaves in search of insects. Unlike the Western Whipbird (*Psophodes nigrogularis*), this species generates a sharp crack of the whip in

its call. Although frequently heard, it inhabits dense forest and is shy and rarely seen. 25cm. e Aus.

VICTORIA'S RIFLEBIRD ▲
(Ptiloris victoriae)

Australia is home to four species of birds of paradise, two of which are also found in New Guinea. This one has a loud rasping 'yaaah'. It is a solitary bird except in the breeding season. The iridescent green and purple of the male glistens in the sunshine as it flies, while the cinnamon-buff chevrons of the female are also striking. It feeds mostly on fruit and insects. 25cm. ne Qld.

REGENT BOWER BIRD ▲

(Sericulus chrysocephalus)
Bowerbird species primarily
feed on fruit, although they
will also eat other plant
material and animals,
including insects and young
birds. Their common name
derives from the bowers that
the males build to attract
breeding females. However,
not all species build a bower;
some decorate a cleared
patch of ground.

The black and yellow male
Regent Bower Bird is one of
Australia's most colourful
birds. It is a rainforest species

with several different calls,
such as 'whit whit', as well
as hisses and chatterings. It
generally eats fruit but also
forages on the ground in
some camping areas. 28cm.
ce NSW to ce Qld.

SATIN BOWER BIRD ▼

(Ptilonohynchus violaceus)
This is one of Australia's most
colourful birds in rainforest
and eucalypt forest. Males
have dark blue iridescent
plumage and females are olive
green with blue eyes. The male
builds a decorated bower in a
small cleared section of
ground, decorating it with any
blue coloured natural or man-
made materials. This species
has a variety of calls, including
a loud 'wee-you'. 33cm. e Vic,
e NSW, e Qld.

SPOTTED CATBIRD ◄

(Ailuroedus melanotis)
This member of the bowerbird
family feeds on fruit and leaves
in rainforests. During the
breeding season its cat-like
wailing is one of the distinctive
sounds of north Qld forests. A
similar species without the
black patch behind the eye,
the Green Catbird (*Ailuroedus
crassirostris*), lives in subtropical rainforests of central-
eastern Australia. 32cm.
ne Qld.

SUPERB LYREBIRD ▼
(Menura novaehollandiae)
This bird is closely allied to
the birds of paradise and
bowerbirds. Individuals, pairs
or small groups scratch the
ground and turn over leaves
in search of insects, small
molluscs and worms. Males
mate with several females
and take no role in nesting or
raising the chicks. At mating
time the male displays on top
of a mound of earth, fanning
its long tail and throwing it
over its head while prancing,
bobbing and weaving. An
excellent mimic, this bird's
repertoire includes songs of
at least 15 birds as well as
man-made sounds such as
axe blows and chainsaws.
95cm. Coastal s Vic to se Qld;
introduced in s Tas.

APOSTLEBIRD ▲
(Struthidea cinerea)
This species was given its
name when it was thought to
move in groups of 12.
Numbers are actually quite
variable. Apostlebirds have a
complex, communal way of
life, with a dominant male,
several mature females, and
immature birds born the
previous year. Birds in flocks
tend to remain close together,
noisily feeding on grubs,
insects, spiders and seeds. The
basin-shaped nest is made
from mud and grass. 33cm.
se SA, nw Vic, NSW, Qld, NT.

AUSTRALIAN MAGPIE ▼
(Gymnorhina tibicen)
This melodious songster
is an excellent mimic and
one of Australia's most
recognised birds. Its back
feathers are coloured
black in NSW and white
in southern Australia. Living
in groups with a dominant
male, it is territorial,
attacking humans that
venture too close to its
nest during the breeding
season. It eats insects, small
reptiles, birds and worms.
44cm. Aus, Tas.

PIED BUTCHERBIRD ➤

(Craticus nigrogularis)

A well-known songster, this butcherbird is regularly heard calling at dawn. Mostly seen in pairs or small groups, it eats small birds and has been known to take canaries out of cages. It also feeds on insects, lizards, small mammals and fruit. Prey items may be stored in the fork of a tree and eaten later in the day. 35cm. Aus.

PIED CURRAWONG ▼

(Strepera graculina)

Many currawongs are altitudinal migrants, spending winter at lower altitudes and summer as breeding pairs in upland forests. This species forms large flocks that harass smaller birds. A loud ringing call of 'curra-wong' is commonly heard throughout its range. It is a successful coloniser of urban areas and may be responsible in part for the disappearance of many small bird species from cities. 46cm. e Aus.

AUSTRALIAN RAVEN ▼

(Corvus coronoides)

This is the largest of five Australian species of ravens and crows. Identification in the field is difficult and may depend on differences in call. This one has a strident rasping call of 'caah caah caaaaah'. It feeds on carrion, insects and fruit, and frequents rubbish dumps. 52cm. s WA, SA, Vic, NSW, Qld, e NT.

Platypus and Echidna

The Platypus and the Echidna are monotreme ('one hole') mammals, named for the common opening through which urine and faeces pass and young are born. Like the other 320 mammal species in Australia, they are warm-blooded and have a four-chambered heart, hair, milk-producing glands, teeth and a muscular diaphragm for breathing. However, they lack whiskers, teeth and external ears. Only three living monotremes survive, two in Australia and the other in New Guinea. Females lay a soft-shelled egg. When the young hatch they lap up milk secreted through ducts on the mother's underbelly.

PLATYPUS ▼
(Ornithorhynchus anatinus)
This species constructs a burrow in the steep vegetated banks of freshwater streams, concealing the entrance behind overhanging vegetation. It mainly feeds at night and at dawn and dusk, using electroreceptors in its 'bill' to locate invertebrate prey on the stream bottom. The female lays two eggs. Males can protect themselves using a spur connected to venom glands on their ankles. 55cm. Coast and GDR sw Vic to ne Qld, Tas.

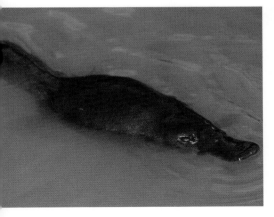

ECHIDNA ▲
(Tachyglossus aculeatus)
The echidna's body is covered with sharp spines and it has an elongated tubular snout. It feeds on ants, termites and beetle larvae, which it locates using its acute sense of smell. The short, powerful forelimbs are used to dig for prey, which it consumes using its long, sticky tongue. Females lay a single egg that is carried in an underbody pouch. 45cm. Aus, Tas.

Kangaroos and Other Marsupials

Marsupial mammals produce embryos that remain in the uterus for a relatively short period, then are born and complete their development in an external pouch, where they suckle milk through teats. Babies are tiny when born, with only the head and forearms well developed. Herbivorous marsupials possess two front teeth; carnivores possess many front teeth. The largest of the carnivores was the Thylacine or Tasmanian Tiger (*Thylacinus cyanocephalus*), a striped species confined to Tas at the time of European settlement but previously widespread across mainland Australia, as indicated by fossils and Aboriginal cave paintings. It generally inhabited open woodlands and grasslands. The Thylacine was hunted to extinction by European colonists, with the last known animal dying in 1936. The species remains the focus of devotees determined to prove that remnant populations still exist in remote parts of Tas. A reward of one million dollars has been offered for its rediscovery.

KOALA ▼
(Phascolarctos cinereus)

This tree-dwelling marsupial feeds almost exclusively on eucalypt leaves. It is a clumsy climber, perhaps indicating that its tree-living existence was adopted recently. The majority of its life is spent sleeping or moving slowly due to a poor-quality diet laced with toxic chemicals. Both sexes are occasionally seen on the ground moving between food trees. Males bellow loudly during the mating season. A single young is carried in a pouch until it is six months old, when it starts riding on its mother's back. 78cm. Coast and GDR Vic to Qld.

COMMON WOMBAT ▲
(Vombatus ursinus)

Generally solitary, this powerful burrower digs extensive burrows at the base of trees or rocks. It generally emerges at dusk to feed on the roots and bark of trees, shrubs, tubers and grasses. A single young attaches to a teat in a pouch that faces backward to prevent entry of dirt. The young leaves the pouch at six months and travels with the mother until weaned at 20 months. 1.1m. se SA, sw Vic, mountainous areas in NSW and s Qld, Tas.

since European settlement. In pastoral country, large mobs feed on grasses and herbs. It also frequents urban areas. Males can occasionally be observed engaged in 'boxing' matches, the winner gaining access to breeding females. Grey Kangaroos feed at night, dusk and dawn in semi-arid scrub, coastal woodlands and forests. 1.3m. e Aus, e Tas.

RED KANGAROO ▲
(Macropus rufus)
This is the largest macropod, a group of marsupials that includes wallabies, tree kangaroos and pademelons, with more than 50 species described. Members of the group vary in size but most have large hind legs and a long, powerfully muscled tail. They are grazers or browsers, and their teeth are designed for cropping and grinding up fibrous plants. Macropods are able to store elastic energy in the tendons of their hindlimbs to power the next hop—an efficient form of locomotion. This gives them the ability to survive on poor-quality food, and to travel long distances with minimal expenditure of energy.

The Red Kangaroo is superbly adapted to central Australia's unpredictable arid environment. It feeds largely at night and is capable of moving large distances to take advantage of green growth after infrequent rainfall. For much of the day it shelters from the sun's rays under a bush. The Red Kangaroo adorns the Australian coat-of-arms. 1.4m. Interior Aus, w of GDR.

EASTERN GREY KANGAROO ◄
(Macropus giganteus)
Populations of this species have increased in numbers

EURO, WALLAROO ▲
(Macropus robustus)
This adaptable species is characterised by a heavy build and shaggy appearance. It occurs most commonly among rocky outcrops and hills, sheltering under overhangs and caves during the day, and moving singly or in pairs to nearby grasslands to forage at night. Males may weigh up to three times more than females. 1.1m. Aus.

a shrub understorey, most frequently with nearby grassland. The forest acts as a refuge during daylight. Tas animals tend to have shaggy dark fur compared to the shorter hair and brighter colours of mainland animals. 92cm. se SA to se Qld, Tas.

AGILE WALLABY ▲
(Macropus agilis)
The most abundant wallaby in the tropics, this species lives in habitats ranging from open forest and grasslands to coastal sand dunes, but especially in areas near water. Primarily a grazer, it will also dig for roots of grasses and eat fallen fruits. Mobs of up to 50 sometimes graze on

fresh green grass in areas regenerating from fire. 85cm. n Aus.

RED-NECKED WALLABY, BENNETT'S WALLABY ▼
(Macropus rufogriseus)
Both a grazer and browser, this species is commonly found in eucalypt forests with

LUMHOLTZ'S TREE KANGAROO ▲
(Dendrolagus lumholtzii)
This macropod has relatively long, strong forelimbs with stout claws; short, broad hind feet with granular pads; and a long tail. These attributes make it an excellent climber, able to exploit the rainforest canopy, feeding on leaves and fruits without competition from other large herbivores. It sleeps during daylight hours with head tucked between legs on a large branch or in dense foliage. 65cm. ne Qld above 800m altitude.

RUFOUS-BELLIED PADEMELON ▼
(Thylogale billardierii)
This medium-sized wallaby occupies a variety of habitats, including rainforest, wet eucalypt forest and coastal heaths. It is a solitary species that uses the forest margins as a refuge during daylight hours. It forms and follows defined runways while foraging for grasses, fruits and fallen leaves. 63cm. Tas.

QUOKKA ▲
(Setonix brachyurus)
One of the first marsupials to be seen by European explorers (1658), the Quokka has two different habitat preferences. On the mainland it lives in densely vegetated habitats, while on Rottnest Island it survives in dry conditions among low vegetation. Quokkas are both browsers and grazers, and can climb low shrubs and trees. 54cm. sw WA.

RED-LEGGED PADEMELON ➤
(Thylogale stigmatica)
This rainforest species lives in well-organised family groups, and will rapidly seek shelter if disturbed. It feeds primarily on fallen fruits and leaves. At night, it will venture to rainforest margins to eat grasses. 54cm. ne NSW to ne Qld.

Kangaroos and Other Marsupials

It is solitary and nocturnal and typically lives in a grass nest hidden under dense cover. If alarmed it will emit a hissing sound before hopping rapidly away with forelimbs tucked against its body. 39cm. ce NSW to ne Qld.

YELLOW-FOOTED ROCK WALLABY ▲
(Petrogale xanthopus)
Fifteen rock-wallaby species are known, some with isolated populations that may represent distinct species. They typically inhabit rocky gullies and boulder fields.

This prettily marked species inhabits scree slopes and low cliffs in several distinct populations scattered across the semi-arid zone. In winter it sometimes basks in the sun. It is an endangered species that can survive without drinking, gaining moisture from herbs and grasses. 65cm. w SA, nw NSW, cs Qld.

SHORT-EARED ROCK-WALLABY ➤
(Petrogale brachyotis)
This gregarious species can sometimes be observed foraging in cloudy weather, but is more typically nocturnal. It feeds on sedges and grasses adjacent to cliffs, gorges and low rocky hills, retreating to caves and overhangs during daylight. 55cm. nw WA, n NT.

RUFOUS BETTONG ➤
(Aepyprymnus rufescens)
The largest of the rat-kangaroos, this species characteristically has a reddish tinge to its belly.

NORTHERN BETTONG ▲

(Bettongia tropica)

As much as 70% of the diet of this animal is truffles, the underground fruiting bodies of fungi. Many forest trees depend on fungi to provide nutrients for growth, and the fungi in turn depend on the bettong for dispersal. When bettongs dig up and eat truffles, many spores pass through their digestive system unharmed, to be dispersed throughout the local environment. 35cm. ne Qld.

COMMON BRUSHTAILED POSSUM ◄

(Trichosurus vulpecular)

Possums are tree-dwelling marsupials with a long tail that is often used for grasping branches. The 26 Australian species include possums, pygmy possums, gliders and cuscuses.

This possum frequents towns and cities, and is the most commonly encountered marsupial in eastern Australia. It shelters by day in tree hollows in its natural habitat, and will also nest in house roofs. The tail is partially prehensile, assisting movement through the tree canopy. Food consists of leaves, flowers and fruits. 50cm. sw WA, se SA, e Aus, n NT.

HERBERT RIVER RINGTAIL POSSUM ▲

(Pseudocheirus herbertensis)

This solitary species moves at night among trees in mountain rainforests above 300m altitude. It eats mostly fruits, flowers and the leaves of rainforest plants. Births occur between May and July. 40cm. ne Qld.

SUGAR GLIDER ▼
(Petaurus breviceps)

Membrane-like skin webbing between wrist and ankle allows this possum to glide up to 90m from tree to tree in eucalypt forest and woodland. Its distinctive 'yip yip' call can be heard at night. It feeds on insects and saps and gums produced by wattles and eucalypts. Up to seven individuals may share a nest hollow, a useful way to conserve body heat during cold weather. 20cm. s Vic to ne Qld, n NT, n WA, Tas.

COMMON RINGTAIL POSSUM ▲
(Pseudocheirus peregrinus)

This social species lives in family groups in both open and closed forests. It is an adept nocturnal climber, making good use of its prehensile tail. During daylight hours it shelters in a nest made from bark, twigs and leaves called a 'drey'. Often seen in suburban areas, it can become quite tame. 38cm. sw Vic to ne Qld, Tas.

EASTERN PYGMY POSSUM ▼
(Cercartetus nanus)

This agile climber has grasping feet and a prehensile tail. It is predominantly a pollen and nectar feeder, possibly playing an important pollinating role for the plants on which it feeds. This small species constructs a number of shredded bark nests, within which it sleeps during winter. 10cm. Coast and ranges se SA to se Qld, Tas.

FEATHERTAIL GLIDER ▼

(Acrobates pygmaeus)

This glider is named for the fringe of stiff hairs that grows either side of the tail. It is the world's smallest gliding mammal, making controlled glides of up to 25m. It is most common in unlogged forests with a high diversity of plant species, ensuring a year-round supply of nectar and saps. 8cm. s Vic to ne Qld.

EASTERN QUOLL ➤

(Dasyurus viverrinus)

The four quoll species have a superficial 'cat-like' appearance, hence were once called 'native cats'. They are primarily nocturnal, spending the daylight hours in dens that can be occupied by several individuals.

The Eastern Quoll feeds mainly on insects, but will also opportunistically eat birds and small mammals, as well as grasses and fruits. Up to 30 young are born, but as there are only six nipples in the pouch, only six young can survive the first hours of birth. The species remains common in Tas, but is regarded as extinct on the mainland following depredation by foxes and other introduced predators. 40cm. Tas.

SPOTTED–TAILED QUOLL, TIGER CAT ▲

(Dasyurus maculatus)

The largest marsupial carnivore on the mainland, this agile climber hunts birds and mammals, often killing its prey with a crushing bite to the back of the head. It is occasionally found in chicken coops, surrounded by feathers and other remains of a favoured prey. 75cm. Coast and ranges sw Vic to ne Qld, Tas.

Kangaroos and Other Marsupials

NUMBAT ▼

(Myrmecobius fasciatus)

The only marsupial adapted to feed exclusively on termites, the Numbat does not have sufficient strength to dig into termite mounds. Rather, it locates shallow runways that radiate from mounds, exposes these, and uses a long sticky tongue to 'lap' up termites. The cryptic coloration of the Numbat provides good camouflage as it forages during the day. 28cm. sw WA.

TASMANIAN DEVIL ▲

(Sarcophilus harrisi)

This is the largest marsupial carnivore. It primarily feeds on carrion, crunching through bone with its extremely powerful jaws; it also hunts insects and small vertebrates. It patrols its defined territory, at night with a rocking gait. 'Devils' are often heard before being seen, especially when several animals are competing over a carcass, with threatening growls and screams. 65cm. Tas.

DUSKY ANTECHINUS ➤

(Antechinus swainsonii)

This is one of about 10 mouse-like marsupial carnivores that are voracious predators of insects, spiders and lizards. This one will also occasionally eat plant material. Mating is a violent affair, with copulation lasting up to six hours. Males generally live for one year, dying after mating, leaving the females and young to feed upon the abundant food available during spring. 19cm. Coast and ranges sw Vic to se Qld, Tas.

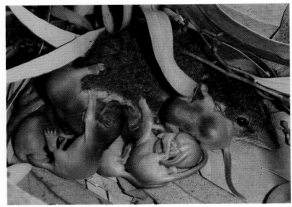

EASTERN BARRED BANDICOOT ◄
(Perameles gunnii)

This grassland species is easily recognised by the three to four pale bars on its hindquarters. It has a very short gestation period of 13 days, one of the shortest of any mammal, and usually gives birth to two or three young. It is now virtually extinct on the mainland. 35cm. sw Vic, Tas.

SOUTHERN BROWN BANDICOOT ▼
(Isoodon obesulus)

Like the other ten bandicoot species, this marsupial has second and third toes of the hindfeet fused for digging, and powerful forelimbs to hold invertebrates, fungi and tubers. It is a solitary, territorial and reclusive mammal that forages at night. It constructs a grass nest in dense cover for shelter during the day. It may raise up to three litters in a year, with births occurring between late winter and late summer. 36cm. s Aus, Tas.

BILBY ▲
(Macrotis lagotis)

Populations of this nocturnal arid-zone bandicoot have contracted greatly due to land clearance and feral animal predation. The species is now largely confined to predator-exclusion zones in acacia scrublands and hummock grasslands. 55cm. c WA to cw NT.

Placental Mammals

Placental mammals have a different reproductive strategy from other mammals. They possess a placenta that provides nourishment for the developing embryo within the mother's uterus. Young are fully formed when born and suckle milk from the mother's mammary glands. The only native placentals in Australia are bats and mice, plus the recently established dingo.

GREY-HEADED FLYING-FOX ▼
(Pteropus poliocephalus)

This is one of a group of 12 large bat species, all with claws on the first and second toes of the forelimb. Most are tropical; those living in temperate regions migrate seasonally in search of food sources. This one eats nectar, blossoms and fruit. When feeding on fruits, it swallows small seeds and juice and spits out the fibre. These bats spend daylight hours in 'camps', which may number tens of thousands of individuals, from which they fly out to forage at dusk. 29cm. Coastal se Vic to ce Qld.

LITTLE NORTHERN FREETAIL
BAT (Mormopterus loriae) ▲

Australia is home to 62 species of small insectivorous bats. They possess one claw on the forelimb and navigate by echolocation. This bat has triangular ears, wrinkled lips and narrow, pointed wings. It flies with rapid wingbeats through open forest and rainforest; however, it sometimes scurries across the ground in pursuit of prey. Tree hollows and to a lesser extent buildings are used for roosting. 55mm. Coast and ranges ne Qld to nw NT.

GHOST BAT ▲
(Macroderma gigas)

This is the only Australian bat that feeds on vertebrate prey, including other bats, small mammals, birds, frogs and lizards, as well as insects. It captures most prey on the ground then takes the victim to a feeding site for consumption. Although widely distributed, Ghost Bats are disturbed easily and regarded as threatened. Females form nursery colonies without males. 11cm. n Aus.

SPINIFEX HOPPING MOUSE ➤
(Notomys alexis)

Sixty-four native and five introduced rodents live in Australia. All have one pair of upper and lower incisors that grow continuously throughout their lives. The group colonised Australia from Indonesia relatively recently (15 million years ago). Since that time different species have evolved to occupy habitats Australia-wide. Like many small desert mammals, populations of this one fluctuate widely with rainfall. It shelters during daylight hours in groups in burrow complexes. It has a kangaroo-like gait, and hops with the body and tail held horizontally. An omnivore, it eats insects and plants, particularly seeds when they are available. It inhabits sandy desert areas. 12cm. c and nw Aus.

DINGO ▲
(Canis lupus dingo)

This dog was probably brought into Australia about 4000 years ago by seafaring peoples from Indonesia. A generalist predator, it eats a wide range of species from kangaroos to small mammals, reptiles and insects. Breeding depends on recent rainfall and the associated presence of prey. A 9600km fence extends across south-eastern Australia to separate dingo populations from pastoral lands. The dingo freely hybridises with domestic dogs. The only pure population remaining is located on Fraser Island, Qld. 1m. Aus.

DUGONG ▲
(Dugong dugon)
This large herbivorous marine mammal lives and feeds in shallow tropical seagrass beds. Females give birth in shallow inshore waters protected from sharks by sandbanks. Aborigines and Torres Strait Islanders are permitted to hunt dugongs using traditional hunting methods. 3m. se Qld to ce WA.

AUSTRALIAN FUR SEAL ▲
(Arctocephalus pusillus doriferus)
This is the most abundant of the ten seal and sea-lion species recorded in Australian waters. All have streamlined body shapes, forelimbs shaped as flippers, and webbed hindlimbs to provide propulsion at sea.

Population numbers of Australian Fur Seals were drastically reduced by commercial sealers in the nineteenth and early twentieth centuries, but numbers have now increased to about 50 000 individuals. Diving to 200m, this species feeds primarily on pelagic fish and octopuses.

The closely related New Zealand Fur Seal (*Arctocephalus forsteri*) is increasingly common in Australia, and other fur seal species, including the animal pictured, breed at Macquarie Island. 2.3m. Vic to s NSW, Tas.

AUSTRALIAN SEA-LION ▼
(Neophoca cinerea)
This is the only seal confined to Australia. Unusually, the period between births is about 18 months, rather than a seasonal cycle of 12 or 24 months. Also, births are not synchronised between breeding females but extend over a five- to seven-month period at a colony; hence there is no fixed breeding season. This species feeds mainly in offshore waters, diving to depths of over 150m in search of fish, lobster and squid. 2.5m. Shark Bay, WA, to se SA.

BOTTLENOSE DOLPHIN ▼

(Tursiops truncatus)

Forty-four dolphin and whale species have been recorded in Australian waters. These fall into two groups: the dolphins and 'toothed' whales, which capture prey in their jaws; and the 'baleen' whales, which use horny plates in their mouths to filter small marine organisms and fish from mouthfuls of seawater.

Bottlenose dolphins have a relatively short beak with curved mouth shaped into a grin, and a grey back blending into a white belly. Individuals approach divers more often than other dolphin species, and enter very shallow water for feeding at Monkey Mia, Shark Bay, WA. This dolphin is often seen following boats in bays and estuaries in groups of 5–20 animals. 4m. Aus, Tas.

SOUTHERN ELEPHANT SEAL ▲

(Mirounga leonina)

This is the largest seal in Australian waters. It belongs to the 'earless' group of true seals rather than the 'eared' sea-lions and fur seals. Adult males weigh up to 4 tonnes. This seal can remain submerged for more than an hour, diving to depths of 1200m in search of squid and fish. Young are weaned at three weeks and then fast for seven weeks before heading out to sea. Elephant Seals once bred in large numbers at King Island, Bass Strait, but that population was exterminated by sealers. They still breed on Macquarie Island, with occasional vagrants in southern Australia. 5m. sw WA to c NSW, Tas.

SOUTHERN RIGHT WHALE ➤

(Eubalaena australis)
This species often head-stands, with its tail flukes above the water. It gained the name 'right whale' because whalers preferred to catch this species above all others—it floated when dead, was easy to approach, and provided a large amount of oil, meat and whalebone. 17.5m. May–Oct sw WA to ce NSW, Tas.

HUMPBACK WHALE ◄

(Megaptera novaeangliae)
During its winter migration to tropical waters this species engages in flipper slapping, lobtailing and breaching, often in sight of land. The migration forms the basis of an important eco-tourism industry along the west and east coasts. Males sing complex songs that are heard by scuba divers. This species is distinguished by its exceptionally long white pectoral fins. 18m. Winter w and e Aus, Tas.

References

Allen, G. R. 1989. *Freshwater Fishes of Australia.* TFH, Sydney.

Allen, G. R. & Swainston, R. 1988. *The Marine Fishes of North-Western Australia.* WA Museum, Perth.

Bennett, J., Harley, D., Worley, M., Donaldson, B., Andrew, D., Geering, D., Povey, A. & Cohen, M. 2000. *Watching Wildlife Australia.* Lonely Planet, Melbourne.

Boland, D. J., Brooker, M. I. H., Chippendale, G. M., Hall, N., Hyland, B. P. M., Johnson, R. D., Kleinig, D. A. & Turner, J. D. 1984. *Forest Trees of Australia.* CSIRO Publishing, Melbourne.

Braby, M. F. 2004. *The Complete Field Guide to Butterflies of Australia.* CSIRO Publishing, Melbourne.

Carwardine, M. 1995. *Whales, Dolphins and Porpoises.* Dorling Kindersley, London.

Carolin, R. & Clarke, P. 1991. *Beach Plants of South Eastern Australia.* Sainty & Associates, Sydney.

Cherikoff, V. 2000. *The Bushfood Handbook.* Cherikoff Pty Ltd, Sydney.

Cogger, H. G. 2000. *Reptiles and Amphibians of Australia.* Reed New Holland, Sydney.

Common, I. F. B. 1990. *Moths of Australia.* Melbourne University Press, Melbourne.

Cronin, L. 1987. *Key Guide to Australian Wildflowers.* Reed, Sydney.

CSIRO (ed.) 1970. *The Insects of Australia.* Melbourne University Press, Melbourne.

Edgar, G. J. 2000. *Australian Marine Life.* Reed New Holland, Sydney.

Egerton, L. (ed.) 2005. *Encyclopedia of Australian Wildlife.* Readers Digest, Sydney.

Gooderham, J. & Tsyrlin, E. 2002. *The Waterbug Book.* CSIRO Publishing, Melbourne.

Gomon, M. F., Glover, J. C. M. & Kuiter, R. H. 1994. *The Fishes of Australia's South Coast.* State Print, Adelaide.

Hawkeswood, T. J. 2003. *Spiders of Australia: An Introduction to their Classification, Biology and Distribution.* Pensoft, Sofia, Bulgaria.

Holliday, I. 2002. *A Field Guide to Australian Trees.* Reed New Holland, Sydney.

Holliday, I. & Watton, G. 1989. *A Field Guide to Australian Native Shrubs.* Lansdowne, Sydney.

Huisman, J. M. 2000. *Marine Plants of Australia.* University of Western Australia Press, Nedlands.

Hutchins, B. & Swainston, R. 1986. *Sea Fishes of Southern Australia.* Swainston, Daglish, WA.

Jones, D. S. & G. J. Morgan 2002. *A Field Guide to Crustaceans of Australian Waters.* Reed New Holland, Sydney.

Kuiter, R. 1993. *Coastal Fishes of South-eastern Australia.* Crawford House, Bathurst, NSW.

Lawrence, J. F. & Britton, E. B. 1994. *Australian Beetles.* Melbourne University Press, Melbourne.

Low, T. 1991. *Wild Food Plants of Australia.* Angus & Robertson, Sydney.

Menkhorst, P. and Knight, F. 2001. *A Field Guide to the Mammals of Australia.* Oxford University Press, Melbourne.

Mirtschin, P. & Davis, R. 1992. *Snakes of Australia.* Hill of Content, Melbourne.

Morecombe, M. & Morecombe, I. 1983. *Discover Australia's National Parks & Naturelands.* Lansdowne, Sydney.

Randall, J. E., Allen, G. R. & Steene, R. C. 1986. *Fishes of the Great Barrier Reef and Coral Sea.* Crawford House, Bathurst, NSW.

Robinson, M. 1993. *A Field Guide to the Frogs of Australia.* Reed New Holland, Sydney.

Simpson, K. & Day, N. 1989. *Field Guide to the Birds of Australia.* Penguin, Melbourne.

Slater P., Slater, P. & Slater, R. 2001. *The Slater Field Guide To Australian Birds.* Reed New Holland, Sydney.

Strahan, R. (ed.) 1995. *The Mammals of Australia.* Reed New Holland, Sydney.

Wilson, S. and Swan, G. 2003. *A Complete Guide to Reptiles of Australia.* Reed New Holland, Sydney.

Websites

Plants
http://florabase.calm.WA.gov.au
http://farrer.riv.csu.edu.au/ASGAP/whereto8.html
http://www.wettropics.gov.au/pa/pa_default.html

Plants and Animals of Western Australia
http://www.calm.WA.gov.au/plants_animals/index.html

Frogs
http://frogsaustralia.net.au
http://frogs.org.au

Reptiles
http://www.kingsnake.com/oz/
http://www.jcu.edu.au/school/tbiol/zoology/herp/herp2.html

Birds
http://www.ausbird.com
http://www.birdsaustralia.com.au
http://www.birdata.com.au

Parks and Gardens
National Parks South Australia—
http://www.denr.sa.gov.au/parks/parks.html
National Parks Queensland—
http://www.epa.qld.gov.au
Australian National Parks—
http://www.atn.com.au/links/parks.html
Department of Environment and Conservation, NSW—http://www.npws.nsw.gov.au
National Parks Northern Territory—
http://www.nreta.nt.gov.au/
National Parks Tasmania—
http://www.parks.tas.gov.au

National Parks Victoria—
http://www.parkweb.vic.gov.au/
Great Barrier Reef Marine Parks Authority—
http://www.gbrmpa.gov.au
Sydney Royal Botanic Gardens—
http://www.rbgsyd.gov.au/

Museums
Australian Museum—
http://www.austmus.gov.au
Museum of Tropical Queensland—
http://www.mtq.qld.gov.au/
Museum of Victoria—
http://www.museum.vic.gov.au/
Queen Victoria Museum and Art Gallery, Tasmania—http://www.qvmag.tas.gov.au
Queensland Museum—
http://www.qmuseum.qld.gov.au
South Australian Museum—
http://www.samuseum.sa.gov.au/
Tasmanian Museum and Art Gallery—
http://www.tmag.tas.gov.au/
Western Australian Museum—
http://www.museum.wa.gov.au/

Marine
Australian Institute of Marine Science:
www.aims.gov.au
Shells of NSW—
http://seashellsofnsw.org.au/index.htmFish
base http://www.fishbase.org/search.cfm

General
Australian's Venomous Creatures and First Aid Procedures—
http://www.avru.unimelb.edu.au/avruweb/creatable.html
IUCN Red List of Threatened Species
http://www.redlist.org/

Index

Index

HOW TO COOK
Crusty Fresh Bread in Your
Breadmaker

Awake Sunday morning to fresh bread aroma
and hot buttered toast!

Carol Palmer

foulsham
LONDON • NEW YORK • TORONTO • SYDNEY

foulsham

Capital Point, 33 Bath Road, Slough, Berkshire, SL1 3UF, England

Foulsham books can be found in all good bookshops and direct from www.foulsham.com

ISBN: 978-0-572-03897-7

You may also be interested in:
How to cook comfort food on a tight budget
How to cook complete meals in your halogen cooker

Printed in Great Britain by Cox & Wyman Ltd, Reading

contents

introduction

The ploy of brewing fresh coffee or baking bread has long been used as a 'welcoming' smell in the home environment. A good idea in theory, but anyone who has ever made their own bread will know that it can be a long drawn-out process that it not always justified by the end results. Cooking a successful loaf can be a rather hit-and-miss affair. There are a number of very important factors that govern the results and we don't all have the time or the energy to spend on something that we can quite easily buy in the supermarket. However, nothing compares to the flavour of home-made bread and now it is possible for even the most inexperienced of cooks to bake their own bread successfully using a breadmaker.

There is a wide range of breadmaking machines now available, which offer a variety of cycles and functions to make breadmaking a pleasure rather than a chore. I have been baking bread by the traditional method for about 20 years, but I am more than impressed with the results I have had from the range of breadmakers I have tested. To get the maximum benefit from the appliance, however, you will probably want to explore beyond the realms of a basic loaf of white bread and this book will help you do just that. Whether you have a penchant for continental-style bread or prefer the traditional bakery favourites, there will be something here for you to try.

Once you have made some of the basic recipes, be bold and try something a little different. None of the recipes is complicated because the breadmaker itself is a simple machine. Eventually, you will feel brave enough to develop your own recipes. But don't think that breadmakers, and indeed this book, are just for special occasions: once you get into the routine of using the machine, you will find that it is a useful tool for every day, whether making sandwiches for the kids or bread for a special buffet.

If you are completely new to the breadmaker, then initially take some time to examine your machine and read the manufacturer's instruction manual. Once you have done this, start by following one of the basic recipes in this book such as white or brown bread. You may need to adjust quantities slightly to suit your particular machine.

Our Menu

Browse Our Menu

Browse through our menu to take your pick of the superb selection on offer.

Our Menu

Basic bread recipes

Basic white bread
A tasty white bread with a crisp top crust
and an airy texture. *p34*

Brown bread
A wholesome brown bread with plenty of flavour
and a tantalising texture. *p36*

Variety crown bread
The ideal loaf for sharing! Seven wholemeal rolls
flavoured with honey cluster together and are topped
with a selection of crunchy seeds. *p38*

Light wholemeal bread
A truly wholesome bread that has a pleasant flavour
and a light, airy texture. *p40*

Granary bread
A traditional granary bread with a grainy,
pleasantly chewy texture. *p42*

Grain breads

Cheese and mint semolina bread

A crumbly semolina bread with fresh mint and strong Cheddar cheese make this loaf a Middle Eastern experience. *p44*

Malted oat loaf

Comfort food at its best. A moist, dark bread that exudes malty flavour. *p46*

Malted bran loaf

Malty moistness and the addition of bran flakes give this loaf depth and appeal. *p48*

Rye bread

A dark, close-textured rye bread. A delicious alternative to wheat-based bread. *p50*

Rye, onion, potato and fennel loaf

Onion and fennel seeds give this dark rye loaf heaps of favour, while potato ensures a smooth, silky texture. *p52*

Carrot and fancy mustard bread

A cornmeal and wheat-based loaf with sweet, moist grated carrot and the kick of mustard. *p54*

Spelt bread with sesame seeds

A traditional Roman spelt flour bread with a deep flavour and thick, crunchy crust. *p56*

Sun-dried tomato and rosemary bread

A taste of Italy! Sun-dried tomatoes meld with rosemary to give an intensely seductive flavour. *p58*

Very light seed and granary loaf

Health food at its best! The nutritional benefits of whole seeds and granary flour but the lightness of a white loaf. *p60*

Mango, banana and seed loaf

Juicy, sweet mango and banana combine with crunchy pumpkin and sunflower seeds and the unmistakeable flavour of cinnamon. *p62*

Oatmeal sourdough bread

The sourdough base and oatmeal give this loaf a truly unique flavour. *p64*

Savoury breads

Tapenade bread

The punchy flavour of olive tapenade in a mixed grain, full-textured bread. *p66*

Courgette and tomato bread

Pan-fried courgette, shallot and tomato laced with aromatic basil make a truly indulgent French-style loaf. *p68*

Chilli avocado bread

A moist avocado and sautéed tomato bread with the heat of chilli. *p70*

Hawaiian bread

Sweet meets savoury when pineapple combines with full-flavoured Cheddar for a bread with a tropical twist. *p72*

Blue cheese and walnut bread

A classic combination of blue cheese and walnuts in light, wholemeal dough. Simply slice and enjoy. *p74*

Cheese and bean bread

Green beans hide in a cheesy bread made with granary flour. *p76*

Fast basil, chive and cheese bread

Enjoy the taste of summer herbs in no time with this rapid cheese-flavoured loaf. *p78*

Ploughman's bread

All the best bits of a ploughman's lunch in a loaf – cheese and pickled onion in a light granary dough. *p80*

Fast ham and chutney bread

A meal in itself! Ham and chutney in wholemeal dough make a substantial snack. *p82*

Sun-dried pepper and basil bread

Enjoy a slice of the Mediterranean when you cut through aromatic basil and sun-dried peppers in a white bread loaf. *p84*

Sage and crispy bacon loaf

Crispy bacon mingles with sage in an airy wholemeal bread. *p86*

Smoked salmon platter

Bite into a thin, crisp dough base lavishly topped
with smoked salmon, Mozzarella cheese, courgette
and tomato for a taste of luxury. *p88*

Potato and goats' cheese bread

A smooth-textured potato bread with the unmistakeable
flavour of goats' cheese. *p90*

Garlic and oregano bread

A pungent garlic and oregano French-style loaf. *p92*

Continental and foreign breads

Fried bread

Individual spelt and wholemeal flour flatbreads sizzled
in hot oil until golden-brown. *p94*

Grissini

Lovely long wholemeal breadsticks –
crunchy and moreish! *p96*

Tikka and coriander corn loaf

A dense cornbread with spicy tikka and refreshing
coriander flavouring. *p98*

Madras flatbread

Indian spiced bread pockets to split and fill.
Lovely hot or cold. *p100*

Dark pumpernickel
Close-textured rye bread enriched and moistened with dark black treacle. *p102*

Brioche
A real taste of France. An enriched sweet, white, soft dough with a golden crust. *p104*

Olive and chilli pitta bread
Red and green chillies mixed with chopped olives make these little pitta breads moist and delicious. *p106*

Basic pizza dough
A basic Italian-style dough to make a sumptuous base for all your favourite pizzas. *p108*

Fennel and smoked salmon pizza
Scandinavian flavours of smoked salmon and fennel team up with Mozzarella on a thin, crisp crust. *p110*

Red pesto and artichoke pizza
Juicy artichoke hearts and red pesto topped with melting Mozzarella on a pizza base. *p111*

Croissants
A flaky crisp crust and a rich, airy dough in these French patisserie classics. *p112*

Salami and brie croissants
Delicious ripe Brie oozes from the fresh croissant dough and perfectly complements the salami slices hidden inside. *p115*

Challah bread

Traditional Jewish white dough bread. Soft-textured, golden-glazed and shaped into an ornate plait. *p116*

French stick

A versatile all-time favourite white bread to enjoy sliced or torn into chunks. *p118*

French bread

Classic crisp-crusted French bread. Split, fill, eat! Lovely warm or cold. *p120*

Rolls and buns

White bread rolls

Fluffy white rolls with a thin, crisp crust. *p122*

Wholemeal bread rolls

Wholemeal flour and white flour make these light-textured rolls a pleasing high-fibre option. *p124*

Shrimp knots

Aromatic lemongrass and salty Chinese shrimp paste add an interesting twist to these knot-shaped rolls. *p126*

Summer herb and onion rolls

Enjoy the flavours of the summertime garden. A medley of garden herbs and chopped shallot flavour mini baton-shaped rolls. *p128*

Cracked wheat granary clovers

These attractive clover-shaped rolls are made
with granary flour and topped with crunchy
cracked wheat. *p130*

Hot cross buns

The aroma of mixed spices and plump dried fruit can
only mean Easter time. A traditional favourite. *p132*

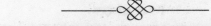

Sweet breads and teatime favourites

Chocolate and raisin bread

Juicy raisins against the backdrop of a chocolate dough
make for a teatime delight. *p136*

Double chocolate and hazelnut bread

Sticky chocolate melds with crunchy hazelnuts –
a real indulgence! *p138*

Cornish clotted cream heavies

West Country clotted cream is the luxury ingredient
in these densely fruity spiced buns. *p140*

Fast orange and cardamom bread

The citrus tang of orange is accentuated by
crushed cardamom seeds in this quick and
easy-to-make loaf. *p142*

Toffee bread

Double toffee delight! An envelope of toffee-flavoured
dough containing a soft toffee filling. *p144*

Fast vanilla bread

Simply vanilla! The unmistakeable flavour of vanilla makes this loaf unique. *p146*

Lemon and lime marmalade bread

Lemon and lime marmalade gives this bread a bitter-sweet zing as well as an interesting texture. *p148*

Teacakes

A traditional English favourite. Enriched dough buns peppered with juicy currants and mixed peel. *p150*

Double banana bread

Fresh banana and dried yoghurt-coated banana give moisture and crunch to this honey-sweetened loaf. *p152*

Milk bread

More than just a loaf! A very soft white bread to make extra-special sandwiches or to serve with good-quality jam. *p154*

Mixed fruit, orange and syrup bread

The king of fruit breads results from the combination of dried mixed fruit, the citrus tang of orange juice and zest and sweet golden syrup. *p156*

about your breadmaker

It is difficult to generalise about your breadmaker as there is now such a wide range of models available on the market. To mention just a few, there are those that bake two small loaves, compact models for your work surface and those that cook a long, large loaf. To complicate matters, many of the instruction manuals recommend slightly different procedures. However, whatever your model, many of the basic features and principles are the same.

It is probably fair to say that they all consist of a removable non-stick bread pan, which is heated by an electric element housed at the base of the machine. Within the bread pan are either one or two paddles/blades which rotate during mixing and kneading. The hot 'oven' atmosphere results from the lid, which is closed when the machine is working.

settings and functions

All the breadmakers I have tested and encountered include such basic programmes as BASIC, WHOLEMEAL/WHEAT and DOUGH. Most now also have FRENCH/CONTINENTAL/SPECIALITY, JAM and CAKE options. Some offer a range of more elaborate choices. To make the vast majority of recipes in this book, it is necessary to have only the basic range of programmes and, as your confidence grows in using your machine, you will enjoy experimenting with different programmes and recipes. However, as a rule of thumb, if you are unsure always use the BASIC cycle. (See the notes on page 20 for choice of cycle.)

Most breadmakers give you a colour crust option so that you can choose the appearance of your final loaf. Some also offer EXTRA BAKE and KEEP WARM functions. The first is useful if your bread is noticeably pale or wet when you go to remove it: the second is used to keep bread warm if that's how you want to eat it. Many loaves taste better warm, but remember that it does affect their cutting quality.

Most of the machines display the cycle you have selected and the time it will take. Generally, they also have a buzzer or beeper that sounds after the first kneading to signify when to add ingredients such as raisins and nuts that you do not wish to become minced up.

The timer option, present on the majority of breadmakers, allows you to delay the time the cycle commences. It is important that you calculate the time that you want the bread to be ready and delay the time until then, rather than the time you want it to start. Your instruction manual will explain how you set this.

the bread pan and paddles

Some bread pans are quite heavy, others relatively lightweight, though the results are not noticeably different. A handle allows you to lift the pan out of the machine to insert the paddles and put in the ingredients. It is essential that you always do this and do not attempt to add ingredients while the pan is still in the machine – if anything gets down the side of the pan, it will cause burning when the machine is switched on and could damage the element. Once the ingredients are in the pan, it can simply be pushed back down into position. Check that it has locked into position or the machine will fail to operate. Similarly, ensure that the paddle or paddles are firmly engaged before you put the ingredients in the pan. It is very difficult to adjust them once the food is in there, and NEVER attempt to adjust them once the machine is switched on, even if they are not turning.

Always wait until the pan and paddles have cooled down before you attempt to clean them. Never use metal or anything abrasive against the pan or paddles as the surface can easily be damaged and bread will then stick to it. Use warm soapy water and a dishcloth, sponge or soft brush to clean the inside. The paddles can be immersed in water, but not the pan. Fill it with water but never place its underside in water – only the inside should require cleaning. In some cases you may simply be able to wipe it with a cloth but, if it is very dirty or the paddles seem stuck, allow the inside to soak for a little while. Normal household washing-up liquid is all that is needed; never use strong cleaners or chemicals.

safety tips

These are common sense, but important enough to mention here:

- Never plug in or operate the machine with wet hands.
- Do not immerse the cord or plug in water.
- The breadmaker should be used on a work surface where it cannot be knocked, but not near sources of heat such as the cooker.
- Keep the machine out of the reach of children.
- Remove the bread pan before adding ingredients, then lock it into position in the machine.
- Use oven gloves to remove the pan.
- Stand the pan on a heatproof surface.
- Do not attempt cleaning until the pan has cooled down.
- Clean up any spills inside the machine itself, for example by the element, when the machine is switched off, unplugged and has cooled down.
- Do not cover the steam vents while in operation.
- Do not attempt to move the machine while it is switched on.
- Follow the manufacturer's instructions carefully.
- Use the breadmaker only for its intended purpose.

how to use your breadmaker

The first thing to reiterate here is **refer to your instruction manual**; though most breadmakers are similar in their operation, there are variations and if these are not taken into account your results may be disappointing. With practice you will develop a safe and effective routine for using your breadmaker.

1 Find a safe place to use your breadmaker.

2 Open the lid and remove the paddle(s) then, using the handle, pull out the bread pan and stand it on a safe, level work surface.

3 Reinsert the paddle(s), checking they are properly engaged.

4 Add the ingredients to the pan in the order listed in the recipe or that recommended in the instruction manual.

NOTE: Some breadmakers recommend adding the dry ingredients first, some the wet: I have tried both methods in a variety of breadmakers and find there is no noticeable difference in the end results. The important factor seems to be keeping the yeast separated from the liquid by the dry ingredients (particularly when delaying the start time). Apart from this, the precise order of adding the ingredients doesn't seem to make a lot of difference.

5 Some manufacturers recommend using tepid water. Although the temperature of the water is essential with the RAPID/FAST cycles, I have found that cold water is just as successful with other cycles.

6 Carefully push the bread pan back down into position in the machine until it clicks into place. Close the lid.

7 Plug in the machine and switch it on at the mains.

8 Set the programme/cycle you require. The instruction booklet will tell you how to do this. You may also have a choice of loaf size and crust colour.

9 Press START.

10 If the recipe includes ingredients that you do not want to become too minced up, such as nuts, raisins and olives, then add them when the beeper/buzzer sounds. Apart from this, avoid opening the machine during a cycle as you will release the heat and affect both the proving and cooking temperatures required.

11 At the end of the cycle press STOP and turn off at the mains. Unplug the machine. Open the lid.

12 Carefully lift out the bread pan using oven gloves and tip the loaf out on a wire rack to cool.

13 Clean the pan as described earlier.

14 If the paddle has become lodged in the base of the loaf, as I found often happened, hook it out using a wooden or tough plastic implement so that the non-stick surface is not damaged. It is easier to do this while the bread is still warm.

15 Slice the bread when cool.

choosing the right setting

Much of this comes with trial and error, but here are some guidelines for the basic range of programmes.

- BASIC: use this for breads that are made from all or a high proportion of strong white bread flour.

- WHOLEMEAL/WHEAT: this cycle is most effective for breads containing wholemeal flour or wholegrain flours such as rye, barley and oats.

- FRENCH/CONTINENTAL/SPECIALITY: use this cycle for French breads, Italian breads or breads with very little or no fat.

- DOUGH: this programme is used for any recipe where the bread is removed from the pan, shaped and then baked in a conventional oven. The dough generally needs a second rising outside the breadmaker.

- SWEET: this cycle can be used for breads with a high proportion of sugar such as fruit loaves and some of the enriched doughs.

some more unusual settings

- RAPID/FAST: very quick cycles that require warm water and fast-acting yeast.

- CAKE: a programme used to bake cakes, which require longer cooking. Good results can be achieved, though the cakes do not have the puffy risen appearance of those cooked by the conventional method.

- JAM: a useful programme for making small quantities of fruit into jam.

- PASTA: a useful programme for Italian food enthusiasts.

the successful loaf

Results in breadmaking vary quite markedly depending on a combination of factors:

* Using the breadmaker correctly.
* The right choice of flour and other ingredients.
* Creating the correct conditions.
* Using the correct techniques.

We have already looked at the correct process for using the breadmaker, so I am now going to look at the choice of ingredients. These are not hard and fast rules, but my own finding from experimenting with various breadmakers and ingredients.

ingredients
flour

To make successful bread you need to choose flour with a high gluten content. These are known as strong flours, such as strong white or strong wholemeal bread flour. Generally speaking, ordinary plain (all-purpose) flours do not have enough gluten to produce a good, well-risen loaf.

I have found that using all wholemeal or wholegrain flour in a recipe produces a rather stodgy, tough bread. The texture is greatly improved by using half white and half wholemeal or wholegrain flour but, of course, this is again a matter of taste.

* Granary flour combined with white bread flour gives a lovely crumbly texture to bread.

* Rye flour has a very low gluten content so needs to be supplemented with a bread flour.

* Spelt flour, derived from a particular variety of the wheat plant, gives good results in the breadmaker and produces an interesting nutty flavour.

* Semolina (cream of wheat) flour also makes an interesting bread and lends itself well to savoury flavourings.

* Buckwheat is not strictly a wheat but is the seed of a rhubarb-type plant. As such, it has no gluten and is

therefore used only as a flavouring, not as the base flour in a recipe.

- Cornmeal adds texture and colour to a standard loaf and is enhanced by spicy flavourings.

- Ordinary plain (all-purpose) or self raising flour should be used in the cake recipes in this book.

grains

Cereal grains such as oats and barley and also bran etc. may be used in their various forms to both enhance the flavour and texture and add to the nutritional value of the bread. However, too large a proportion of these ingredients may result in heavy bread.

yeast

Yeast produces carbon dioxide when it is given warmth, time, food and moisture and is essential to make bread. Traditional active dried yeast is used in breadmakers, and I recommend this for all but the RAPID/FAST programmes, for which you must use fast-activating yeast. Fresh yeast is not suitable for use in a breadmaker.

Traditional active dried yeast is the ordinary dried yeast you would normally mix with warm water before adding to the dough, but it is added neat to breadmakers and gives good results. Some manufacturers say fast-acting yeast is suitable for ordinary as well as RAPID/FAST programmes, others that it reacts too quickly and results in a bread that is too 'airy'.

sourdough

Some recipes, particularly some traditional or foreign ones, require a sourdough starter. If you wish to make use of this, make up a small batch and keep it on hand. Simply mix a cup of flour with a cup of water and stir in a pinch of yeast. Place in a large plastic or glass container and leave unrefrigerated for about a week. The yeast gets to work and produces a small bubbling cauldron! Use some of the sourdough starter at least once a week and replace with equal quantities of flour and water, mixed. After the initial week, the mixture can be stored in the fridge for about two weeks, but ensure it is at room temperature before you use it.

sweeteners

Most recipes require a small amount of sweetener of some description to feed the yeast if not to flavour the dough. Some instruction manuals recommend caster (superfine) sugar as it mixes in easily. However, I have used granulated sugar successfully in most of my recipes. Brown sugar may also be used. Alternatively, some recipes use honey, which gives a very delicate sweetness, or golden (light corn) syrup. Be fairly accurate in measuring the sweetener or you may end up with a bland or sickly bread.

You may also like to experiment with malt extract, which is a syrup extracted from dried sprouted barley. This adds a sweetness to the bread as well as contributing a malty flavour. It is available from health food shops.

salt

Salt is included in all the bread recipes as it is essential for adding flavour as well as contributing to the final risen structure of the loaf. As it has a slowing effect on the activity of the yeast, too much salt will kill the yeast, while too little would make the dough rise so fast that it may collapse before it is baked.

fat

Fat has a shortening property, which gives bread its slightly crumbly texture and also improves its keeping properties. It may be added in the form of oil, margarine, butter or lard (shortening). Oil is easily incorporated in the breadmaker. Sunflower oil contributes little flavour to the bread, while extra virgin oil gives a lovely tang to Italian and continental-style bread. It is fine to use margarine suitable for cooking, butter or lard, but ensure that it is softened before being put in the bread pan or it may not mix in properly.

liquids

The recipes in this book include a range of liquids from water and milk to cider, beer and fruit juice. Most recipes use dried milk powder (non-fat dry milk) and water, which combine in the mixing process to give milk. Ordinary milk can also be used but is not recommended if you wish to use the timer function for a delayed start. It is important that the quantity of liquid used in the recipe is correct, or there can be problems with the shape and texture of the final loaf. Unfortunately, this tends to vary not only from recipe to recipe but also according to the breadmaker you have, the flour used and the cycle selected. Trial and error is really the only answer.

eggs

Eggs help to give an enriched dough and a more 'cakey' texture. Use fresh eggs and add the liquid ingredients. It is not advisable to use them with the timer function to delay the start time.

baking techniques

Having looked at the basic ingredients for breadmaking, it is important to explain some of the techniques and helpful hints for successful baking with the breadmaker. These are as follows:

- Always add ingredients in the order listed OR ensure that the yeast does not come in contact with the liquid as it will start to ferment too quickly.

- Ensure that the quantities you use suit the capacity of your breadmaker.

- 'Knock back' means giving the dough a few small punches to knock out air pockets.

- Don't over-work dough once it comes out of the machine, simply shape it.

- Don't over-flour work surfaces as this will dry out the dough and give an unpleasant, heavy texture.

- Ensure that baking (cookie) sheets are lightly greased with either a little oil or a smear of margarine or lard (shortening). Do not over-grease as this will give your bread an unpleasant flavour.

- 'Proving' dough means putting it in a warm place to allow it to rise. Generally, the dough should nearly double in size. Never put the dough anywhere hot as this would kill the yeast: similarly, do not put the dough anywhere cold or in a draught as this can kill the yeast or radically slow its action.

- Always completely cover proving dough. Use either a tea towel (dish cloth) or lightly greased clingfilm (plastic wrap) or place the dough inside a greased polythene bag.

- Always remove the covering from the dough before it is placed in the oven.

- Ensure that your oven is preheated before putting in the dough.

- Remove bread from the baking tin as soon as possible to prevent it going soggy.

- Bread slices better once it is cool.

- You can vary any of the oven-baked loaves by glazing them to give a shiny finish, or sprinkling them with nuts, seeds or herbs for extra flavour and texture. There are glazing and topping suggestions on page 121.

timings

Timings vary tremendously between different machines so it is not possible to give useful recipe times; for example, the BASIC programme can take 2½ hours in one machine and 4 hours in another. However, this will give you some ideas of the average length of time a programme should take.

- BASIC: 2½ hours
- WHOLEMEAL/WHEAT: 2¾ hours
- FRENCH/CONTINENTAL/SPECIALITY: 2¾ hours
- RAPID/FAST: 1–2 hours
- SWEET: 1½ hours
- CAKE: 2½ hours
- JAM: 1 hour
- PASTA: 15 minutes

problems and solutions

Be prepared for a few mishaps! Even if you have followed the recipe meticulously, as mentioned previously, breadmakers, their cycles and the ingredients do vary so you may have to make some adjustments. Here are a few common problems and their solutions.

Problem	Causes	Solution
Sunken top	Too wet	Reduce liquid by 15 ml/1 tbsp or increase flour by 30 ml/2 tbsp
Mushroom top	Bread has risen too quickly	Reduce yeast by 1.5 ml/¼ tsp or increase salt slightly
Uneven top	Too little moisture	Add 15 ml/1 tbsp water or reduce flour by 30 ml/2 tbsp
Bread has risen too much	Liquid too hot	Use tepid or cold water
	Too much yeast	Measure ingredients accurately
	Too much liquid	Measure ingredients accurately
Bread soggy in the middle	Too much syrup from canned fruit	Drain canned fruit thoroughly
	Too high a proportion of rich ingredient (e.g. nuts and grains)	Reduce amount of rich ingredient
Bread has large air holes	Too much liquid or liquid added too hot	Measure accurately and use tepid or cold water
Bread overbrowned	Too much sugar in mixture	Reduce the amount of sugar or sugary ingredients
Bread texture too dense	Not enough liquid	Add an extra 15 ml/1 tbsp water

your breadmaker storecupboard

The range of ingredients you can use in your breadmaker is limitless, though there are obviously some that form the basis of most bread recipes. The following list gives only a guide to the basic ingredients you may need and also some that I have found useful for flavouring breads. Your choice will depend on your taste and your spirit of adventure.

dried and packets

- Strong white bread flour
- Strong wholemeal bread flour
- Strong brown bread flour
- Malted granary flour
- Spelt wheat flour
- Rye flour
- Barley flour
- Buckwheat flour
- Cornmeal
- Semolina (cream of wheat)
- Barley flakes
- Cracked wheat
- Wheatgerm
- Rolled oats
- Oatmeal
- Traditional active dried yeast
- Fast-acting dried yeast
- Salt
- Sugar: granulated, caster (superfine) and brown
- Dried mixed fruit (fruit cake mix)
- Raisins
- No-need-to-soak dried apricots
- No-need-to-soak dried peaches

- No-need-to-soak dried pears
- Dried figs
- Walnut pieces
- Almonds: ground, flaked (slivered) and whole blanched
- Dried milk powder (non-fat dry milk)
- Sesame seeds
- Sunflower seeds
- Pumpkin seeds

cans and bottles
- Stoned (pitted) olives
- Canned anchovies
- Bottled tapenade
- Canned pineapple

herbs, flavourings and condiments
- Peppercorns
- Garlic purée (paste)
- Tomato purée
- Chutney
- Soy sauce
- Vinegar
- Chilli powder
- Curry paste
- Dried herbs: oregano, basil, mint, thyme, parsley etc.
- Spices: nutmeg, cinnamon, ground ginger, mixed (apple-pie) spice etc.
- Honey
- Peanut butter
- Strawberry jam (conserve)
- Golden (light corn) syrup
- Mustard powder
- Wholegrain mustard

- Sunflower oil
- Olive oil
- Cocoa (unsweetened chocolate) powder
- Plain (semi-sweet) chocolate
- Pesto
- Malt extract
- Vanilla essence (extract)
- Caraway seeds

fridge and freezer

- Fresh herbs: basil, thyme, parsley, sage, mint, coriander (cilantro) etc.
- Eggs
- Milk
- Butter
- Margarine
- Lard (shortening)
- Garlic
- Onions
- Potatoes
- Strong Cheddar cheese
- Blue cheese
- Cream cheese
- Parmesan cheese
- Bacon
- Ham
- Oranges
- Lemons
- Limes
- Bananas (stored in a cool place)

notes on the recipes

The following are guidelines to help you with the recipes. The breadmaker manuals and books I have studied all vary in whether they use weighed ingredients or cup measures.

I have attempted to give both options for all the recipes, but certain variations occur in translating one to another. It is important therefore to follow one or the other and also to make adjustments to quantities if you find this necessary for your specific breadmaker.

- Do not mix metric, imperial and American measures.

- All spoon measures are level: 1 tsp = 5 ml; 1 tbsp = 15 ml.

- Eggs are medium. If you use a different size, adjust the amount of added liquid accordingly.

- Thoroughly prepare fruit and vegetables before you start to assemble your ingredients. NEVER add fruits to the breadmaker without removing the stones first.

- Ensure that flour, yeast and fresh ingredients are in date and in good condition.

- Always use fresh herbs where possible, but if you replace them with dried use only half the amount. Dried versions of some herbs, such as parsley and coriander (cilantro), bear little resemblance to fresh and should not be used.

- Can and packet sizes are approximate.

- Thoroughly drain canned foods before adding to the breadmaker, but read the recipe to see if liquid should be reserved.

- Use good-quality oil such as sunflower or olive. Where the recipe specifies olive oil, extra virgin gives the best flavour.

- Ensure that margarine is suitable for cooking and that butter and margarine are softened before adding to the breadmaker.

- Use your discretion when substituting ingredients in recipes.

- Always preheat a conventional oven and cook on the centre shelf. Fan ovens do not require preheating.

- Oven temperatures vary so baking times have to be approximate. Adjust cooking times and temperatures according to manufacturer's instructions.

- Do not use perishable ingredients such as milk and eggs when using the timer to delay the start time.

- Only use fast-acting yeast in the RAPID recipes.

- Measure ingredients carefully but make a note on your recipe if you have found it necessary to adjust quantities.

- Loaf sizes are designed to give an approximate guide.

storing your bread

Ideally, eat your bread on the day that you make it. Allow it to cool first on a wire rack, then slice with a very sharp bread knife. However, if this is not possible, you can store bread either in a sealed plastic bag or closely wrapped in clingfilm (plastic wrap), then placed in an airtight container or in the fridge. Home-made bread dries out more quickly than the commercial variety, so it is important to wrap it well.

Bread also stores well in the freezer. Allow it to cool thoroughly, then wrap well in clingfilm and place in the freezer. Defrost at room temperature for a couple of hours before eating.

Bread that has dried out can either be used in desserts such as bread and butter pudding and bread pudding or be made into crumbs and used as a coating for food or in stuffing mixtures.

basic bread
recipes

Some basic bread recipes to whet your appetite and give you a feel for how your breadmaker works. These are straightforward recipes that are delicious in their own right, but once you have a feel for the basic techniques, experiment by adding your own flavourings.

basic
white bread

I have given separate quantities for small, medium and large loaves so you have accurate amounts whatever size you choose.

MAKES 1 SMALL, MEDIUM OR LARGE LOAF
BASIC SETTING

water	150 ml/¼ pt/⅔ cup
dried milk powder (non-fat dry milk)	15 ml/1 tbsp
caster (superfine) sugar	15 ml/1 tbsp
salt	2.5 ml/½ tsp
sunflower oil	30 ml/2 tbsp
strong white bread flour	225 g/8 oz/2 cups
traditional active dried yeast	5 ml/1 tsp

MAKES 1 MEDIUM LOAF
BASIC SETTING

water	300 ml/½ pt/1¼ cups
dried milk powder (non-fat dry milk)	30 ml/2 tbsp
caster (superfine) sugar	20 ml/1½ tbsp
salt	5 ml/1 tsp
sunflower oil	45 ml/3 tbsp
strong white bread flour	350 g/12 oz/3 cups
traditional active dried yeast	7.5 ml/1½ tsp

MAKES 1 LARGE LOAF
BASIC SETTING

water	400 ml/14 fl oz/1¾ cups
dried milk powder (non-fat dry milk)	60 ml/2 tbsp
caster (superfine) sugar	45 ml/3 tbsp
salt	7.5 ml/1½ tsp
sunflower oil	60 ml/4 tbsp
strong white bread flour	450 g/1 lb/4 cups
traditional active dried yeast	10 ml/1 tsp

1 Place all the ingredients in the bread pan in the order listed. Place the pan in the breadmaker, ensuring that it is locked into position.

2 Close the lid, select the BASIC setting and press START.

3 When the cycle is complete, carefully remove the pan using oven gloves. Tip out the loaf on to a cooling rack and allow to cool before slicing.

brown bread

I have given separate quantities for small, medium and large loaves so you don't have to do any calculating.

MAKES 1 SMALL LOAF
BASIC SETTING

water	150 ml/¼ pt/⅔ cup
dried milk powder (non-fat dry milk)	15 ml/1 tbsp
caster (superfine) sugar	15 ml/1 tbsp
salt	2.5 ml/½ tsp
sunflower oil	30 ml/2 tbsp
strong brown bread flour	225 g/8 oz/2 cups
traditional active dried yeast	5 ml/1 tsp

MAKES 1 MEDIUM LOAF
BASIC SETTING

water	300 ml/½ pt/1¼ cups
dried milk powder (non-fat dry milk)	30 ml/2 tbsp
caster (superfine) sugar	20 ml/1½ tbsp
salt	5 ml/1 tsp
sunflower oil	45 ml/3 tbsp
strong brown bread flour	350 g/12 oz/3 cups
traditional active dried yeast	7.5 ml/1½ tsp

MAKES 1 LARGE LOAF
BASIC SETTING

water	400 ml/14 fl oz/1¾ cups
dried milk powder (non-fat dry milk)	60 ml/2 tbsp
caster (superfine) sugar	45 ml/3 tbsp
salt	7.5 ml/1½ tsp
sunflower oil	60 ml/4 tbsp
strong brown bread flour	450 g/1 lb/4 cups
traditional active dried yeast	10 ml/1 tsp

1 Place all the ingredients in the bread pan in the order listed. Place the pan in the breadmaker, ensuring that it is locked into position.

2 Close the lid, select the BASIC setting and press START.

3 When the cycle is complete, carefully remove the pan using oven gloves. Tip out the loaf on to a cooling rack and allow to cool before slicing.

variety crown bread

This loaf is made up of individual rolls with different toppings. Choose from those suggested – or use your imagination!

MAKES 1 SMALL LOAF
DOUGH SETTING

water	300 ml/½ pt/1¼ cups
olive oil	40 ml/2½ tbsp
dried milk powder (non-fat dry milk)	30 ml/2 tbsp
honey	20 ml/1½ tbsp
salt	5 ml/1 tsp
strong white bread flour	100 g/4 oz/1 cup
spelt flour	100 g/4 oz/1 cup
strong wholemeal bread flour	100 g/4 oz/1 cup
traditional active dried yeast	7.5 ml/1½ tsp
For the toppings	
milk for brushing	a little
choose a few from the following: sesame seeds, poppy seeds, sunflower seeds, cracked wheat, pumpkin seeds, grated cheese, crushed peanuts	

1 Place all the ingredients in the bread pan in the order listed. Place the pan in the breadmaker, ensuring that it is locked into position.

2 Close the lid, select the DOUGH setting and press START.

3 When the cycle is complete, carefully remove the pan using oven gloves and tip the dough out on to a lightly floured work surface.

4 Knock back the dough, then divide into seven equal-sized pieces. Roll each piece into a smooth ball.

5 Arrange the rolls on a lightly greased baking (cookie) sheet with one roll in the middle and the others closely packed surrounding it.

6 Brush the surface of the rolls with milk, then scatter your selected toppings over the rolls so that people will be able to choose the topping they like.

7 Cover loosely with lightly greased clingfilm (plastic wrap) and leave in a warm place to prove for about 20 minutes.

8 Bake in a preheated oven at 220°C/425°F/gas mark 7/ fan oven 200°C for about 20–25 minutes.

light wholemeal bread

I use half-and-half strong white bread flour and wholemeal flour here as using just wholemeal results in a rather heavy loaf.

MAKES 1 SMALL LOAF
WHOLEMEAL SETTING

water	150 ml/¼ pt/⅔ cup
dried milk powder (non-fat dry milk)	15 ml/1 tbsp
caster (superfine) sugar	15 ml/1 tbsp
salt	2.5 ml/½ tsp
sunflower oil	30 ml/2 tbsp
strong white bread flour	100 g/4 oz/1 cup
wholemeal bread flour	100 g/4 oz/1 cup
traditional active dried yeast	5 ml/1 tsp

MAKES 1 MEDIUM LOAF
WHOLEMEAL SETTING

water	300 ml/½ pt/1¼ cups
dried milk powder (non-fat dry milk)	30 ml/2 tbsp
caster (superfine) sugar	20 ml/1½ tbsp
salt	5 ml/1 tsp
sunflower oil	40 ml/2½ tbsp
strong white bread flour	175 g/6 oz/1½ cups
wholemeal bread flour	175 g/6 oz/1½ cups
traditional active dried yeast	7.5 ml/1½ tsp

MAKES 1 LARGE LOAF
WHOLEMEAL SETTING

water	400 ml/14 fl oz/1¾ cups
dried milk powder (non-fat dry milk)	60 ml/2 tbsp
caster (superfine) sugar	45 ml/3 tbsp
salt	7.5 ml/1½ tsp
sunflower oil	60 ml/4 tbsp
strong white bread flour	225 g/8 oz/2 cups
wholemeal bread flour	225 g/8 oz/2 cups
traditional active dried yeast	10 ml/1 tsp

1 Place all the ingredients in the bread pan in the order listed. Place the pan in the breadmaker, ensuring that it is locked into position.

2 Close the lid, select the WHOLEMEAL setting and press START.

3 When the cycle is complete, carefully remove the pan using oven gloves. Tip out the loaf on to a cooling rack and allow to cool before slicing.

granary bread

Serve this lovely textured bread with a good-flavoured British cheese, a tomato or two and home-made chutney or pickles.

 MAKES 1 MEDIUM LOAF
WHOLEMEAL SETTING

water	300 ml/½ pt/1¼ cups
dried milk powder (non-fat dry milk)	30 ml/2 tbsp
caster (superfine) sugar	20 ml/1½ tbsp
salt	5 ml/1 tsp
sunflower oil	40 ml/2½ tbsp
strong white bread flour	175 g/6 oz/1½ cups
granary flour	175 g/6 oz/1½ cups
traditional active dried yeast	6 ml/1¼ tsp

1 Place all the ingredients in the bread pan in the order listed. Place the pan in the breadmaker, ensuring that it is locked into position.

2 Close the lid, select the WHOLEMEAL setting and press START.

3 When the cycle is complete, carefully remove the pan using oven gloves and tip the loaf out on to a cooling rack and allow to cool before slicing.

grain breads

A selection of bread recipes using an assortment of different grains. Dabble with wheat, oats, barley and a range of flours to discover the different flavours and textures they produce. Visit any good wholefood or health food store to discover other unusual grains and flours you may like to try.

cheese and mint semolina bread

An unusual Middle Eastern-style bread that makes a good accompaniment to the spicy soups and stews from this part of the world.

MAKES 1 LARGE LOAF
BASIC SETTING

water	300 ml/½ pt/1¼ cups
sunflower oil	45 ml/3 tbsp
fresh mint leaves	a good handful
salt	7.5 ml/1½ tsp
sugar	7.5 ml/1½ tsp
strong Cheddar cheese	100 g/4 oz/1 cup, grated
semolina (cream of wheat) flour	400 g/14 oz/3½ cup
traditional active dried yeast	10 ml/2 tsp

1 Place all the ingredients in the bread pan in the order listed. Place the pan in the breadmaker, ensuring that it is locked into position.

2 Close the lid, select the BASIC setting and press START.

3 When the cycle is complete, carefully remove the pan using oven gloves and tip the loaf out on to a cooling rack and allow to cool before slicing.

malted oat loaf

A healthy bread with a wonderfully crumbly texture and malty flavour. Enjoy it with fresh fruit and strong cheese.

MAKES 1 MEDIUM LOAF
BASIC SETTING

water	350 ml/¾ pt/1⅓ cups
sunflower oil	30 ml/2 tbsp
malt extract	30 ml/2 tbsp
dried milk powder (non-fat dry milk)	60 ml/4 tbsp
salt	7.5 ml/1½ tsp
strong white bread flour	300 g/11 oz/2¾ cups
rolled oats	175 g/6 oz/1½ cups
traditional active dried yeast	10 ml/2 tsp

1 Place all the ingredients in the bread pan in the order listed. Place the pan in the breadmaker, ensuring that it is locked into position.

2 Close the lid, select the BASIC setting and press START.

3 When the cycle is complete, carefully remove the pan using oven gloves and tip the loaf out on to a cooling rack and allow to cool before slicing.

malted bran loaf

This is lovely sliced and buttered at teatime. Rolled bran flakes are available from health food stores.

MAKES 1 MEDIUM LOAF
BASIC SETTING

water	350 ml/¾ pt/1⅓ cups
sunflower oil	30 ml/2 tbsp
malt extract	30 ml/2 tbsp
dried milk powder (non-fat dry milk)	60 ml/4 tbsp
salt	7.5 ml/1½ tsp
strong white bread flour	300 g/11 oz/2¾ cups
rolled bran flakes	175 g/6 oz/1½ cups
traditional active dried yeast	5 ml/1 tsp

1 Place all the ingredients in the bread pan in the order listed. Place the pan in the breadmaker, ensuring that it is locked into position.

2 Close the lid, select the BASIC setting and press START.

3 When the cycle is complete, carefully remove the pan using oven gloves and tip the loaf out on to a cooling rack and allow to cool before slicing.

rye bread

This is quite a dense, heavy rye bread that is excellent for using as a tasty base for open sandwiches.

MAKES 1 MEDIUM LOAF
WHOLEMEAL SETTING

water	250 ml/8 fl oz/1 cup
margarine	15 ml/1 tbsp
caster (superfine) sugar	5 ml/1 tsp
salt	10 ml/2 tsp
strong white bread flour	225 g/8 oz/2 cups
rye flour	225 g/8 oz/2 cups
traditional active dried yeast	7.5 ml/1½ tsp

1 Place all the ingredients in the bread pan in the order listed. Place the pan in the breadmaker, ensuring that it is locked into position.

2 Close the lid, select the WHOLEMEAL setting and press START.

3 When the cycle is complete, carefully remove the pan using oven gloves. Tip the loaf out on to a cooling rack and allow to cool before slicing.

rye, onion, potato and fennel loaf

A moist, close-textured bread that lends itself equally well as an accompaniment to cheese and pickles as soups and stews.

MAKES 1 MEDIUM LOAF
WHOLEMEAL SETTING

water	250 ml/8 fl oz/1 cup
sunflower oil	30 ml/2 tbsp
vinegar	60 ml/4 tbsp
salt	7.5 ml/1½ tsp
sugar	30 ml/2 tbsp
fennel seeds	30 ml/2 tbsp
large onion	1, grated
raw unpeeled boiling potato	1, grated
strong white bread flour	350 g/12 oz/3 cups
rye flour	100 g/4 oz/1 cup
traditional active dried yeast	10 ml/2 tsp

1 Place all the ingredients in the bread pan in the order listed. Place the pan in the breadmaker, ensuring that it is locked into position.

2 Close the lid, select the WHOLEMEAL setting and press START.

3 When the cycle is complete, carefully remove the pan using oven gloves and tip the loaf out on to a cooling rack and allow to cool before slicing.

carrot and fancy mustard bread

Try this well-flavoured bread with soup or grilled (broiled) meat or fish – and do experiment with different mustards.

MAKES 1 SMALL LOAF
WHOLEMEAL SETTING

water	300 ml/½ pt/1¼ cups
carrots	275 g/10 oz/1⅔ cups, grated
tomato and basil mustard with honey or your favourite mustard	60 ml/4 tbsp
sunflower oil	20 ml/1½ tbsp
caster (superfine) sugar	20 ml/1½ tbsp
salt	5 ml/1 tsp
strong white bread flour	225 g/8 oz/2 cups
strong wholemeal bread flour	100 g/4 oz/1 cup
yellow cornmeal	50 g/2 oz/½ cup
traditional active dried yeast	7.5 ml/1½ tsp

1 Place all the ingredients in the bread pan in the order listed. Place the pan in the breadmaker, ensuring that it is locked into position.

2 Close the lid, select the WHOLEMEAL setting and press START.

3 When the cycle is complete, carefully remove the pan using oven gloves and tip the loaf out on to a cooling rack and allow to cool before slicing.

spelt bread with sesame seeds

This bread has a thick crispy crust and a pronounced wheaty flavour. The dough is quite runny and needs to be poured.

MAKES 2 SMALL LOAVES
DOUGH SETTING

water	400 ml/14 fl oz/1¾ cups
honey	15 ml/1 tbsp
salt	7.5 ml/1½ tsp
margarine	15 ml/1 tbsp
strong white bread flour	225 g/8 oz/2 cups
spelt flour	225 g/8 oz/2 cups
traditional active dried yeast	7.5 ml/1½ tsp
sesame seeds	30 ml/2 tbsp

1 Place all the ingredients in the bread pan in the order listed. Place the pan in the breadmaker, ensuring that it is locked into position.

2 Close the lid, select the DOUGH setting and press START.

3 When the cycle is complete, carefully remove the pan using oven gloves and pour the dough into two lightly greased 450 g/1 lb loaf tins.

4 Sprinkle with the sesame seeds, cover loosely with lightly greased clingfilm (plastic wrap) and leave in a warm place to prove for 15 minutes.

5 Bake in a preheated oven at 190°C/375°F/gas mark 5/ fan oven 170°C for about 45 minutes.

6 Tip the loaf out on a cooling rack and allow to cool before slicing.

sun-dried tomato and rosemary bread

A really 'gutsy' bread and a good accompaniment to grilled (broiled) meat or fish. Oregano or thyme could be used.

MAKES 1 MEDIUM LOAF
WHOLEMEAL SETTING

sun-dried tomatoes	100 g/4 oz
warm water	250 ml/8 fl oz/1 cup
olive oil	30 ml/2 tbsp
fresh rosemary sprigs	a good handful
salt	7.5 ml/1½ tsp
sugar	15 ml/1 tbsp
strong white bread flour	375 g/13 oz/3¼ cups
rolled oats	125 g/4½ oz/1 cup + 2 tbsp
traditional active dried yeast	5 ml/1 tsp

1 Soak the tomatoes in the warm water for 15 minutes. Allow to cool.

2 Place the tomatoes and the soaking water in the bread pan and add the remaining ingredients in the order listed. Place the pan in the breadmaker, ensuring that it is locked in position.

3 Close the lid, select the WHOLEMEAL setting and press START.

4 When the cycle is complete, carefully remove the pan using oven gloves and tip the loaf out on to a cooling rack and allow to cool before slicing.

very light seed and granary loaf

This recipe gives a smallish amount of dough, but don't increase the quantities as it rises so well it fills a standard breadmaker.

MAKES 1 MEDIUM LOAF
WHOLEMEAL SETTING

water	300 ml/½ pt/1¼ cups
dried milk powder (non-fat dry milk)	15 ml/1 tbsp
brown sugar	40 ml/2½ tbsp
salt	5 ml/1 tsp
sunflower oil	30 ml/2 tbsp
strong white bread flour	225 g/8 oz/2 cups
granary flour	100 g/4 oz/1 cup
sesame seeds	15 ml/1 tbsp
pumpkin seeds	15 ml/1 tbsp
sunflower seeds	15 ml/1 tbsp
traditional active dried yeast	6 ml/1¼ tsp

1 Place all the ingredients in the bread pan in the order listed. Place the pan in the breadmaker, ensuring that it is locked into position.

2 Close the lid, select the WHOLEMEAL setting and press START.

3 When the cycle is complete, carefully remove the pan using oven gloves and tip the loaf out on to a cooling rack and allow to cool before slicing.

mango, banana and seed loaf

This moist tea bread is as good for breakfast as it is for afternoon tea! Serve as it is or with butter and honey.

MAKES 1 LARGE LOAF
BASIC SETTING

sun-dried mango	100 g/4 oz/1 cup
cold water	300 ml/½ pt/1¼ cups
sunflower oil	15 ml/1 tbsp
banana	1, mashed
salt	5 ml/1 tsp
sugar	30 ml/2 tbsp
dried milk powder (non-fat dry milk)	30 ml/2 tbsp
strong white bread flour	450 g/1 lb/4 cups
ground cinnamon	5 ml/1 tsp
traditional active dried yeast	5 ml/1 tsp
pumpkin seeds	25 g/1 oz/¼ cup
sunflower seeds	25 g/1 oz/¼ cup

1 Soak the mango in enough warm water to cover for about 15 minutes.

2 Place all the remaining ingredients except the seeds in the bread pan in the order listed. Place the pan in the breadmaker, ensuring that it is locked into position.

3 Close the lid, select the BASIC setting and press START.

4 Drain the water from the mango. Add the mango and seeds at the buzzer or after the first kneading.

5 When the cycle is complete, carefully remove the pan using oven gloves and tip the loaf out on to a cooling rack and allow to cool before slicing.

oatmeal sourdough bread

These quantities give the right size loaf for my family as it is quite filling, but you could increase the measures proportionally.

MAKES 1 SMALL LOAF
WHOLEMEAL SETTING

milk	150 ml/¼ pt/½ cup
oatmeal	100 g/4 oz/1 cup
sourdough starter	60 ml/4 tbsp
water	60 ml/4 tbsp
honey	5 ml/1 tbsp
salt	2.5 ml/½ tsp
strong white bread flour	175 g/6 oz/1½ cups
traditional active dried yeast	5 ml/1 tsp

1 Place all the ingredients in the bread pan in the order listed. Place the pan in the breadmaker, ensuring that it is locked into position.

2 Close the lid, select the WHOLEMEAL setting and press START.

3 When the cycle is complete, carefully remove the pan using oven gloves and tip the loaf out on to a cooling rack and allow to cool before slicing.

savoury breads

This chapter offers a whole host of ideas for savoury breads – the problem is knowing when to stop experimenting with flavours! Strong flavours work well in bread and it is important to remember that the flour tends to absorb and dilute flavours, so be bold and use strong cheeses, punchy herbs and spices and lingering flavours.

tapenade bread

I like to use an olive, lemon and garlic tapenade for this bread, but you can use your own particular favourite.

MAKES 1 LARGE LOAF
WHOLEMEAL SETTING

water	300 ml/½ pt/1¼ cups
olive oil	20 ml/1½ tbsp
sugar	5 ml/1 tsp
salt	5 ml/1 tsp
freshly ground black pepper	2.5 ml/½ tsp
tapenade	90 ml/6 tbsp
strong white bread flour	225 g/8 oz/2 cups
strong wholemeal bread flour	100 g/4 oz/1 cup
granary flour	75 g/3 oz/¾ cup
traditional active dried yeast	10 ml/2 tsp

1 Place all the ingredients in the bread pan in the order listed. Place the pan in the breadmaker, ensuring that it is locked in position.

2 Close the lid, select the WHOLEMEAL setting and press START.

3 When the cycle is complete, carefully remove the pan using oven gloves and tip the loaf out on to a cooling rack and allow to cool before slicing.

courgette and tomato bread

This is a moist bread, best eaten warm from the oven with either grilled (broiled) meat or a large chunk of Brie.

MAKES 1 LARGE LOAF
FRENCH OR BASIC SETTING

For the flavouring

olive oil	15 ml/1 tbsp
shallot	1, chopped
courgette (zucchini)	1, diced
large tomatoes	2, sliced
tomato purée (paste)	30 ml/2 tbsp
basil leaves	10, torn
salt and freshly ground black pepper	

For the dough

water	100 ml/3½ fl oz/½ cup
olive oil	30 ml/2 tbsp
sugar	10 ml/2 tsp
salt	7.5 ml/1½ tsp
ground black pepper	2.5 ml/½ tsp
strong white bread flour	400 g/14 oz/3½ cups
traditional active dried yeast	10 ml/2 tsp

1 To make the flavouring, heat the oil in a frying pan. Add the shallot and courgette and cook gently until softened.

2 Stir in the tomato slices and continue to cook until pulpy.

3 Stir in the tomato purée and basil and season to taste.

4 Place the mixture in the bread pan, then add all the dough ingredients in the order listed. Place the pan in the breadmaker, ensuring that it is locked in position.

5 Close the lid, select the FRENCH or BASIC setting and press START.

6 When the cycle is complete, carefully remove the pan using oven gloves and tip the loaf out on to a cooling rack and allow to cool before slicing.

chilli avocado bread

A moist Mexican-style bread – with a good chilli kick – that is ideal for serving with dips or spare ribs.

MAKES 1 LARGE LOAF
FRENCH OR BASIC SETTING

water	175 ml/6 fl oz/¾ cup
olive oil	20 ml/1½ tbsp
avocado pear	1, skinned and stoned (pitted)
cold fried tomatoes	75 g/ 3 oz
sugar	10 ml/2 tsp
salt	5 ml/1 tsp
freshly ground black pepper	2.5 ml/½ tsp
chilli powder	10 ml/2 tsp
strong white bread flour	350 g/12 oz/3 cups
malted granary flour	75 g/3 oz/¾ cup
traditional active dried yeast	10 ml/2 tsp

1 Place all the ingredients in the bread pan in the order listed. Place the pan in the breadmaker, ensuring that it is locked into position.

2 Close the lid, select the FRENCH or BASIC setting and press START.

3 When the cycle is complete, carefully remove the pan using oven gloves and tip the loaf out on to a cooling rack and allow to cool before slicing.

hawaiian bread

Choose a really strong cheese for this recipe, such as a Cheddar, for maximum flavour to complement the sweet pineapple.

MAKES 1 MEDIUM LOAF
BASIC SETTING

can of pineapple pieces	225 g/8 oz/small, drained and juice reserved
sunflower oil	30 ml/2 tbsp
strong cheese	175 g/6 oz/1½ cups, grated
salt	5 ml/1 tsp
strong white bread flour	350 g/12 oz/3 cups
traditional active dried yeast	7.5 ml/1½ tsp
small slices of ham	6, chopped

1 Make up the reserved pineapple juice to 175 ml/6 fl oz/ ¾ cup with water. Pour into the bread pan, then add all the remaining ingredients except the ham in the order listed. Place the pan in the breadmaker, ensuring it is locked into position.

2 Close the lid, select the BASIC setting and press START.

3 Add the ham at the buzzer or after the first kneading.

4 When the cycle is complete, carefully remove the pan using oven gloves and tip the loaf out on to a cooling rack and allow to cool before slicing.

blue cheese and walnut bread

The classic and classy combination of blue cheese and walnuts – delicious with cold meats or with cheese and fresh fruit.

MAKES 1 LARGE LOAF
WHOLEMEAL SETTING

water	350 ml/12 fl oz/1⅓ cups
butter	25 g/1 oz/2 tbsp
strong blue cheese	175 g/6 oz/1½ cups, crumbled
caster (superfine) sugar	15 ml/1 tbsp
dried milk powder (non-fat dry milk)	15 ml/1 tbsp
salt	7.5 ml/1½ tsp
strong white bread flour	225 g/8 oz/2 cups
strong wholemeal bread flour	225 g/8 oz/2 cups
traditional active dried yeast	7.5 ml/1½ tsp
walnuts	100 g/4 oz/1 cup

1 Place all the ingredients except the nuts in the bread pan in the order listed. Place the pan in the breadmaker, ensuring that it is locked into position.

2 Close the lid, select the WHOLEMEAL setting and press START.

3 Add the nuts at the buzzer or after the first kneading.

4 When the cycle is complete, carefully remove the pan using oven gloves and tip the loaf out on to a cooling rack and allow to cool before slicing.

cheese and bean bread

Choose a really strong-flavoured cheese for this recipe, such as a farmhouse Cheddar or one of the newish salty Cornish cheeses.

MAKES 1 LARGE LOAF
BASIC SETTING

water	300 ml/½ pt/1¼ cups
sunflower oil	45 ml/3 tbsp
strong cheese	175 g/6 oz/1½ cups, grated
wholegrain mustard	30 ml/2 tbsp
dried milk powder (non-fat dry milk)	45 ml/3 tbsp
salt	7.5 ml/1½ tsp
sugar	20 ml/1½ tbsp
strong white bread flour	350 g/12 oz/3 cups
granary flour	75 g/3 oz/¾ cup
traditional active dried yeast	7.5 ml/1½ tsp
cold cooked French (green) beans	175 g/6 oz, chopped

1 Place all the ingredients except the beans in the bread pan in the order listed. Place the pan in the breadmaker, ensuring that it is locked into position.

2 Close the lid, select the BASIC setting and press START.

3 Add the beans at the buzzer or after the first kneading.

4 When the cycle is complete, carefully remove the pan using oven gloves and tip the loaf out on to a cooling rack and allow to cool before slicing.

fast basil, chive and cheese bread

This bread is made using the RAPID cycle. You must use fast-acting yeast and warm water for the loaf to be successful.

 MAKES 1 MEDIUM LOAF
RAPID SETTING

warm water	300 ml/½ pt/1¼ cups
sunflower oil	45 ml/3 tbsp
strong cheese	175 g/6 oz/1½ cups, grated
fresh basil leaves	good handful
fresh chives	60 ml/4 tbsp, snipped
dried milk powder (non-fat dry milk)	30 ml/2 tbsp
salt	5 ml/1 tsp
sugar	10 ml/2 tsp
strong white bread flour	350 g/12 oz/3 cups
fast-acting yeast	7.5 ml/1½ tsp

1 Place all the ingredients in the bread pan in the order listed. Place the pan in the breadmaker, ensuring that it is locked into position.

2 Close the lid, select the RAPID setting and press START.

3 When the cycle is complete, carefully remove the pan using oven gloves and tip the loaf out on to a cooling rack and allow to cool before slicing.

ploughman's bread

This bread makes an ideal lunch with plenty of strong Cheddar cheese. Try using other pickles such as gherkins (cornichons).

MAKES 1 LARGE LOAF
BASIC SETTING

water	375 ml/13 fl oz/1½ cups
sunflower oil	15 ml/1 tbsp
salt	5 ml/1 tsp
sugar	15 ml/1 tbsp
dried milk powder (non-fat dry milk)	15 ml/1 tbsp
pickled onions	100 g/4 oz, halved
Cheddar cheese	175 g/6 oz/1½ cups, grated
strong white bread flour	225 g/8 oz/2 cups
granary flour	225 g/8 oz/2 cups
traditional active dried yeast	7.5 ml/1½ tsp

1 Place all the ingredients in the bread pan in the order listed. Place the pan in the breadmaker, ensuring that it is locked into position.

2 Close the lid, select the BASIC setting and press START.

3 When the cycle is complete, carefully remove the pan using oven gloves and tip the loaf out on to a cooling rack and allow to cool before slicing.

fast ham and chutney bread

It is important to use fast-acting yeast and warm water for this recipe, which uses the RAPID setting, to be successful.

MAKES 1 MEDIUM LOAF
RAPID SETTING

warm water	300 ml/½ pt/1¼ cups
sunflower oil	45 ml/3 tbsp
chutney	90 ml/6 tbsp
slices of ham	8, chopped
dried milk powder (non-fat dry milk)	30 ml/2 tbsp
salt	5 ml/1 tsp
sugar	10 ml/2 tsp
strong white bread flour	225 g/8 oz/2 cups
strong wholemeal bread flour	100 g/4 oz/1 cup
fast-acting yeast	7.5 ml/1½ tsp

1 Place all the ingredients in the bread pan in the order listed. Place the pan in the breadmaker, ensuring that it is locked in position.

2 Close the lid, select the RAPID setting and press START.

3 When the cycle is complete, carefully remove the pan using oven gloves and tip the loaf out on to a cooling rack and allow to cool before slicing.

sun-dried pepper and basil bread

The sun-dried peppers make this a very 'punchy' bread. It is best eaten with a selection of cheeses and cold meats.

 MAKES 1 LARGE LOAF
FRENCH OR BASIC SETTING

water	150 ml/¼ pt/⅔ cup
milk	15 ml/1 tbsp
caster (superfine) sugar	7.5 ml/1½ tsp
salt	7.5 ml/1½ tsp
black pepper	2.5 ml/½ tsp
olive oil	45 ml/3 tbsp
sun-dried peppers	50 g/2 oz
fresh basil leaves	a good handful
strong white bread flour	450 g/1 lb/4 cups
traditional active dried yeast	5 ml/1 tsp

1 Place all the ingredients in the bread pan in the order listed. Place the pan in the breadmaker, ensuring that it is locked in position.

2 Close the lid, select the FRENCH setting if you have it otherwise the BASIC setting and press START.

3 When the cycle is complete, carefully remove the pan using oven gloves and tip the loaf out on to a cooling rack and allow to cool before slicing.

sage and crispy bacon loaf

Lovely with cheese, salad or poached fish. To save time, you could use crumbled ready-cooked crispy bacon rashers.

MAKES 1 LARGE LOAF
WHOLEMEAL SETTING

water	300 ml/½ pt/1¼ cups
butter	15 ml/1 tbsp
fresh sage leaves	a good handful
streaky bacon rashers (slices)	8, grilled (broiled) and chopped
salt	7.5 ml/1½ tsp
black pepper	1.5 ml/¼ tsp
sugar	10 ml/2 tsp
strong white bread flour	250 g/9 oz/2¼ cups
strong wholemeal bread flour	250 g/9 oz/2¼ cups
traditional active dried yeast	5 ml/1 tsp

1 Place all the ingredients in the bread pan in the order listed. Place the pan in the breadmaker, ensuring that it is locked in position.

2 Close the lid, select the WHOLEMEAL setting and press START.

3 When the cycle is complete, carefully remove the pan using oven gloves and tip the loaf out on to a cooling rack and allow to cool before slicing.

smoked salmon platter

Enjoy large wedges of this with a tomato and basil salad or cut into smaller pieces for a party buffet.

**MAKES 1 LARGE LOAF
DOUGH SETTING**

For the dough

water	300 ml/½ pt/1¼ cups
olive oil	45 ml/3 tbsp
salt	7.5 ml/1½ tsp
sugar	7.5 ml/1½ tsp
strong white bread flour	450 g/1 lb/4 cups
traditional active dried yeast	10 ml/2 tsp

For the topping

tomato purée (paste)	30 ml/2 tbsp
large red onion	1, sliced
courgette (zucchini)	1, sliced
large tomato	1, sliced
smoked salmon	175 g/6 oz, cut into ribbons
fresh basil leaves	a good handful, torn
Mozzarella cheese	100 g/4 oz/1 cup, grated
coarse salt and freshly ground black pepper	

1 To make the dough, place all the ingredients in the bread pan in the order listed. Place the pan in the breadmaker, ensuring that it is locked into position.

2 Close the lid, select the DOUGH setting and press START.

3 When the cycle is complete, carefully remove the pan using oven gloves and tip the dough out on to a lightly floured work surface. Knock back the dough, then roll out to line a 30 x 20 cm/12 x 8 in baking (cookie) sheet.

4 To make the topping, spread the tomato purée over the dough, then arrange the remaining ingredients over, finishing with Mozzarella and seasoning.

5 Cover with lightly greased clingfilm (plastic wrap) and leave in a warm place to prove for 10 minutes, then bake in a preheated oven at 220°C/425°F/gas mark 7/ fan oven 200°C for 15 minutes.

potato and goats' cheese bread

Try this warm with grilled (broiled) meat or fish or a tomato salad. Try a range of goats' cheeses to find your favourite.

MAKES 1 LARGE LOAF
WHOLEMEAL SETTING

water	300 ml/½ pt/1¼ cups
egg	1
cold mashed potato	175 g/6 oz/1 cup
hard goats' cheese	175 g/6 oz/1½ cups, grated
sunflower oil	20 ml/1½ tbsp
dried milk powder (non-fat dry milk)	45 ml/3 tbsp
salt	5 ml/1 tsp
freshly ground black pepper	2.5 ml/½ tsp
sugar	15 ml/1 tbsp
strong white bread flour	400 g/14 oz/3½ cups
traditional active dried yeast	10 ml/2 tsp

1 Place all the ingredients in the bread pan in the order listed. Place the pan in the breadmaker, ensuring that it is locked in position.

2 Close the lid, select the BASIC setting and press START.

3 When the cycle is complete, carefully remove the pan using oven gloves and tip the loaf out on to a cooling rack and allow to cool before slicing.

garlic and oregano bread

This is a very garlicky bread with a good measure of oregano. It makes a wonderful accompaniment to soups, stews and steak.

MAKES 1 LARGE LOAF
FRENCH OR BASIC SETTING

water	200 ml/7 fl oz/1 cup
salt	7.5 ml/1½ tsp
olive oil	30 ml/2 tbsp
strong white bread flour	450 g/1 lb/4 cups
fresh oregano leaves	good handful
large garlic cloves	4, crushed
traditional active dried yeast	5 ml/1 tsp

1 Place all the ingredients in the bread pan in the order listed. Place the pan in the breadmaker, ensuring that it is locked in position.

2 Close the lid, select the FRENCH setting if you have it or otherwise the BASIC setting and press START.

3 When the cycle is complete, carefully remove the pan using oven gloves and tip the loaf out on to a cooling rack and allow to cool before slicing.

continental and foreign breads

This chapter deals with some exciting breads from around the world and demonstrates how easy it is to get tasty and authentic results using the breadmaker. These breads make ideal accompaniments to foreign and exotic meals.

fried bread

An Indian-style bread that lends itself well to dhals, hot or mild curries and many other spicy Asian dishes.

MAKES 8
DOUGH SETTING

water	300 ml/½ pt/1¼ cups
olive oil	40 ml/2½ tbsp
dried milk powder (non-fat dry milk)	30 ml/2 tbsp
honey	20 ml/1½ tbsp
salt	5 ml/1 tsp
strong white bread flour	100 g/4 oz/1 cup
spelt flour	100 g/4 oz/1 cup
strong wholemeal bread flour	100 g/4 oz/1 cup
traditional active dried yeast	7.5 ml/1½ tsp
oil for shallow-frying	

1 Place all the ingredients in the bread pan in the order listed. Place the pan in the breadmaker, ensuring that it is locked in position.

2 Close the lid, select the DOUGH setting and press START.

3 When the cycle is complete, carefully remove the pan using oven gloves and tip the loaf out on to a lightly floured work surface.

4 Knock back the dough, then divide into eight equal-sized pieces. Roll them out to give very flat ovals.

5 Cover loosely with clingfilm (plastic wrap) and leave in a warm place to prove for about 10 minutes.

6 Heat about 30 ml/2 tbsp of oil in a frying pan and fry the ovals a few at a time for about 3 minutes on each side.

7 Drain on kitchen paper (paper towels) and eat while still warm.

grissini

These Italian-style breadsticks are brilliant for munching on when you're peckish, as well as for serving with dips.

MAKES 25
DOUGH SETTING

For the dough

water	300 ml/½ pt/1¼ cups
olive oil	40 ml/2½ tbsp
dried milk powder (non-fat dry milk)	30 ml/2 tbsp
honey	20 ml/1½ tbsp
salt	5 ml/1 tsp
strong white bread flour	100 g/4 oz/1 cup
spelt flour	100 g/4 oz/1 cup
strong wholemeal bread flour	100 g/4 oz/1 cup
traditional active dried yeast	7.5 ml/1½ tsp

For the topping

milk for brushing	a little
coarse salt	
sesame seeds	

1 To make the dough, place all the ingredients in the bread pan in the order listed. Place the pan in the breadmaker, ensuring that it is locked into position.

2 Close the lid, select the DOUGH setting and press START. When the cycle is complete, carefully remove the pan using oven gloves and tip the dough out on to a lightly floured work surface.

3 Knock back the dough and divide into 25 equal-sized pieces. Roll each into a long stick about 30 cm/12 in long. Brush each stick with milk, then sprinkle with either salt or sesame seeds.

4 Place on a lightly greased baking (cookie) sheet. Cover loosely with lightly greased clingfilm (plastic wrap) and leave in a warm place to prove for about 10 minutes.

5 Bake in a preheated oven at 220°C/425°F/gas mark 7/ fan oven 200°C for about 5–10 minutes until golden.

tikka and coriander corn loaf

A close-textured, full-flavoured bread with the fresh taste of coriander (cilantro). Use to mop up casseroles and stews.

 MAKES 1 MEDIUM LOAF
BASIC SETTING

water	375 ml/13 fl oz/1½ cups
sunflower oil	20 ml/2½ tbsp
tikka paste	45 ml/3 tbsp
chopped fresh coriander	30 ml/2 tbsp
salt	5 ml/1 tsp
sugar	5 ml/1 tsp
strong white bread flour	275 g/10 oz/2½ cups
cornmeal	75 g/3 oz/¾ cup
traditional active dried yeast	7.5 ml/1½ tsp

1 Place all the ingredients in the bread pan in the order listed. Place the pan in the breadmaker, ensuring that it is locked in position.

2 Close the lid, select the BASIC setting and press START.

3 When the cycle is complete, carefully remove the pan using oven gloves and tip the loaf out on to a cooling rack and allow to cool before slicing.

madras flat bread

Spicy little pitta-type breads that can be eaten warm, split and filled with salad, kebabs or your favourite fillings.

MAKES 4
DOUGH SETTING

For the dough	
water	300 ml/½ pt/1¼ cups
Madras curry powder	60 ml/4 tbsp
dried milk powder (non-fat dry milk)	30 ml/2 tbsp
caster (superfine) sugar	20 ml/1½ tbsp
salt	5 ml/1 tsp
sunflower oil	30 ml/2 tbsp
strong white bread flour	350 g/12 oz/3 cups
traditional active dried yeast	6 ml/1¼ tsp
For the topping	
Madras curry paste	30 ml/2 tbsp

1 To make the dough, place all the ingredients in the bread pan in the order listed. Place the pan in the breadmaker, ensuring that it is locked into position.

2 Close the lid, select the DOUGH setting and press START.

3 When the cycle is complete, carefully remove the pan using oven gloves and tip the dough out on to a lightly floured work surface. Knock back the dough, then divide into four equal-sized pieces. Flatten each out to an oval.

4 Spread the curry paste all over the surface of the dough.

5 Place on a lightly greased baking (cookie) sheet, cover with lightly greased clingfilm (plastic wrap) and leave in a warm place to prove for about 20 minutes.

6 Bake in a preheated oven at 200°C/400°F/gas mark 6/ fan oven 180°C for about 15 minutes.

dark pumpernickel

A close-textured dark rye bread that is excellent with a range of continental cheeses and cold deli-style meats.

MAKES 1 MEDIUM LOAF
WHOLEMEAL SETTING

water	150 ml/¼ pt/⅔ cup
sunflower oil	15 ml/1 tbsp
black treacle (molasses)	30 ml/2 tbsp
salt	5 ml/1 tsp
dried milk powder (non-fat dry milk)	45 ml/3 tbsp
strong white bread flour	300 g/11 oz/2¾ cups
cornflour (cornstarch)	25 g/1 oz/¼ cup
rye flour	100 g/4 oz/1 cup
traditional active dried yeast	7.5 ml/1½ tsp

1 Place all the ingredients in the bread pan in the order listed. Place the pan in the breadmaker, ensuring that it is locked in position.

2 Close the lid, select the WHOLEMEAL setting and press START.

3 When the cycle is complete, carefully remove the pan using oven gloves and tip the loaf out on to a cooling rack and allow to cool before slicing.

brioche

This is a wonderful rich breakfast bread, which can be dunked into your coffee. Alternatively use to mop up syrup.

MAKES 1 SMALL LOAF
BASIC SETTING

water	120 ml/4 fl oz/½ cups
eggs	2
salt	2.5 ml/½ tsp
sugar	45 ml/3 tbsp
strong white bread flour	225 g/8 oz/2 cups
traditional active dried yeast	5 ml/1 tsp
butter	120 g/4½ oz/¾ cup, softened

1 Place all the ingredients except the butter in the bread pan in the order listed. Place the pan in the breadmaker, ensuring that it is locked in position.

2 Close the lid, select the BASIC setting and press START.

3 Start adding the butter about 5 minutes into the kneading process, adding 15 ml/1 tbsp at a time and giving it a chance to mix in. Close the lid.

4 When the cycle is complete, switch off the machine, open the lid and allow the loaf to cool inside for about 30 minutes.

5 Carefully remove the pan using oven gloves and tip the loaf out on to a cooling rack and allow to cool before slicing.

olive and chilli pitta bread

These full-flavoured pitta breads make a wonderful lunch when filled with Feta cheese and lettuce or slices of tomato.

MAKES 12
DOUGH SETTING

water	300 ml/½ pt/1¼ cups
salt	7.5 ml/1½ tsp
sugar	7.5 ml/1½ tsp
olive oil	20 ml/1½ tbsp
red chilli	1, seeded and halved
green chilli	1, seeded and halved
strong white bread flour	450 g/1 lb/4 cups
traditional active dried yeast	7.5 ml/1½ tsp
mixed stoned (pitted) olives	100 g/4 oz

1 Place all the ingredients except the olives in the bread pan in the order listed. Place the pan in the breadmaker, ensuring that it is locked into position.

2 Close the lid, select the DOUGH setting and press START. Add the olives at the first buzzer or after the first kneading.

3 When the cycle is complete, carefully remove the pan using oven gloves and tip the dough out on to a lightly floured work surface.

4 Knock back the dough, divide into 12 equal-sized pieces and roll into balls. Roll each out to a flat oval and place on a lightly greased baking (cookie) sheet.

5 Cover with lightly greased clingfilm (plastic wrap) and leave in a warm place to prove for about 30 minutes.

6 Bake in a preheated oven at 200°C/400°F/gas mark 6/ fan oven 180°C for about 10–15 minutes.

basic
pizza dough

Use this recipe to make the pizza dough, then shape and top it how you choose. The two recipes that follow give some ideas.

MAKES 1 LARGE PIZZA BASE
DOUGH SETTING

water	250 ml/8 fl oz/1 cup
olive oil	30 ml/2 tbsp
dried milk powder (non-fat dry milk)	15 ml/1 tbsp
salt	7.5 ml/1½ tsp
sugar	30 ml/2 tbsp
strong white bread flour	450 g/1 lb/4 cups
traditional active dried yeast	10 ml/2 tsp

1 Place all the ingredients in the bread pan in the order listed. Place the pan in the breadmaker, ensuring that it is locked into position.

2 Close the lid, select the DOUGH setting and press START.

3 When the cycle is complete, carefully remove the pan using oven gloves and tip the dough out on to a lightly floured work surface.

4 Knock back the dough and roll out to the required shape.

5 Place on an oiled baking (cookie) sheet, cover with lightly greased clingfilm (plastic wrap) and leave in a warm place to prove for 15 minutes.

6 Top with your chosen ingredients and leave to rest for a further 15 minutes.

7 Bake in a preheated oven at 200°C/400°F/gas mark 6/ fan oven 180°C for 10–15 minutes.

fennel and smoked salmon pizza

Elegant smoked salmon, aniseed-scented fennel and mild, melting Mozzarella cheese make a brilliantly stylish pizza topping.

MAKES 1 LARGE PIZZA
DOUGH SETTING FOR PIZZA BASE

large red onion	1, thinly sliced
medium fennel bulb	1, sliced
olive oil	5 ml/1 tsp
prepared uncooked pizza base	1
wholegrain mustard	60 ml/4 tbsp
smoked salmon	175 g/6 oz, cut into ribbons
Mozzarella cheese	175 g/6 oz, grated

1 Put the onion, fennel and oil in a lidded saucepan and cook over a moderate heat for 10–15 minutes until very soft.

2 Spread the pizza base with the mustard, top with the onion and fennel mixture and arrange the salmon ribbons over the top. Sprinkle the Mozzarella over. Leave to rest for 15 minutes.

3 Bake in a preheated oven at 200°C/400°F/gas mark 6/fan oven 180°C for about 15 minutes.

red pesto and artichoke pizza

If you wish, canned asparagus could be used in place of the artichoke hearts – or even fresh asparagus when in season.

MAKES 1 LARGE PIZZA
DOUGH SETTING FOR PIZZA BASE

prepared uncooked pizza base	1
red pesto	90 ml/6 tbsp
can of artichoke hearts	400 g/14 oz/large, drained and sliced
Mozzarella cheese	175 g/6 oz, grated

1 Spread the pizza base with the pesto, top with the artichoke hearts and sprinkle the Mozzarella over. Leave to rest for 15 minutes.

2 Bake in a preheated oven at 200°C/400°F/gas mark 6/fan oven 180°C for about 15 minutes.

croissants

Making perfect croissants takes time, but the breadmaker takes the strain out of mixing and kneading and gives good results.

MAKES 8 LARGE CROISSANTS
DOUGH SETTING

water	375 ml/13 fl oz/1½ cups
dried milk powder (non-fat dry milk)	60 ml/4 tbsp
sugar	60 ml/4 tbsp
salt	10 ml/2 tsp
sunflower oil	60 ml/4 tbsp
strong white bread flour	450 g/1 lb/4 cups
traditional dried yeast	10 ml/2 tsp
butter	225 g/8 oz/1 cup, chilled
egg	1, beaten
water	10 ml/2 tsp

1 Place all the ingredients except the butter, egg and water in the bread pan in order listed. Place the pan in the breadmaker, ensuring that it is locked into position.

2 Close the lid, select the DOUGH setting and press START.

3 Meanwhile, place the butter between two sheets of greaseproof (waxed) paper and roll out to a 23 cm/9 in square. Return to the fridge.

4 When the cycle is complete, carefully remove the pan using oven gloves and tip the dough out on to a lightly floured work surface.

5 Knock back the dough, then roll out to a 30 cm/12 in square. Arrange the butter diagonally across the centre of the dough and bring the corners of the dough to meet in the middle so that all the butter is covered.

6 Put the dough in the freezer for 5 minutes, then roll it out to a 50 x 25 cm/20 x 10 in rectangle. Fold in both ends to meet in the middle, then fold one half over the other. Return to the freezer for 15 minutes.

7 Repeat the rolling and folding process with the rested dough, then return to the freezer for a further 15 minutes.

8 Finally, roll the rested dough out to a 12.5 cm/5 in wide strip. Cut the strip into 12.5 cm/5 in squares, then cut each in half diagonally to give triangles. Roll out each to stretch it by about a third.

9 Mix together the egg and water and use to brush over each triangle. Roll up the dough from the wide base and coil the ends round to form crescents.

10 Brush the surface with egg wash, then leave in a warm place to prove for a further 20 minutes.

11 Bake at 220°C/425°F/gas mark 7/fan oven 200°C for 10–15 minutes until golden and puffy. Eat warm or cold.

salami and brie croissants

You can do plenty of variations with this recipe, changing the Brie to any kind of cheese you like, and the salami to ham or other meats.

MAKES 8 LARGE CROISSANTS
DOUGH SETTING

water	375 ml/13 fl oz/1½ cups
dried milk powder (non-fat dry milk)	60 ml/4 tbsp
sugar	60 ml/4 tbsp
salt	10 ml/2 tsp
sunflower oil	60 ml/4 tbsp
strong white bread flour	450 g/1 lb/4 cups
traditional dried yeast	10 ml/2 tsp
butter	225 g/8 oz/1 cup, chilled
salami	8, small, thin slices
Brie or other similar cheese	8 slices
egg	1, beaten
water	10 ml/2 tsp

1 Follow the method instructions 1 to 8 for croissants.

9 Mix together the egg and water and use to brush over each triangle. Lay a slice of salami, then a slice of cheese on each one, then roll up from the wide base and coil the ends round to form crescents.

10 Brush the surface with egg wash, then leave in a warm place to prove for a further 20 minutes.

11 Bake at 220°C/425°F/gas mark 7/fan oven 200°C for 10–15 minutes until golden and puffy.

challah bread

A rich dough formed into an attractive plait and finished with an egg glaze. This traditional Jewish bread is best eaten warm.

MAKES 1 LARGE LOAF
DOUGH SETTING

For the dough

water	200 ml/7 fl oz/1 cup
egg	1
kosher margarine	15 ml/1 tbsp
caster (superfine) sugar	5 ml/1 tsp
salt	2.5 ml/½ tsp
strong white bread flour	450 g/1 lb/4 cups
traditional active dried yeast	7.5 ml/1½ tsp

For the glaze

egg	1, beaten
water	10 ml/2 tsp

1 To make the dough, place all the ingredients in the bread pan in the order listed. Place the pan in the breadmaker, ensuring that it is locked into position.

2 Close the lid, select the DOUGH setting and press START.

3 When the cycle is complete, carefully remove the pan using oven gloves and tip the dough out on to a lightly floured work surface. Knock back the dough, cut off a third and reserve.

4 Roll the large piece of dough into a sausage about 30 cm/12 in long. Twist slightly, then place on a lightly greased baking (cookie) sheet. Mix together the egg and water for the glaze and brush over the dough.

5 Divide the remaining dough into three pieces and roll each to about the same length as the big sausage. Plait the three pieces, then lay on top of the sausage on the baking sheet. Cover with lightly greased clingfilm (plastic wrap) and leave in a warm place to prove for about 25 minutes.

6 Bake in a preheated oven at 200°C/400°F/gas mark 6/ fan oven 180°C for 30 minutes.

french stick

It's worth making soup just as an excuse to eat this bread! Baguettes use the same dough and are given as a variation.

MAKES 1 MEDIUM LOAF
DOUGH SETTING

water	250 ml/8 fl oz/1 cup
dried milk powder (non-fat dry milk)	30 ml/2 tbsp
salt	5 ml/1 tsp
sugar	15 ml/1 tbsp
strong white bread flour	350 g/12 fl oz/3 cups
traditional active dried yeast	5 ml/1 tsp

1 Place all the ingredients in the bread pan in the order listed. Place the pan in the breadmaker, ensuring that it is locked into position.

2 Close the lid, select the DOUGH setting and press START.

3 When the cycle is complete, carefully remove the pan using oven gloves and tip the dough out on to a lightly floured work surface. Knock back the dough, then roll into a long stick.

4 Place on a lightly greased baking (cookie) sheet. Cover loosely with lightly greased clingfilm (plastic wrap) and leave in a warm place to prove for 20–30 minutes.

5 Bake in a preheated oven at 220°C/425°F/gas mark 7/ fan oven 200°C for about 20 minutes.

variation

Baguettes: follow the recipe as above, but at step 4 shape into about six equal-sized portions and roll into long torpedo shapes. When cooled, split and butter and fill with cold meat or cheese and salad.

french bread

A popular accompaniment and a must for picnics and buffets. Cut into slices – or just pull off and eat warm chunks!

MAKES 1 MEDIUM LOAF
FRENCH SETTING

water	250 ml/8 fl oz/1 cup
dried milk powder (non-fat dry milk)	30 ml/2 tbsp
salt	5 ml/1 tsp
sugar	15 ml/1 tbsp
strong white bread flour	350 g/12 oz/3 cups
traditional active dried yeast	5 ml/1 tsp

1 Place all the ingredients in the bread pan in the order listed. Place the pan in the breadmaker, ensuring that it is locked in position.

2 Close the lid, select the FRENCH setting and press START.

3 When the cycle is complete, carefully remove the pan using oven gloves and tip the loaf out on to a cooling rack and allow to cool before slicing.

rolls and buns

Most of the bread recipes in this book can be adjusted to make rolls, but this chapter concentrates on rolls and buns and explains the techniques of shaping.

You can also ring the changes by experimenting with different glazes and toppings.

Suggested glazes: oil, melted butter, egg (1 yolk beaten with 10 ml/2 tsp water), milk, salt (5 ml/1 tsp mixed with 30 ml/2 tbsp water).

Suggested toppings: sunflower seeds, poppy seeds, sesame seeds, rolled oats, crushed peanuts, cracked wheat, grated or crumbled cheese, a sprinkling of dried herbs.

white bread rolls

You just can't beat a warm roll straight from your breadmaker. Use this basic bread roll recipe to create your favourite shapes.

MAKES 8–12
DOUGH SETTING

water	300 ml/½ pt/1¼ cups
dried milk powder (non-fat dry milk)	30 ml/2 tbsp
caster (superfine) sugar	20 ml/1½ tbsp
salt	5 ml/1 tsp
sunflower oil	40 ml/2½ tbsp
strong white bread flour	350 g/12 oz/3 cups
traditional active dried yeast	6 ml/1¼ tsp

1 Place all the ingredients in the bread pan in the order listed. Place the pan in the breadmaker, ensuring that it is locked into position.

2 Close the lid, select the DOUGH setting and press START.

3 When the cycle is complete, carefully remove the pan using oven gloves and tip the dough out on to a lightly floured work surface. Knock back the dough, divide into 8–12 equal-sized pieces and shape as you wish.

4 Place on a lightly greased baking (cookie) sheet. Cover loosely with clingfilm (plastic wrap) and leave in a warm place to prove for about 30 minutes.

5 Bake in a preheated oven at 220°C/425°F/gas mark 7/ fan oven 200°C for 10–15 minutes depending on size.

wholemeal bread rolls

I think using some plain white flour makes the best wholemeal rolls. If you like them slightly heavier, try using all wholemeal flour.

MAKES 8–12
DOUGH SETTING

water	300 ml/½ pt/1¼ cups
dried milk powder (non-fat dry milk)	30 ml/2 tbsp
caster (superfine) sugar	20 ml/1½ tbsp
salt	5 ml/1 tsp
sunflower oil	40 ml/2½ tbsp
strong white bread flour	100 g/4 oz/1 cup
strong wholemeal bread flour	225 g/8 oz/2 cups
traditional active dried yeast	6 ml/1¼ tsp

1 Place all the ingredients in the bread pan in the order listed. Place the pan in the breadmaker, ensuring that it is locked into position.

2 Close the lid, select the DOUGH setting and press START.

3 When the cycle is complete, carefully remove the pan using oven gloves and tip the dough out on to a lightly floured work surface. Knock back the dough, divide into 8–12 equal-sized pieces and shape as you wish.

4 Place on a lightly greased baking (cookie) sheet. Cover loosely with clingfilm (plastic wrap) and leave in a warm place to prove for about 30 minutes.

5 Bake in a preheated oven at 220°C/425°F/gas mark 7/ fan oven 200°C for 10–15 minutes depending on size.

shrimp knots

These little rolls have a distinctly Oriental taste. They are a wonderful accompaniment to Chinese soups and many noodle dishes.

MAKES 6
DOUGH SETTING

water	300 ml/½ pt/1¼ cups
olive oil	40 ml/2½ tbsp
Chinese shrimp paste	7.5 ml/1½ tsp
chopped lemongrass	30 ml/2 tbsp
dried milk powder (non-fat dry milk)	40 ml/2½ tbsp
sugar	40 ml/2½ tbsp
salt	7.5 ml/1½ tsp
strong white bread flour	350 g/12 oz/3 cups
traditional active dried yeast	7.5 ml/1½ tsp

1 Place all the ingredients in the bread pan in the order listed. Place the pan in the breadmaker, ensuring that it is locked into position.

2 Close the lid, select the DOUGH setting and press START.

3 When the cycle is complete, carefully remove the pan using oven gloves and tip the dough out on to a lightly floured work surface.

4 Knock back the dough, then divide into six equal-sized pieces. Roll out each into a long sausage, then form each one into a loose knot.

5 Place on a lightly greased baking (cookie) sheet. Cover loosely with lightly greased clingfilm (plastic wrap) and leave in a warm place to prove for about 20 minutes.

6 Bake in a preheated oven at 220°C/425°F/gas mark 7/ fan oven 200°C for about 10–15 minutes.

summer herb and onion rolls

Use a mixture of seasonal herbs to flavour these rolls. Serve as an accompaniment or split and buttered or drizzled with olive oil.

MAKES 10
DOUGH SETTING

For the dough

water	300 ml/½ pt/1¼ cups
sunflower oil	45 ml/3 tbsp
dried milk powder (non-fat dry milk)	30 ml/2 tbsp
honey	10 ml/2 tsp
salt	5 ml/1 tsp
mixed fresh herb leaves	large handful
shallot	1, chopped
strong white bread flour	225g/8 oz/2 cups
strong wholemeal bread flour	100 g/4 oz/1 cup
traditional active dried yeast	6 ml/1¼ tsp
For the glaze	
egg	1, beaten
water	10 ml/2 tsp

1 To make the dough, place all the ingredients in the bread pan in the order listed. Place the pan in the breadmaker, ensuring that it is locked into position.

2 Close the lid, select the DOUGH setting and press START.

3 When the cycle is complete, carefully remove the pan using oven gloves and tip the dough out on to a lightly floured work surface.

4 Knock back the dough and divide into 10 equal-sized pieces. Roll each into a smooth ball, then roll and lengthen slightly to form batons.

5 Place on a lightly greased baking (cookie) sheet, cover with lightly greased clingfilm (plastic wrap) and leave in a warm place to prove for about 20 minutes.

6 To make the glaze, mix together the egg and water and brush all over the rolls. Bake in a preheated oven at 220°C/425°F/gas mark 7/fan oven 200°C for about 10–15 minutes. Eat warm or cold.

cracked wheat granary clovers

Sesame, sunflower or pumpkin seeds could be used instead of cracked wheat to make the topping for these attractive rolls.

MAKES 8
DOUGH SETTING

For the dough

water	300 ml/½ pt/1¼ cups
dried milk powder (non-fat dry milk)	30 ml/2 tbsp
caster (superfine) sugar	20 ml/1½ tbsp
salt	5 ml/1 tsp
sunflower oil	40 ml/2½ tbsp
strong white bread flour	175 g/6 oz/1½ cups
granary flour	175 g/6 oz/1½ cups
traditional active dried yeast	6 ml/1¼ tsp

For the topping

milk for brushing	a little
cracked wheat	50 g/2 oz/½ cup

1 To make the dough, place all the ingredients in the bread pan in the order listed. Place the pan in the breadmaker, ensuring that it is locked into position.

2 Close the lid, select the DOUGH setting and press START.

3 When the cycle is complete, carefully remove the pan using oven gloves and tip the dough out on to a lightly floured work surface.

4 Knock back the dough, then divide into eight equal-sized pieces. Divide each into three small portions and roll each into a smooth ball.

5 Place the three balls close together on a lightly greased baking (cookie) sheet to resemble a clover leaf. Repeat with the remaining balls.

6 Brush the top of each clover with a little milk, then sprinkle with the cracked wheat.

7 Cover loosely with lightly greased clingfilm (plastic wrap) and leave in a warm place to prove for about 20 minutes.

8 Bake in a preheated oven at 200°C/400°F/gas mark 6/ fan oven 180°C for about 10–15 minutes.

hot cross buns

A traditional Easter favourite, warmly spiced and bursting with fruit, is made easy with the breadmaker. Try them lightly toasted.

MAKES 8–10
DOUGH SETTING

For the dough	
warm milk	150 ml/¼ pt/⅔ cups
egg	1
butter	30 ml/2 tbsp
caster (superfine) sugar	30 ml/2 tbsp
salt	2.5 ml/½ tsp
strong white bread flour	350 g/12 oz/3 cups
ground cinnamon	5 ml/1 tsp
mixed (apple-pie) spice	2.5 ml/½ tsp
traditional active dried yeast	7.5 ml/1½ tsp
dried mixed fruit (fruit cake mix)	100 g/4 oz/⅔ cup
For the glaze	
egg	1, beaten
water	10 ml/2 tsp

1 To make the dough, place all the ingredients except the dried fruit in the bread pan in the order listed. Place the pan in the breadmaker, ensuring that it is locked into position.

2 Close the lid, select the DOUGH setting and press START. Add the dried fruit at the buzzer or after the first kneading.

3 When the cycle is complete, carefully remove the pan using oven gloves and tip the dough out on to a lightly floured work surface.

4 Knock back the dough and divide into 8–10 equal-sized pieces. Shape into smooth balls and cut a cross on the top of each with a sharp knife.

5 Place on a lightly greased baking (cookie) sheet. Cover with lightly greased clingfilm (plastic wrap) and leave in a warm place to prove for about 20 minutes.

6 To make the glaze, mix together the egg and water and brush all over the surface of the buns.

7 Bake in a preheated oven at 190°C/375°F/gas mark 5/ fan oven 170°C for about 15 minutes.

sweet breads and teatime favourites

This chapter offers a wide range of ideas for sweet breads to suit all tastes. There are some delicious breads using chocolate and fruits, as well as some traditional old favourites such as teacakes and milk bread.

chocolate and raisin bread

A rich chocolate dough generously loaded with raisins. A wonderful accompaniment to your morning coffee or afternoon tea!

MAKES 1 MEDIUM LOAF
BASIC SETTING

water	300 ml/½ pt/1¼ cups
sunflower oil	20 ml/1½ tbsp
chocolate spread	75 ml/5 tbsp
dried milk powder (non-fat dry milk)	45 ml/3 tbsp
salt	5 ml/1 tsp
sugar	90 ml/6 tbsp
strong white bread flour	350 g/12 oz/3 cups
cocoa (unsweetened chocolate) powder	20 ml/1½ tbsp
traditional active dried yeast	7.5 ml/1½ tsp
raisins	100 g/4 oz/⅔ cup

1 Place all the ingredients except the raisins in the bread pan in the order listed. Place the pan in the breadmaker, ensuring that it is locked in position.

2 Close the lid, select the BASIC setting and press START. Add the raisins at the buzzer or after the first kneading.

3 When the cycle is complete, carefully remove the pan using oven gloves and tip the loaf out on to a cooling rack and allow to cool before slicing.

double chocolate and hazelnut bread

Chocolate and hazelnuts (filberts) are very good companions, but walnuts, pecans or almonds could be substituted for a change.

MAKES 1 MEDIUM LOAF
BASIC SETTING

water	300 ml/½ pt/1¼ cups
sunflower oil	20 ml/1½ tbsp
chocolate and hazelnut spread	90 ml/6 tbsp
dried milk powder (non-fat dry milk)	30 ml/2 tbsp
salt	5 ml/1 tsp
sugar	30 ml/2 tbsp
strong white bread flour	350 g/12 oz/3 cups
traditional active dried yeast	7.5 ml/1½ tsp
plain (semi-sweet) chocolate	75 g/3 oz, broken into squares
hazelnuts	100 g/4 oz/1 cup

1 Place all the ingredients except the chocolate and nuts in the bread pan in the order listed. Place the pan in the breadmaker, ensuring that it is locked in position.

2 Close the lid, select the BASIC setting and press START. Add the chocolate and the nuts at the buzzer or after the first kneading.

3 When the cycle is complete, carefully remove the pan using oven gloves and tip the loaf out on to a cooling rack and allow to cool before slicing.

cornish clotted cream heavies

These rich buns have a close texture, similar to a scone (biscuit). They are delicious eaten warm, or cooled and toasted.

MAKES 8
DOUGH SETTING

saffron strands	2.5 ml/½ tsp
milk	30 ml/2 tbsp
clotted cream	100 g/4 oz/½ cup, warmed
butter	30 ml/2 tbsp
egg	1
salt	2.5 ml/½ tsp
sugar	50 g/2 oz/¼ cup
ground cinnamon	2.5 ml/½ tsp
strong white bread flour	350 g/12 oz/3 cups
traditional active dried yeast	10 ml/2 tsp
dried mixed fruit (fruit cake mix)	75 g/3 oz/½ cup

1 Place all the ingredients in the bread pan except the dried fruit in the order listed. Place the pan in the breadmaker, ensuring that it is locked into position.

2 Close the lid, select the DOUGH setting and press START. Add the dried fruit at the buzzer or after the first kneading.

3 When the cycle is complete, carefully remove the pan using oven gloves and tip the dough out on to a lightly floured work surface. Knock back the dough and divide into eight equal-sized pieces. Roll each into a smooth ball, then flatten very slightly.

4 Place on a lightly greased baking (cookie) sheet, cover with lightly greased clingfilm (plastic wrap) and leave in a warm place to prove for about 30 minutes.

5 Bake in a preheated oven at 200°C/400°F/gas mark 6/ fan oven 180°C for about 15 minutes.

fast orange and cardamom bread

This bread is made using the RAPID setting, and fast-acting yeast and warm water must be used for the bread to be successful.

MAKES 1 MEDIUM LOAF
RAPID SETTING

cardamom pods	15 ml/1 tbsp
oranges	2, grated zest and juice
butter	25 g/1 oz/2 tbsp, softened
salt	5 ml/1 tsp
sugar	60 ml/4 tbsp
strong white bread flour	350 g/12 oz/3 cups
fast-acting yeast	7.5 ml/1½ tsp

1 Crush the cardamom pods and discard the husks.

2 Make up the orange juice to 300 ml/½ pt/1¼ cups with warm water.

3 Place the cardamom seeds and orange liquid in the bread pan and add the remaining ingredients in the order listed. Place the pan in the breadmaker, ensuring that it is locked in position.

4 Close the lid, select the RAPID setting and press START.

5 When the cycle is complete, carefully remove the pan using oven gloves and tip the loaf out on to a cooling rack and allow to cool before slicing.

toffee bread

With its chewy toffee pieces and a soft toffee fudge filling, this is a very naughty but nice bread for adults and kids alike!

**MAKES 1 MEDIUM LOAF
DOUGH SETTING**

warm milk	150 ml/¼ pt/⅔ cup
egg	1
butter	25 g/1 oz/2 tbsp
caster (superfine) sugar	30 ml/2 tbsp
salt	7.5 ml/1½ tsp
strong white bread flour	350 g/12 oz/3 cups
fast-acting yeast	7.5 ml/1½ tsp
hard toffees	8, broken into small pieces
toffee fudge spread	75 ml/5 tbsp

1 Place all the ingredients in the bread pan except the toffees and toffee spread in the order listed. Place the pan in the breadmaker, ensuring that it is locked into position.

2 Close the lid, select the DOUGH setting and press START.

3 When the cycle is complete, carefully remove the pan using oven gloves and tip the dough out on to a lightly floured work surface. Knock back the dough, then knead in the toffee pieces.

4 Roll out to a little larger than a sheet of A4 paper, then spread with the toffee spread. Fold in half and seal the edges.

5 Place on a lightly greased baking (cookie) sheet, cover with lightly greased clingfilm (plastic wrap) and leave in a warm place to prove for about 20 minutes.

6 Bake in a preheated oven at 200°C/400°F/gas mark 6/ fan oven 180°C for about 15 minutes.

fast
vanilla bread

This is made using the RAPID setting. The success of the bread depends on using fast-acting yeast and warm water.

 MAKES 1 MEDIUM LOAF
RAPID SETTING

vanilla pod	1
warm milk	300 ml/½ pt/1¼ cups
butter	30 ml/2 tbsp, softened
salt	5 ml/1 tsp
sugar	90 ml/6 tbsp
strong white bread flour	350 g/12 oz/3 cups
fast-acting yeast	10 ml/2 tsp

1 Slit the vanilla pod lengthways and scrape the seeds into the milk.

2 Warm the milk with the vanilla seed until just simmering, then remove from the heat and allow to cool until it reaches blood temperature.

3 Pour into the bread pan with the vanilla seed, then add all the remaining ingredients in the order listed. Place the pan in the breadmaker, ensuring that it is locked in position.

4 Close the lid, select the RAPID setting and press START.

5 When the cycle is complete, carefully remove the pan using oven gloves and tip the loaf out on to a cooling rack and allow to cool before slicing.

lemon and lime marmalade bread

A white loaf with a citrus tang. It's at its very best eaten sliced and buttered while still warm from the breadmaker.

**MAKES 1 MEDIUM LOAF
BASIC SETTING**

water	300 ml/½ pt/1¼ cups
sunflower oil	40 ml/2½ tbsp
lemon and lime marmalade	75 ml/5 tbsp
dried milk powder (non-fat dry milk)	30 ml/2 tbsp
salt	5 ml/1 tsp
strong white bread flour	350 g/12 oz/3 cups
traditional active dried yeast	7.5 ml/1½ tsp

1 Place all the ingredients in the bread pan in the order listed. Place the pan in the breadmaker, ensuring that it is locked in position.

2 Close the lid, select the BASIC setting and press START.

3 When the cycle is complete, carefully remove the pan using oven gloves and tip the loaf out on to a cooling rack and allow to cool before slicing.

teacakes

Serve these fruity teacakes warm from the oven, split and buttered, or allow to cool and toast and butter later.

 MAKES ABOUT 8
DOUGH SETTING

For the dough

warm milk	150 ml/¼ pt/⅔ cup
egg	1
butter	30 ml/2 tbsp
caster (superfine) sugar	30 ml/2 tbsp
salt	7.5 ml/1½ tsp
strong white bread flour	350 g/12 oz/3 cups
traditional active dried yeast	7.5 ml/1½ tsp
currants	100 g/4 oz/⅔ cup
chopped mixed (candied) peel	30 ml/2 tbsp

For the glaze

egg	1, beaten
water	10 ml/2 tsp

1 To make the dough, place all the ingredients except the currants and peel in the bread pan in the order listed. Place the pan in the breadmaker, ensuring that it is locked into position.

2 Close the lid, select the DOUGH setting and press START. Add the currants and peel at the buzzer or after the first kneading.

3 When the cycle is complete, carefully remove the pan using oven gloves and tip the dough out on to a lightly floured work surface. Knock back the dough, then divide into eight equal-sized pieces. Shape into small balls, then flatten slightly.

4 Place on a lightly greased baking (cookie) sheet, cover with lightly greased clingfilm (plastic wrap) and leave in a warm place to prove for about 20 minutes.

5 To make the glaze, mix together the egg and water and brush all over the surface of the teacakes.

6 Bake in a preheated oven at 220°C/425°F/gas mark 7/ fan oven 200°C for about 15 minutes.

double banana bread

A delicious bread flavoured with fresh banana and with added texture from banana chips. Eat warm with butter and honey.

MAKES 1 MEDIUM LOAF
BASIC SETTING

water	300 ml/½ pt/1¼ cups
sunflower oil	30 ml/2 tbsp
honey	10 ml/2 tsp
large banana	1, mashed
dried milk powder (non-fat dry milk)	30 ml/2 tbsp
salt	5 ml/1 tsp
strong white bread flour	350 g/12 oz/3 cups
wheatgerm	45 ml/3 tbsp
traditional active dried yeast	7.5 ml/1½ tsp
yoghurt-coated dried banana	100 g/4 oz/⅔ cup

1 Place all the ingredients except the dried banana in the bread pan in the order listed. Place the pan in the breadmaker, ensuring that it is locked in position.

2 Close the lid, select the BASIC setting and press START. Add the dried banana at the buzzer or after the first kneading.

3 When the cycle is complete, carefully remove the pan using oven gloves and tip the loaf out on to a cooling rack and allow to cool before slicing.

milk bread

Use this recipe to make a moist, rich loaf ideal for the most sumptuous of sandwiches and for spreading with jam.

MAKES 1 LARGE LOAF
BASIC SETTING

warm milk	250 ml/8 fl oz/1 cup
egg	1
butter	50 g/2 oz/¼ cup
caster (superfine) sugar	60 ml/4 tbsp
salt	10 ml/2 tsp
strong white bread flour	450 g/1 lb/4 cups
traditional active dried yeast	10 ml/2 tsp

1 Place all the ingredients in the bread pan in the order listed. Place the pan in the breadmaker, ensuring that it is locked in position.

2 Close the lid, select the BASIC setting and press START.

3 When the cycle is complete, carefully remove the pan using oven gloves and tip the loaf out on to a cooling rack and allow to cool before slicing.

mixed fruit, orange and syrup bread

Simply slice, spread with butter and enjoy with a cup of tea – in particular elegantly fragrant Earl Grey tea.

MAKES 1 LARGE LOAF
BASIC SETTING

oranges	4, finely grated zest and juice
sunflower oil	60 ml/4 tbsp
golden (light corn) syrup	60 ml/4 tbsp
salt	5 ml/1 tsp
dried milk powder (non-fat dry milk)	60 ml/4 tbsp
strong white bread flour	450 g/1 lb/4 cups
traditional active dried yeast	10 ml/2 tsp
dried fruit (fruit cake mix)	100 g/4 oz/⅔ cup

1 Place all the ingredients except the dried fruit in the bread pan in the order listed. Place the pan in the breadmaker, ensuring that it is locked in position.

2 Close the lid, select the BASIC setting and press START. Add the dried fruit at the buzzer or after the first kneading.

3 When the cycle is complete, carefully remove the pan using oven gloves and tip the loaf out on to a cooling rack and allow to cool before slicing.

index